Happy Birthday I
All my love
Louise.
Nov 1991 x x x

AGAINST THE ODDS

AGAINST THE ODDS

The Life of Group Captain
Lionel Rees,
VC, OBE, MC, AFC.

W. Alister Williams

BRIDGE BOOKS, WREXHAM, CLWYD

First published in Great Britain by
BRIDGE BOOKS
61 Park Avenue
Wrexham, Clwyd.
LL12 7AW

1989

ISBN 1 872424 00 7

Printed and bound by WBC Print Ltd.,
Bristol and Maesteg.

To
Gwilym
whose kindness, generosity and enthusiasm
made this book possible
Diolch o'r galon

CONTENTS

LIST OF ILLUSTRATIONS

INTRODUCTION

Whilst visiting the town of Caernarfon to carry out research for a book on the Welsh recipients of the Victoria Cross, I was approached by the 'keyholder' of one of the local churches who mentioned the name of Brabazon Rees, VC, and asked me whether I knew anything about the man. Despite the fact that I am originally from a village less than four miles outside the town, I had to admit that I had never heard the name before. I soon discovered that I was not the only one who was ignorant of the town's only VC; it appeared that everyone that I spoke to was in the same position. Further research increased my appetite to know more about this man and gradually, the pieces began to fall into place and a story emerged of an extraordinary individual.

As a child I had grown up on a diet of flying heroes. Names like Ball, Bader and Lindbergh took me (if I might be excused the pun) on flights of romantic fancy to the far reaches of my imagination. Here, on my very own doorstep, was Lionel Rees, a real hero of the air, a man who thrived on challenges who devoted his life to pitting his wits, skills and abilities against any odds. This was as true of his service life as it was later when, as a civilian, he accepted the challenge of the sea and sailed, single-handed, across the Atlantic. He was a man who was interested in anything and everything which went on around him, who was side-tracked onto all manner of new courses, giving the impression of being an eccentric

1

and yet is remembered by those who knew him as a totally sane, rational man.

His story was a very difficult one to put together as, although he died less than thirty-five years ago, the information appears to have died with him. I was compelled to seek data in the most obscure places and, from what was available, I then rebuilt the story. The difficulties began with Rees' own personality which was a very private one which did not crave publicity (I am sure that he would be horrified to think that his life story is now in print) and the records which have survived are few and far between. So often, when tracking down information, I have followed an avenue which has promised to be fruitful only to discover that the one page or picture which I need is the one that is missing. It has felt at times as if someone has gone ahead of me removing all data that might be of value. I have encountered ignorance, racial prejudice, illiteracy and even a hint of financial greed during the course of my searches but, despite all of these, I think the story that I have uncovered is worthy of record, if for no other reason than my contention that Rees was the first official fighter pilot of the Royal Flying Corps, the first of the original 'few' who arrived in France in 1915 and laid the foundations for the thousands who were to follow them in aerial combats from Flanders to the Falklands. Their machines were underpowered, lightly armed and very fragile but they dared to embark upon building the tradition of aerial combat which has made the Royal Air Force the envy of the world. I hope that the finished story helps to fill a gap in the earliest history of aerial warfare as well as placing on permanent record the story of a very remarkable Welshman.

Introduction

During the course of my researches I was very privileged to meet or correspond with a number of fascinating people and to them all I wish to extend my gratitude for the kind assistance which they gave to a total stranger. However, without wishing in any way to deprecate the contribution made by all those who have assisted me, I must draw particular attention to a few who warrant a very special thank you.

First and foremost, I must acknowledge the enormous debt which I owe to Wing Commander Gwilym H Lewis, DFC, the one-time 'baby' of No 32 Squadron, RFC, who is the last survivor of the original airmen who joined Rees at Netheravon in 1916 - a fact of which he is justifiably very proud. I hope that I am not presuming too much when I say that I now include him and his delightful wife, Mrs Christian Lewis, amongst my friends; from the very first time that I contacted them on the telephone they have shown me nothing but kindness, encouragement and courtesy and, were it not for them, this book would never have been produced. My one apology to them is that it has taken so long to finish the research and I hope that they are not too disappointed with the 'end product'. Wing Commander Lewis has, very kindly, given me permission to quote quite extensively from his own letters to his father written in 1916 which formed the basis of his book 'Wings Over the Somme', published in 1976 and which I recommend to anyone interested in military aviation during the Great War.

I would also like to thank Lionel Rees' family who, when I visited the Bahamas during the course of my research, made every effort to assist me. In particular, I must thank Olvin Rees and his wife Val who kindly accepted a stranger into their home and allowed me to prise open the door of their 'family cupboard' not knowing what skeletons I might find.

I must also take this opportunity to express my gratitude to that most prolific and knowledgeable writer of aviation history, Chaz Bowyer. Whenever I have turned to him for assistance he has been more than generous in terms of knowledge, advice and photographs. Anyone interested in the history of the RAF owes him a debt of gratitude and, on behalf of us all, I say a most sincere thank you.

Finally, I must thank my wife Susan who, whilst acting as unpaid editor, managed to turn my peculiarities of phrasing into an intelligable text. I cannot begin to praise her enough for her ability to have Lionel Rees to breakfast, lunch, tea and supper every day for several years, without a penny extra on the housekeeping.

W Alister Williams

Wrexham, 1989

ACKNOWLEDGEMENTS

In addition to those individuals whom I have already mentioned in my introduction, I would like to acknowledge my most sincere thanks to the following organisations and individuals who have given me information, materials and perhaps, most importantly, their time and advice. If I have omitted to mention anyone I trust that they will accept my apologies and an assurance that such an oversight was entirely unintentional. What use I have made of their information is also my own responsibility and any errors which may have crept in are mine alone.

RAF Air Historical Branch (particularly Air Commodore H A Probert, MBE, MA); RAF Museum, Hendon; RAF College, Cranwell (particularly Miss Jean Buckberry); RAF Personnel Records; RAF Regiment Museum; No 11 Squadron, RAF (particularly Wing Commander S N Bostock); RMA, Sandhurst; Royal Artillery Institution; Imperial War Museum; Commonwealth War Graves Commission; Royal Archives, Windsor Castle; National Library of Wales; The British Library; Wrexham Public Library; Gwynedd Archives Service (Caernarfon); Bahamas Record Office (Nassau); Lloyd's Register of Shipping; The Law Society; The Probate Registry; Public Record Office (Kew); British High Commission, Nassau (particularly Mr Michael Holmes and Mr Alan Greenwood); Royal Welsh Yacht Club, Caernarfon (particularly Mr Neville Thomas); the Elms Preparatory School; Eastbourne College (particularly Mr Harral); The British Museum; National Library of Congress, Washington DC; United States Air Force; United States Coastguard; Institute of Archaeology, Hebrew University, Jerusalem; Royal Geographical Society; Institute of Archaeology, London University; Mr Alex Revell; Rev. J M Hutcheson; Mrs M Lightbourn; Mr J A McKinney; the late Mr Stanley Toogood and Mrs Mary Toogood; Mr R Beach; Professor Cyrus Sharer; Wing Commander William Fry, MC; Lady Joan Portal; Mr Lester Brown, DFC; Mr Willie de M P Davids, OBE; Air Chief Marshal Sir Walter Dawson, KCB, CBE, DSO; Marshal of the Royal Air Force Sir Dermot Boyle, GCB, KCVO, KBE, AFC; Air Vice-Marshal Sir Geoffrey Worthington, KBE, CB; Air Vice-Marshal Hugh Brookes, CB, CBE, DFC; Air Marshal Sir Edward Chilton, KBE, CB; Air Marshal Alan Gilmore, CB, CBE; Air Vice-Marshal Wilfred Freebody, CB, CBE, AFC; Wing Commander H E Rossiter; Air Marshal Sir Richard Jordan, KCB, DFC; Air Vice-Marshal George Chamberlain, CB, OBE; Air Vice-Marshal John Franks, CB, CBE, AFRAeS; Air Commodore T B Prickman, CB, CBE; Squadron Leader Dudley Apthorpe; Air Commodore E L S Ward, CB, DFC; Air Chief Marshal Sir Theodore McEvoy, KCB, CBE, AFRAeS; Mr Michael Brindle-Selle; Dr Dov Gavish; Mrs Aline McLaughlen; Dr F G Walton-Smith, PhD, DSc, DS; Miss Denise Dane; Mr H E Jones; Mr Philip Farrington; Mr John Winton; Dr David Kennedy; Mr Barrington Gray; Mr M C A Macdonald; Dr Alison Betts; Miss Jayne Mason; Mr Dave Mason; Mr Gwynne Belton; Mr Michael Schmeelke; Miss Liz Davies; Mr Nigel Hughes and Mr Huw Evans of Clwyd Computers.

CHAPTER I
A Caernarfon Childhood
(1884 - 1914)

The ancient fortress town of Caernarfon stands on a small peninsula between the River Seiont and the Menai Straits, against the backdrop of the Snowdonia mountain range. Traditionally, it had served as a market town for a rather impoverished area where the population had scratched a living from the poor soil of their small upland farms, but, by the turn of the nineteenth century, the district was undergoing dramatic changes as the effects of the industrial revolution reached this remote corner of North Wales and the town became increasingly important as a seaport for the rapidly expanding slate industry. The final restoration of peace in Europe after the defeat of Republican France, allowed the pace of this expansion in the town's trade to increase and, although many industries underwent a devastating slump after 1815, this was not the case in the slate industry as the lack of building caused by the war resulted in an upsurge in the construction industry and by 1825, the quarries of Caernarfonshire were commencing a period of unprecedented expansion. This change in the local economy brought with it an influx of outsiders from other parts of Wales and indeed from every corner of the British Isles; men who brought with them not only their industrial skills, but also an alien culture and alien traditions which were quickly assimilated by the local

9

population so that this corner of the principality developed a unique social composition.

Some of the immigrants came to add their sweat to that of the former dispossessed agricultural labourers in the quarries and mines, whilst others came to seek employment and fortune in the rapidly expanding businesses which were established to service this new found prosperity. As well as being the economic centre of the region, Caernarfon developed into the cultural and political capital of North Wales and it was in this atmosphere that the great Welsh romantic and nationalistic revival took root and flowered.

Amongst the outsiders was James Rees, born in Carmarthen in 1803 and already a man experienced in the ways of the world having left his native south-west Wales for London where he was trained as a printer and had become a master of his trade. His arrival in Caernarfon in 1831 was as a result of his appointment as foreman printer with the firm of R M Preece and Co, publishers of a new newspaper *The Carnarvon and Denbigh Herald*. With him came his young wife Anne, a native of Bristol and an outsider in a predominantly monoglot Welsh region. Superficially, there was little to suggest that the couple were any different to the hundreds of others who had moved into the area but James found the atmosphere ideal for his temperament and quickly began to create his own little niche in the limited social life of the town. When the *Herald* changed hands in 1832, and became the property of William Potter and Co, Rees stayed on under the new management and became an indispensable part of the business.

The economic and social forces in Caernarfon were perfect for the newspaper and it soon became the focus of radical views throughout North Wales and the success which came quickly was due in no small measure to the talent and enterprise of the intelligent, ambitious and very capable Mr Rees. By 1835, his opinion was being sought by the leading Liberal figures in the county and he played an important role in the election of Major General Sir Love Jones-Parry as Member of Parliament for Caernarfon Boroughs. The election was a close-run thing and paved the way for the radical tradition of Caernarfon's future parliamentary representation.

In 1840, William Potter retired and James Rees succeeded him as the editor and publisher of the 'Herald' which went from strength to strength. Aware of the increasing political conscience of his compatriots and realising that an English language newspaper was failing to reach a high proportion of the local population, he founded a second publication in 1854, *Y Herald Cymraeg* which proved to be an immediate success and became the focus of Welsh Liberal opinion for nearly a century.

Rees' status in the community and his commitment to the future of the town of Caernarfon was clearly reflected by his election to the Council, his appointment to the honoured position of Alderman and his service as Mayor in 1856-57 and 1872-74. In his maturity, he appears as a typical Victorian patriarch, a man proud of his humble beginnings and of the success which he had made of his chosen path through life. Whether he was presiding over the weekly publication of his newspapers, serving on the Borough Council or as a Baliff in the Court or simply as head of his family, he was confident that his opinion carried weight.

In the tradition of the time, the Rees family grew

substantially in numbers. Their first child, Walter John, was born in 1834 and, at regular intervals, a further four sons and three daughters arrived to fill the substantial stone built house which the family had acquired in Castle Street. One by one, the sons followed their father into the publishing business and one of them, James Wilmot Rees (born in 1837) established his own business in Monmouthshire, being recorded at the age of twenty-four as the proprietor of the *Star of Gwent*. Tragically, however, when James Rees retired in 1871, only one of his sons, Charles Herbert, was still alive and, although he ran the business for a short time, his heart was not in it and the newspapers were sold to John Evans of Caellenor, Caernarfon.

In 1878, Anne Rees died and her passing had a great effect upon James' health and, although often unwell, he did his utmost to fulfil his varied public duties in the town. In mid-June 1880, he was taken seriously ill and was confined to his bed where his condition deteriorated and he died during the afternoon of 21 June. His obituary, published in the *Herald* said of him:

"There can be no doubt that his labours, his energy and his perseverance in the conduct of 'The Carnarvon and Denbigh Herald' and 'Y Herald Cymraeg' proved of inestimable good to the Liberal Party in North Wales for many years. When the former was started, Liberalism was but a contemptible term with the landed proprietors and men of wealth in Wales: but it was Mr Rees' fortunate lot to see his newspapers and the principles they invariably advocated become not only popular, but successful as well, as witness the last election."

James Rees' funeral was strictly private but, as a mark of respect and an indicator of the esteem with which he was held by his fellow townsmen, the town bell tolled for most of the morning, flags flew at half-mast on all public (and many private) buildings and most shop windows were either shuttered or had their blinds drawn. He had travelled a long and successful road since his arrival in the town half a century earlier and had created a secure social and financial foundation for his descendants.

The death of James Rees meant that Charles, his only surviving son, was now the head of the family. Educated at Caernarfon and Liverpool, he had trained as a solicitor after the sale of the family business and, one month after his father's death, he was admitted into the profession and, rather than join an established business, he opened his own office at the family home, Plas Llanwnda, Castle Street. One year later, aged thirty-four, he married Leonora Maria, the daughter of Smith William Davids of Twthill, Caernarfon, a quarry agent to the Penrhyn Slate Quarries. Resident with the newlyweds were Kate and Ethel Rees, the widow and daughter of James Wilmot, Charles' older brother.

On 31 July, 1884, the family in Castle Street celebrated the birth of a son who was christened Lionel Wilmot Brabazon. The boy's first name appears to have been a personal choice on the part of his parents but, his second name was undoubtedly in remembrance of his late uncle, whilst the third was a link with his mother's maternal ancestors, the Brabazon family, the Earls of Meath in Ireland. Two years later, the birth of a daughter, Muriel Brabazon, completed the family. The legal practice appears to have prospered and the two children grew up in a secure middle-class environment, each devoted to the other; Lionel always there to protect his younger sister and Muriel hero-worshipping her older brother. Lionel grew into a strong, intelligent, good-looking but rather shy boy who seems to have been happy with his own company. He found it difficult to make friends but, those that he did make, remained so for the rest of his life.

He loved his home town and always regarded himself as a Caernarfon boy or 'hogyn o'r Dre' and, at the end of the nineteenth century, the town was a marvellous place for a small boy to grow up in, teeming with life as it did with small trains bringing the slates from Dyffryn Nantlle to the quay where they were loaded aboard ships for export to Europe and North America. His maternal grandfather had been one of the Trustees of the Carnarvon Harbour Board[1] which had transformed the town's quayside. There can be little doubt that Lionel, along with countless other small boys, must have appreciated their predecessors' enterprise as they sat enthralled, listening to the fanciful tales of the sea and distant ports told by tough sailors in the shadow of Edward I's great castle. Each day, the small ships would pass out of the estuary into the Menai Straits carrying not only their cargos but also the dreams of the youths who watched them sail by. A small boy could run in less than a minute from the Rees home to the promenade which flanked the Straits and in two minutes, could run from there to the Slate Quay on the River Seiont. It was here and in the Aber Woods across the river, that Lionel's young imagination evoked images of adventures in faraway places and he must surely have come closer to fulfilling his dreams than any of his contemporaries in Caernarfon.

His natural intelligence, coupled with an enquiring mind, fascinated by all things mechanical, made him a respected but isolated member of his peer group. It was to him that other boys came when a dispute or a problem seemed insoluable. In addition to this, there can be little doubt that Lionel was also influenced by his environment and the varied activities in the town. His father, in addition to his legal practice, was also an officer in the 3rd Volunteer Battalion, Royal Welch Fusiliers, and a long standing member of the Royal Welsh Yacht Club and it was therefore, probably in early childhood, that his future course in life was charted, not by ambitious parents but by his own experience and inclinations. One can even see the seeds of the future aviator being sown in the days before the development of powered flight. A life-long friend, Griffith Lloyd-Jones later recalled:

"In those far off days there were several large families living within the walls and their natural playground was the promenade where the flying of kites was very much in vogue.

Lionel's box-kite, made by himself, was always sailing so very much higher than any of the paper ones flown by the rest of us. I, as a very small boy flying a very small kite, hero-worshipped this much bigger boy, three years older than I, who also possessed the largest ever dog, an immense Newfoundland, of which I was rather frightened until Lionel told him to be friendly, after which he even allowed me to ride on his back."

W G Thomas of Caernarfon recalled a ten year old Lionel Rees who, having been given a camera as a gift, used his kite to attempt to take an aerial photograph of the town.

His formal education began in 1891, when he was enrolled as a boarder at the Elms Preparatory School, Colwell, Worcestershire. A small school, catering for some fifty boys, the Elms was situated amidst the Malvern Hills and placed great emphasis on physical as well as academic excellence and it was here that he probably first acquired a passion for formal games which was to remain with him throughout his life. He left the school in 1895 and, three years later, became a pupil at Eastbourne College, Sussex, an establishment where he was to spend some of the happiest years of his life.

Outside the classroom, he threw himself into every aspect of school activity and represented Blackwater House and the school at rugby football, running and shooting. He became a prefect, Head of House and a Sergeant in the Officer Training Corps before leaving in March, 1901. That summer, he obtained first class passes in Arithmetic and Additional Mathematics in the Oxford and Cambridge Lower School Certificate Examination with further second class passes in Latin, French, Geography, Mechanics and Physics. Although it is doubtful whether he ever made any close friends at Eastbourne, there can be no question that it held a special place in his affections, a fact clearly demonstrated by a generous donation which he made to the school later in life. Lionel certainly appears to have delighted in the surrogate family which boarding school provided, possibly relishing his independence from parental control, in particular that of his domineering father.

It was whilst at Eastbourne that he decided upon a military career and he was placed in the specialised Army Class in order that he might prepare for the entrance examination to one of the military academies. Some pupils undoubtedly used these classes as a means of escaping from the rigours of the traditional public school 'classical' education. This was certainly not the case with Lionel as there can be little doubt that the choice of an army career was anything other than a positive decision. He clearly had the aptitude to succeed in both the academic and practical aspects of school life and a career as an army officer offered perhaps the best possibility of making full use of his talents whilst also providing a continuation of the school atmosphere which he so obviously enjoyed. There is no evidence that he ever considered any other career and certainly he never seems to have expressed any desire to follow in his father's legal footsteps and Charles Rees could hardly object to his son's choice when he himself was a serving officer in the Volunteers.

Having settled on a military career, his aim of being accepted for training at Woolwich is clearly indicative of how he saw his future. A commission in the cavalry or the infantry held no appeal for him despite the fact that entry into either was considerably easier than it was into the Royal Engineers or Royal Artillery. Woolwich offered the promise of adventure, physical challenge and a high degree of academic achievement. Traditionally, the two corps, which drew their junior officers from 'the shop' (as Woolwich was affectionately called) were the choice of men of intelligence who intended making the service their profession.

Entry into the Royal Military Academy was by examination for which the competition was high. Three sections or classes had to be sat of which two were compulsary in all their elements. Class I (compulsory) covered Mathematics (including Arithmetic, Algebra, Euclid and Plane Trigonometry), Latin, French or German and English History. Class II (candidates had to choose any two) included Higher Mathematics, French or German, Greek, English Composition, Chemistry, Physics, Physical Geography and Geology. Class III (compulsory) dealt with freehand drawing and Geometric drawing. As the examination was the same for both

Woolwich and Sandhurst, selection for the former was made by picking those with the highest grades whilst the remaining candidates that had passed would be offered places at Sandhurst. Rees passed into the RMA an inconspicuous 62nd out of an entry of 80 and realised that he had a great deal of hard work ahead of him if he was to have any say regarding which corps, either Engineers or Artillery, he was to enter in two years time.

Each day commenced with reveille at 6.15 am and the cadets paraded at 7.15 am. Within an hour, they had to breakfast and be either at their desks for the first subject of the day (in the junior year this was invariably Mathematics) or parading for outdoor instruction in such subjects as field fortification and military topography. At noon, cadets were given an hour of drill, riding or gymnastics followed by lunch parade at 1.15 pm when they were all carefully inspected by the corporals; a single speck of dust usually being rewarded by extra drill. By 2.15 pm, the cadets were again outside where, for a further hour, they participated in drill, riding or artillery exercises after which they were allowed a two-hour break which they were expected to spend either in personal study, playing games or making use of the workshops. At 5.15 pm, they began two hours of classroom instruction in French or German and Drawing or, in the case of senior classes, Chemistry, Physics, Tactics, Military Administration and Law. After dinner, each cadet had to involve himself in private study, dance practice or additional voluntary subjects in the workshops. At 10 pm, a final roll call was taken and the day ended.

In addition to his academic work, Rees exhibited his usual flair for competetive sports and, whilst at the

Academy, he earned something of a reputation as an athlete. At the Royal Military Tournament held on Derby Day 1903, he represented the Academy in the Sabre versus Sabre competition, taking the first prize. During his two years at the RMA, Rees worked hard at his studies and in the final examinations he passed 16th out of 83 candidates. Such was his success that he was awarded the Tombs Memorial Prize, given annually to the artillery cadet achieving the highest marks in the finals. Although the prize was worth £56, its greatest value to a newly-commissioned officer was the possible kudos which it might bring as the award entitled the recipient to have his name recorded on a panel in the dining-room at Woolwich by way of inspiration to future generations of cadets - he also hoped it would become engraved in the memories of those senior to him in the service and thereby enhance his career.

Whether Rees had failed to gain sufficiently high marks for entry into the Royal Engineers or whether the Royal Artillery had always been his first choice was not recorded and neither was the reason for his decision to take a commission in the Royal Garrison Artillery. Certainly, as the 'Tombs' cadet of 1903, the choice of any branch of the artillery was open to him and traditionally, the Royal Field Artillery was regarded as the elite unit of the corps. A career in the RFA was however regarded as being best suited to a young man who had sufficient private resources to afford the social life which was synonymous with service in that branch. The RGA on the other hand attracted those young men of limited means who wished to follow as inexpensive a career as possible whilst still serving in a highly professional unit. Although the Rees family were financially secure, they were not wealthy and therefore monetary considerations may have had a part to play in Lionel's choice. Another, possibly more decisive factor was the belief that 'Garrison' gunners had far more opportunity for active service, being almost continuously engaged at the sharp end of Britain's minor imperial conflicts throughout the world, particularly on the north-west frontier of India. Finally, a third factor which may well have influenced his decision was the question of equestrian skills. Having an urban upbringing, Lionel had little experience of horsemanship and, indeed, the Riding Certificate issued to him at the Riding Establishment, Woolwich, states that, after 111 lessons in Military Equitation "L W B Rees... is a fair rider". The RFA were the horse worshippers of the gunners and anyone who was less than skilled as a rider would do well to avoid them. A few years later, another Woolwich cadet made the same decision and, in his memoirs published over forty years later, he commented on his choice [2]:

"I ought to have realized the overwhelming importance of horse worship throughout the British Army of that day, and above all its importance in the 'Gunners' ... I was fond of horses and riding myself, but I foolishly never realised till too late how vital it was for an aspiring gunner subaltern to affect an adoration bordering on the fanatical for that intelligent quadruped. To select deliberately the 'unhorsey' branch of the regiment was in those days to commit the unforgiveable sin. It was very doubtful whether any of us who started life in that unfashionable branch (ROYAL GARRISON ARTILLERY) ever lived this stigma down throughout our service, as can be seen by the low proportion of 'Gambardiers' as compared to Field and Horse Gunners who rose to really high command ... it seems unlikely that all the great commanders should have gone into the horsey branch and all the 'duds' into the other ! "

Commissioned as 2nd Lieutenant, Royal Garrison

Artillery on 23 December, 1903, Rees spent six months at the Depot before being posted to No 9 Company, RGA, Gibraltar where he spent four uneventful years learning the skills of his profession. In accordance with the 'time-served' tradition of promotion, he became a Lieutenant after two years, a rank in which he was to remain until the outbreak of war in 1914. Unlike many others who served on 'The Rock', Rees liked the station and was captivated by its dissimilarity to anywhere that he had previously known. Although of immense strategical importance. guarding as it did the entrance to the Mediterranean and the route to the East, life in Gibraltar was not too demanding and, after a time, became rather tedious for anyone with a taste for adventure. Realising that he enjoyed the heat and the exotic nature of an overseas posting, Rees determined to make the most of the potential for travel which military service offered.

In 1908, he was serving with No 50 Company, RGA, in Sierra Leone, West Africa, but returned to Britain on six months leave in July, 1909 after which he joined No 10 Company on Spike Island, Cork, Ireland. Whilst there he attended the 1910 and 1911 courses at the School of Gunnery, Shoeburyness and obtained a "Very Good" pass in the examinations in both years and was deemed to be sufficiently proficient in the use of quick-firing guns to pass as an instructor. In July, 1911, he went on a two month pre-embarkation leave and, on his return, was posted back to West Africa on secondment to the Native Local Artillery, Sierra Leone Company.

It was during this time that he acquired two great passions. The first, a love of discipline and training, was probably inherent within him but only manifested itself at the time when idleness could easily have become lethargy leading in turn to incompetence. The second was a love of the tropics. The so-called 'White Man's Grave' that was West Africa seemed to awaken in Rees a certain romantic streak and, like others before him, he was enthralled by what he saw and found the challenge of surviving in the tropics invigorating. Although he was probably unaware of this attraction at the time, it was to draw him back time and time again in the future.

It was in West Africa that Rees first encountered and grew to admire and respect the native, black population. The men under his command, although very different to the British soldiers he had been accustomed to, had their own qualities and Rees, together with the other British officers in the colony, turned them into an efficient military force, probably a match for any comparable European unit serving in the tropics.

But, however rewarding it may have been to train men in the skills and standards of the Royal Artillery and to see them carry out their duties efficiently on exercises and manoeuvres, it lacked excitment and when Rees returned to Britain at the end of 1912 his mind was receptive to the offer of a new challenge. It came in the form of a frail, under-powered flying machine.

CHAPTER II
No. 7 Squadron, RFC
(1914 - 15)

When Louis Bleriot made his somewhat unsteady landing in the grounds of Dover Castle in July 1909, he achieved more than the first crossing of the English Channel by a heavier-than-air machine, he also ended Britain's isolated position as an island off the coast of Europe. Despite the enormous advances which had taken place in the infant science of aeronautics which was admirably illustrated by this achievement, the British government failed to recognise the importance and, when it discovered that, during the course of that same year, the British taxpayer had already contributed £2,500 towards experiments with flying machines, it decided that enough was enough and cancelled any further expenditure. At the same time Germany was spending £40,000 per annum on military aviation.

Two years later, the situation had not improved and the Chief of the Imperial General Staff is on record as having declared that "Aviation is a useless and expensive fad advocated by a few individuals whose ideas are unworthy of attention." Fortunately, not all those in authority agreed with this viewpoint and during the spring of 1911 the army set up an Air Battalion of the Royal Engineers comprising No. 1 Company, equipped with airships, based at South Farnborough, and No. 2 Company, equipped with heavier-than-air machines, based at Larkhill on Salisbury Plain. Fear of Germany's plans for the future and the ever increasing sums of money which she was expending on military aviation, led the British government at last to set up a committee to investigate the position of military flying in Britain which, after careful deliberations, published its findings in February, 1912. The most important of its proposals was that a 'Flying Corps' should be established by the amalgamation of those units of the Army and the Navy which were already 'dabbling' in flying. The new corps was to have five sections; a Military Wing, a Naval Wing, a Reserve, a Central Flying School (at Upavon) and an Aircraft Factory (at Farnborough) with the latter being responsible for the design, development and manufacture of machines for the entire Corps. With a speed almost unprecedented in official circles the recommendations were accepted and, within one month, the Corps was granted the Royal Warrant (allowing its name to be prefixed with 'Royal') and had come into being on 13 May, 1912.

Initially, the Royal Flying Corps (RFC) was to have a strength of seven squadrons each of which would have twelve aeroplanes with two pilots for each machine. The total establishment for the Corps was to be 364 pilots of which half would be commissioned officers. In addition, the Central Flying School would have a further twelve officers and sixty-six NCOs and men who would be responsible for training a total of 180 pilots each year. After training, the pilots would serve in either the Military or Naval Wings. The first Commanding Officer of the new force was Captain (Temporary Major) Frederick H Sykes of the 15th Hussars [1].

Although the government had clearly stipulated that

both Naval and Military flying was to be developed within the framework of the new corps, the Royal Navy very quickly began to show their independence and, after only a few months, they adopted the title Royal Naval Air Service (RNAS) which was accepted as the official title of a seperate unit in the summer of 1914.

In September 1912, the army held its first manoeuvres in which the RFC was invited to participate and, despite being under very close scrutiny, the aviators acquitted themselves well and the success of the winning side was due in no small measure to the invaluable information supplied to its staff officers by the reconnaissance pilots. A War Office memorandum issued afterwards stated:

> "There can no longer be any doubt as to the value of airships and aeroplanes in locating an enemy on land and obtaining information which would otherwise only be obtained by force."

At the end of the year, the War Office declared its support for the expansion of the RFC and actively encouraged officers already serving with other units to learn to fly and, if necessary, to transfer to the RFC. One such officer was Lieutenant Lionel Rees on home leave from West Africa.

The governing body of British flying was the Royal Aero Club and it was this organisation that supervised all initial flying training, both civil and military, and issued the certificate which indicated an individual's competence at controlling a flying machine. These courses cost the budding aviator about £70 - £80, which if they passed and were accepted for service with the RFC, was fully refundable. If they failed the government had been put to no unnecessary expense! On 7 January, Rees was awarded the Royal Aero Club Certificate No. 392 after successfully completing a course of instruction at the Bristol School at Larkhill. It was an event which, although of little apparent importance at the time, was to have a profound effect upon his life.

Although qualified as a civilian pilot, Rees did not go on to complete his training at the Central Flying School and thereby gain entry into the RFC. Instead, he served for two months in the Adjutant's Department at the School of Gunnery before, once again, being posted to the tropics on secondment to the Nigeria Regiment, West African Frontier Force. Whether this was from choice or because there were no vacancies at the Central Flying School or because the Royal Artillery would not release him is unrecorded and he remained in Nigeria until the following summer when he again returned to Britain. During this leave Britain went to war with Germany and, after eleven years of peacetime soldiering Rees saw the opportunity of active service and immediately volunteered for the RFC. The novelty of flying appealed to his sense of adventure and, if he was accepted and the Corps expanded, his opportunities for promotion would be greatly enhanced. His application was accepted, subject to the proviso that his flying abilities met the standards laid down by the RFC and so, on 10 August, 1914, he commenced the short five week course at the Central Flying School which would qualify him to serve as a military pilot. He completed the course early and on 12 September, was awarded Certificate No. 221 and was imediately seconded to the RFC as a Flying Officer with No. 7 Squadron. He later recalled:

"Everybody was most anxious to get to the front, as all our friends were there, and we did not like being left in England. Looking back it is very funny to remember how we tried to get all the flying we could and how we called people who had even a few more minutes flying than ourselves, 'Air Hogs'. After about four weeks we were all split up, some of us going to the front - lucky men - others remaining as instructors and others, amongst whom I found myself, being posted to reserve squadrons.

When we joined these squadrons we had done very little cross-country flying. On the first morning, I was sent to land on another aerodrome. Having done this fairly successfully I thought I had now really become an aviator. On the way back, I had trouble with my engine control and eventually my engine stopped at a height of 6,000 feet. Knowing nothing of the difficulty of judging a long, straight glide, I thought I could just reach my aerodrome and came in over the sheds with about a foot to spare. On landing, instead of being congratulated on my judgement as I had expected, my Flight Commander said "Don't ever risk your machine again in that manner."

This altered my outlook on aviation and in future I never risked my machine again."

The British Expeditionary Force (BEF) had begun its embarkation for France on 9 August and, two days later, the Headquarters of the RFC had left Farnborough en route for Amiens which it reached on the 13th. On the same day, Nos. 2 and 3 Squadrons and two flights of No. 4 Squadron flew the Channel from Dover and were joined at Amiens by No. 5 Squadron two days later, the whole force being under the command of Brigadier General Sir David Henderson, KCB, DSO [2].

The RFCs front-line strength was sixty-three machines which were armed with neither bomb nor gun, all being intended for purely reconnaissance work. However, it was only a matter of days before individual pilots and observers began to carry rifles (which were stripped down to reduce their weight) and pistols with them on patrol with a view to discouraging any enemy machine which they might chance across. Inexperienced though they were, the pioneers of British aerial power very quickly began to build up a reputation to be proud of and in his despatch dated 7 September, the Commander-in-Chief of the BEF Sir John French stated:

"I wish particularly to bring to your Lordship's notice the admirable work done by the Royal Flying Corps ... their skill, energy and perseverance have been beyond all praise. They have furnished me with the most complete and accurate information, which has been of incalculable value to the conduct of operations. Fired at constantly by both friend and foe, and not hesitating to fly in any kind of weather, they have remained undaunted throughout. Further, by actually fighting in the air, they have succeeded in destroying five enemy machines."

By early October, the hard pressed units of the RFC already in France were desperately in need of reinforcement and No. 6 Squadron, equipped with 6 BE2s, 2 BE8s and 4 Henri Farmans, was ordered at very short notice to Belgium where it was to assist in the attempt to relieve Antwerp. Due to the haste with which the squadron went overseas and its remoteness from the remainder of the RFC, its Commanding Officer, Major Becke, soon found himself in difficulties regarding spares and supplies and he therefore wrote to the Officer Commanding RFC Military Wing at Farnborough requesting materials. As a consequence of this, Rees received the following order dated 11 October, 1914:

"To Lieutenant Rees.
You and No.97 Sergeant H Austin and No. 1346 2/A.M. J Hunnisett, will entrain at North Camp, South Eastern Station, at 7-13 am on Monday, the 12th instant, en route for Folkestone and _____ . On arrival at North Camp Station you will ensure that the truck containing the stores for No.6 Squadron is put on the train. You will also see that when you change at Redhill and

Tonbridge that the truck accompanies you. You will arrive at Folkestone Harbour at 11-9 am where you will report to the Embarkation Staff Officer and hand in your permits and embark with the stores. On arrival at _____ you will ascertain where No.6 Squadron is, and deliver over to the Officer Commanding No.6 RFC or an officer of No. 6 Squadron, the stores you have brought. You will find out from him what other stores he requires, and return with Sergeant Austin and with the list.

You will leave 2/A.M. Hunnisett with No. 6 Squadron. Before leaving you will endeavour to find a suitable place for an Aircraft Park. You will then return to England with all possible speed."

To Belgium went the following message:

"I propose to start a small Aircraft Park mainly with a view to supplying you in the field. Lieutenant Rees and Sergeant Austin will probably form nucleus. It will consist of Motor Repair Lorry and Flight Repair Lorry with most of the stores to keep you a month in the field. This will form your A.P. Stores."

Rees and his companions embarked from Folkestone on the afternoon of 12 October, bound for Ostend. It was not the glamorous entry into the war that he had hoped for, arriving at the front in command of a truck with one sergeant and one air mechanic and with orders to return to England "... with all possible speed". It was however, better than remaining at South Farnborough as who knew what might transpire once he was across the Channel !

No. 6 Squadron was located on a cycle racing track near the sea front at Ostend from where the pilots were flying some seventy miles north-east to obtain reports on the deteriorating situation at Antwerp. No sooner had Rees arrived at Ostend Harbour than he was advised to re-embark for England as the Germans had broken through and it would only be a matter of hours before they were in Ostend. Undeterred, he managed to reach the squadron and made arrangements for the stores to be delivered from the docks before settling down for the night, rolled in a blanket on the race track pavillion floor "... at least I was in France [sic] and the Germans were only a few inches away."

The following morning, reconnaissance patrols were sent up to locate the advancing enemy forces but, despite perfect visibility, no sightings were made but in view of the increasing danger of the squadron being overrun, it was decided to move the airfield further down the coast the next morning.

" Next morning all the machines flew back to Dunkirk. One machine had engine trouble and we saw it disappearing down the main street at Ostend. We sent a light tender after it and found it had managed to reach the water and there it was with the tide rising round it. We took out the engine and instruments and then burnt the machine so the Huns could not use it. [3]

Shortly before the squadron started away from Ostend a funny old Taube appeared. Everybody started firing at it except ourselves, who were armed only with revolvers, although the machine was clearly out of range. It was at a great height ! - we thought so then - it must have been 5,000 feet up.

Although I was in the Royal Flying Corps I had never seen the Corps on the move before and I was greatly taken by the way all vehicles were lined up, ready for the road. On a certain whistle sound all the men fell in and the sergeant major made certain that everything was left clean and that nothing had been left behind. At the next whistle sound, everybody got aboard his allotted vehicle and then we started.

The road was lined with troops going both ways and with refugees from Ostend. We left the race-course at noon, and the Germans came in at 4 pm ... I was given a seat on a light tender and travelled that way for the next few days."

As he was supernumerary and therefore without his own aeroplane, Rees' activities during the retreat from

Belgium were officially confined to the ground, and he busied himself by serving as quartermaster to the squadron. It was quite obvious that it was impossible for him to establish an aircraft park until the situation stabilised and the squadron found a more permanent home; he therefore interpreted his orders as being to remain with No. 6 Squadron.

After one day at Dunkirk they were on the move again and six machines and a large number of personnel and vehicles left immediately for Ypres and Poperinghe. The remaining officers (Rees amongst them), NCOs and men, along with three machines and several vehicles remained at Dunkirk until the following morning when they moved to Boulogne. It was at this time that Rees made his first war patrol as an observer but, as it was not an officially sanctioned flight, no documentation exists to pinpoint the date or the pilot's name. Indeed, the only reference to it is in a note made by Rees himself:

"I was taken up as an observer over the lines and saw all the villages burning as the Huns advanced and all the little bits of trenches here and there. The machines we flew then were slow and bad climbers, and the pilots did not like anyone wearing a heavy coat."

During the third week of October, the activity in No. 6 Sqaudron intensified as more and more patrols were mounted to try and ascertain the exact location of the front line and the logistical situation behind the German front.

On 20 October, Rees arrived at Poperinghe in command of the squadron transport which had been left at Boulogne. No sooner had they arrived than the squadron received orders to hold itself in readiness to move to RFC Headquarters at St Omer as soon as it was relieved by No. 4 Squadron which event occurred the next day. For Rees, this was the end of his sojourn at the front as there was no longer any need of a separate aircraft park for No. 6 Sqaudron which had now joined the main RFC force and, on 22 October, he embarked for England where he rejoined his unit.

No. 7 Squadron had originally been formed at Farnborough in May 1914 under the command of Major J M Salmond [4] but had been broken up three months later in order that other, more senior units could be brought up to full strength before embarking with the BEF. Its formation had resumed on 24 September and when Rees rejoined in October it was well on the way to becoming a fully operational squadron. His days with No. 7, however, were limited as, on the last day of the month, after nearly eight years as a Lieutenant, he was promoted to the rank of Captain which meant that he was eligable for the command of a Flight and, as none was available in the squadron, he could expect a further posting in the near future.

Fears of German air-raids on Britain had prompted the authorities to station aircraft around London, more in an attempt to placate public opinion than as a serious attempt to either deter or destroy the enemy. The main effort in this defensive plan was the responsibility of the RNAS who had units of both land and sea planes based in the Thames estuary and in Kent. The RFC was however, given its part to play in the scheme with units at Hounslow and Joyce Green [5].

" In the event of an aerial attack on London the Officers on duty at the two bases will be informed, and they will take steps to attack the hostile aircraft.

The OC South Farnborough, will also be informed in order that he may prepare to despatch re-inforcements from other squadrons."

The plan was that two machines would be flown to Hounslow and another two to Joyce Green each evening and remain there until morning when they would be flown back to South Farnborough but, by mid-November, the fact that no such air attacks had been carried out by the Germans prompted the War Office to withdraw the four RFC machines at Hounslow and Joyce Green. This decision was too precipitated and, on 21 December at 1 pm, an enemy seaplane crossed the Kent coast and dropped two 20lb bombs into the sea near Dover Pier. Three days later, a Taube dropped one bomb near Dover Castle but, with the exception of a few shattered windows, there was no real damage caused. In both instances, the raiders were well on their way home before any defending aircraft could take off and attempt an interception. Fearing further attacks, the RNAS set up standing patrols in the Dover area and the RFC resumed the stationing of machines at Hounslow and Joyce Green, The first RNAS patrol took off at 8 am on 25 December but the next German raider made landfall further north, a little over four hours later.

At 12.20 pm, just as the unwary population of SE England began to settle down for their first festive lunch of the war, a Friedrichshafen seaplane was seen crossing over Sheerness in the Thames estuary at a height of about 7,000 feet. Several anti-aircraft batteries opened fire but to no avail. From Eastchurch on the Isle of Sheppey and Grain on the north side of the Medway, two RNAS machines took off but failed to catch the intruder which reduced its height to about 4,000 feet and continued on its course westwards over Gravesend, Tilbury and Dartford. Ahead of it went telephone messages and the War Office ordered machines up from Joyce Green, Farnborough and Brooklands in the hope that one of them might be able to intercept the German as he turned for home.

The German pilot, Oberleutnant-zur-see Stephan Prondzynski, having reached the London sunburb of Erith near Bexley and no doubt feeling that he had chanced his arm far enough, decided to reverse his course and begin the long journey home. By this time, the air defences, such as they were, were fully alerted and anti-aircraft batteries at Cliffe Fort opened fire and, either in an attempt to lighten his load and increase speed or out of sheer awkwardness, the German dropped two bombs on Cliffe Station, fortunately causing little significant damage. At Farnborough, Rees was one of the pilots ordered to attempt an interception.

" I was fog-bound at Farnborough [and] . . . had great difficulty in obtaining any alcohol on Christmas Day as none of the public houses would sell me any. Eventually, I managed to get a bottle of gin which I put in the water jacket of my gun to prevent the water freezing.

The pilot of one of our machines was adjusting the controls of his machine when suddenly the raider appeared over the aerodrome [Joyce Green]. The pilot and mechanic immediately jumped aboard, the gunner [6] gave them a gun, somebody started the engine, and away they went. Both the raider and our machine were fired on by the anti-aircraft guns all the way down the Thames. The machines exchanged shots, and chips were seen to fly off the raider. Unfortunately, the gunner's hands got frost bitten and he could no longer work the gun, so our machine had to return and allow the raider to escape. I believe the machine failed to reach Germany." [7]

Insult was later added to injury when an old Thames

barger, on seeing the British aircraft approaching the airfield, dived into his cabin and re-appeared with a duck gun with which he promptly opened fire. Fortunately, he did no damage, other than to the pilot's ego, and the Vickers made a safe landing. Indeed, squadrons defending the capital were always in greater danger of sustaining casualties from flying accidents than they were from enemy action and Rees later recorded two such incidents which happened to members of No. 7 Squadron during that first winter of trial and error.

" One machine went up over London and saw the lights [of the city] 4,000 feet down. The pilot ran into a rain cloud and very shortly afterwards, the lights of London were above him - the aneroid showed forty feet only. Chimneys loomed up in front and the pilot turned sharply and crashed into a bank. He took his electric torch out of his pocket and looked at the observer's seat, only to find him gone. On searching round the machine he suddenly saw the observer sitting on the ground with an enormous Zep. bomb under each arm.

A second machine went up, directly the pilot and observer were out of sight of the aerodrome, the engine failed. The machine made for the Thames or rather for where they thought the river ought to be, and hit the marshes on the bank. The machine crashed in a ditch which had in it about one foot of water. Again the observer was missing from his seat, and was seen lying on his back in one foot of water apparently swimming.

'Is the water deep ?' asked the pilot.

'Seven feet deep and no bottom' replied the observer, who went on kicking hard. "

Rees, like his fellow pilots had no success in intercepting any German raiders but he did manage to equal their record for accidents when he made his first crash-landing as a result of his engine stopping "with a bang" whilst flying over the Kent countryside early in 1915. Looking round he saw that he was over what appeared to be a heavily wooded area and then he spotted one large, clear field. With difficulty he made his approach and touched down on the ground which was partly covered with snow. As the Vickers rolled over the surface, he saw an elderly lady watching his progress from behind a fence which was directly ahead of him and in the path of the machine. As he was heading straight towards her and the machine had no brakes, he was compelled to take avoiding action by turning quickly. This caused two tyres to come off the wheels of his undercarriage which resulted in the machine tipping up and coming to a halt with its nose in the ground. Unhurt, Rees climbed out of the cockpit and went to apologise to the spectator. Before he could say anything she called out that he had done remarkably well as she thought he was going to run into her. Despite this vision of impending doom hurtling towards her, the lady had made no attempt to move away, believing implicitly in Rees' skill as a pilot. Such is the faith engendered by blissful ignorance.

In February 1915, Rees was posted to take command of a flight in a new squadron about to be formed at Netheravon, Wiltshire and rumour had it that this new unit was destined for France. At last, he was legitimately en route for the front, it was now only a question of time.

CHAPTER III
No. 11 Squadron, RFC
(1915)

The new aggressive style of aerial warfare which made its appearance over the Western front during the latter days of 1914 and for which the RFC airmen were probably more responsible than the Germans, demanded the creation of a new type of unit. The result was No. 11 Squadron, the RFC's first fighter squadron, officially formed on 14 February 1915, to which Rees was posted as its very first officer. Arriving at Netheravon, a brick-built former cavalry camp on Salisbury Plain, he became the RFC's first officially recognised 'fighter pilot', the forerunner of an elite group of combatants who were to carve a special niche in the public's affection in two world wars. He was given command of 'A' Flight and was joined by Captain 'Pip' Playfair (commanding 'B' Flight) [1] and Captain C C Darley (commanding 'C' Flight). Command of the squadron was given to Major A G Board [2].

Originally equipped with the Bristol Scout D and Vickers Bullet D, No. 11 Squadron was quickly re-equipped with Geoffrey de Havilland's Vickers Fighting Biplane, designated the FB5 and commonly referred to as the 'Gunbus', a strongly constructed two-seater machine powered by a 100 hp Gnome Monosoupape pusher engine. The positioning of the engine in the rear of the aircraft gave the observer, who sat in the forward cockpit, a clear field of fire for his single, stripped .303 Lewis machine-gun. In addition, the crew carried one stripped Lee Enfield rifle, two revolvers and up to four Hale's hand grenades. Despite its maximum speed, in level flight, of only 65 - 70 mph, the FB5 was seen as a formidable fighting machine.

A J Insall, who joined the squadron as an observer recalled [3]:

" ... the VFB had no vices, and it is doubtful whether anybody ever killed himself in one; if he did, it must have been extremely merited ... the Vickers Fighter was a wonderful aeroplane." [4]

Both pilot and observer were fully exposed to the elements and, in the back of their minds must have been the thought that, if they should be forced to land, the engine positioned behind them had an unpleasant habit of breaking loose and crushing the trapped crew.

"It was bitterly cold there, huddled up and entirely passive, with scarcely more protection from the wind of our own making than that afforded to a ship's figurehead facing an Arctic gale, and my hands and feet ... lost all sense of feeling, while my knees were just solid areas of bent leg. Elsewhere, circulation was normal and the mediocre amount of movement the confines of my cell allowed me was all I needed to make life bearable."[5]

The Vickers took 16 minutes to climb to 5,000 feet and could, if the headwind was strong enough, find forward progress impossible. It was even known to fly backwards, an extremely uncomfortable sensation at any time but particularly so when operating on the wrong side of the front line !

No. 11 was brought up to full strength in aircrew, ground staff and equipment, a total of 157 personnel,

thirty-two motor vehicles and six motor c[...] and [...]
commenced a period of intensive training [...] was to
last until July. When King George V visi[...] the Central
Flying School at nearby Upavon on 23 [...] 1915, the
squadron was decreed to be in a state of sufficient
readiness to participate in the proceedings and
consequently, six machines landed at the CFS where they
were inspected by the King and, when he left by car to
journey to Bulford, they took off to provide an aerial
escort, probably the first in history. What transpired
however, was not quite in accordance with the plans that
had been carefully drawn up. Lieutenant Ditchfield
recalled:

"I'm afraid it was a ragged escort as our engines had the habit of
koncking [sic] out frequently or missing on half the cylinders which
meant we could not keep together (I won't say in formation) and
three of the six had to break off and go home."[6]

An inauspicious start to the squadron's public service
but the problems with the Monosoupape engine were
legendary and they were certainly not solved before the
pilots went on active service. Manufactured by the
Seguin brothers in Paris the engine was ideal in theory
and, for its day, was rated as a high performance engine
and revolutionary in its design but, under the stress of
regular use, it developed a tendency to fail at the most
awkward moments. Part of the problem was the
inexperience of the maintenance crews who had to
service the engine under the most difficult and primitive
conditions. Throughout its service career, it never lost its
reputation for unreliability.

A few weeks after the embarrassment of the Royal
escort, the same six machines flew cross-country to

Oxford where they landed without incident; the greatest threat on that occasion coming from the civilian population who turned out to greet them and who threatened to destroy the machines in their desire for souvenirs. As their efficiency improved, the day drew ever closer when the squadron would be sent to France.

Although officially on record as being present on the Western Front from 25 July 1915, the bulk of No. 11 Squadron did not leave Netheravon until Sunday, 27 July, taking off at 6.55 am and flying at a height of 4,500 feet to Folkestone where, two hours later, only six of the twelve machines landed; the 'jinxed' engines having caused the others to make forced landings. Later the same day, the survivors left England enroute for the British Army Headquarters at St Omer, France but again the unpredictable engines took their toll and only two machines reached their destination. Fortunately, this disasterous crossing had not resulted in any injuries to either men or machines and it was felt that a delay of two days would enable the stragglers to catch up. Rees, with his brief experience of active service, was sent on ahead (accompanied by E Batten, an Air Mechanic) to prepare for the squadron's arrival at Vert Galant [7], south of Doullens. He however, was not exempted from the engine trouble which had plagued the remainder of the squadron and, as he flew south, he had to make a forced landing near Fruges where hasty repairs were carried out. Taking off again he was forced to make a second landing at Beauval where the aircraft's skids became entangled in some corn which pitched it forward onto its nose. Although both skids were broken, neither Rees nor Batten received any injury and they were able to continue their journey after temporary repairs had been effected.

Third time lucky, they reached Vert Galant without further incident. After making arrangements with the OC No. 4 Squadron (who were then the occupants of the airfield) for the allocation of quarters for No. 11 Squadron, Rees joined Batten and assisted in the repairing of the Vickers.

The following morning, as the ground crews and some of the observers arrived from St Omer, Rees took off and headed eastwards. Having climbed to his patrol height, he spotted a British reconnaissance machine returning from a mission with a Fokker monoplane climbing beneath its tail. Rees flew as fast as he could and managed to position himself behind the German where, although still out of effective range, his observer opened fire in an attempt to warn the unsuspecting British pilot of the danger and also in the hope that he might distract the German pilot. The tactic worked and the Fokker turned to confront the Vickers whereupon Rees dived into the attack, thinking that he had an easy target. Suddenly, the German opened fire from a gun fixed to fire forwards, taking him completely by surprise, breaking one of the main spars and piercing another. Despite the fact that he fully expected the wing to collapse at any moment, Rees made no attempt to break away in order that his observer could open fire. The German was hit and suddenly the monoplane dived, almost vertically, through the clouds. As he could not hope to follow, Rees turned for home where later that day, a report arrived to the effect that a German monoplane had been seen to crash behind the enemy lines.

When No. 11 Squadron landed at Vert Galant on the morning of 29 July, they found their "... senior Flight Commander ... covered in oil and happy as Larry,

41

working like a navvy on his machine, which had already collected a sprinkling of scars from a scrap."[8] Thus, the tone of the squadron was established, earning Rees the honour of being the first fighter pilot to take part in an aerial combat and destroy an enemy machine, a fact that came as no surprise to the junior members of the squadron. His experience and age had already made him the focus of attention and this, coupled with his aggressive philosophy of "When you see the Hun, go for him" had enhanced his reputation long before their departure from Netheravon. Insall recalled:

"L W B Rees had a tremendous influence on the RFC, in the way that in other squadrons Lanoe Hawker VC, Harvey-Kelly and Lewis to name three only out of three score, had, and in our case Rees' mantle fell first on H A Cooper, and from Cooper's shoulders on to those of Ball. Had L W B Rees been a few years younger. Captain Rees was one of those rare men who are born leaders, who never flap, and who believe essentially in precept - and who never despise the novice. Rees it was, also, who taught us in No. 11 Squadron that our cardinal rule of behaviour on the battlefront must always adhere to the Flying Corps' watchword: 'Go in to the attack ! Whenever you see the Hun, no matter where he is, be he alone or accompanied, go for him, and shoot him down.' Of commanding appearance and stature, possessed, I should say, of the most captivating eye-twinkle of any officer whom I can recall, Rees was respected and liked by all those who came into contact with him. I was never in his flight, and yet I never passed him by without receiving some smiling acknowledgement of my existence."[9]

The squadron had arrived in France under the command of Major G W P Dawes [10] "...a quite well known character and well versed in the art of keeping his Squadron's nose a little bit ahead of the next one's." Undoubtedly, a man of exceptional talents in command of a group of gifted individuals, he recognised that the untried role of a fighter squadron was different to anything experienced by any other unit which had served in France up to that date. He therefore permitted his officers a degree of flexibility as they struggled to establish a style of their own. Such a style of command suited Rees as he set about putting his training, experience and theories into practice. The men under Dawes' command were pioneers in aerial warfare who, if successful, would show the way for others to follow in the weeks and months to come. Errors would undoubtedly be made and some might have to pay a heavy price for the experience gained but, in making such mistakes, valuable lessons would be learned for the future.

The squadron had already lost members in fatal accidents whilst training at Netheravon but such events were accepted as an occupational hazard of flying. Accidents were expected as were losses in combat but it was hard to accept those losses which could easily have been avoided, forced upon the individuals concerned by an apparently mindless military hierarchy who had little knowledge or understanding of flying. Lieutenant Ditchfield recalled, nearly forty years later, one particularly unfortunate death:

"One day ... a dense fog settled over our drome at Vert Gallant (sic) visibility 20 yards, Major Dawes received a phone message from headquarters (where possibly the sun was shining) ordering him to despatch a plane at once over the line as Jerry machines had been reported. He explained to headquarters that flying was impossible in such conditions only to have his head snapped off, telling him to damn well obey orders and kill one of his pilots OR ruin his [own] career . He obeyed orders as one is taught to do and the young second lieutenant that he chose did likewise knowing he was going to his death.

We watched him rev up and start forward into the fog and we
heard him die 200 yards away. What a waste !"[11]

Vert Galant was an established airfield, situated on
the main Amiens to Doullens road which cut through the
centre of the aerodrome. Administration and quarters
were centred around a number of farm buildings and,
although some servicemen had a roof over their heads,
most were accommodated in bell-tents. By no stretch of
the imagination could the airfield be regarded as
luxurious for either men or machines. No. 4 Squadron
(who left for Baizieux shortly after the arrival of No.11)
had not cut the grass and the canvas hangers left much to
be desired. There was barely enough room to land safely
and then only if the pilot made a good landing and the
clover was wet enough to slow the machine down before
it ran downhill, without brakes, towards the sheds.

The squadron's role was to provide "...aggressively
defensive patrols over the 3rd Army Front, from Bary-
sur-Somme to Gommecourt, and using hand-held wooden
cameras, provide aerial photographs of the front and rear
of the German lines." In addition, they were to act as
escorts for the BE2 squadrons, mount reconnaissance
patrols behind enemy lines and serve as artillery
observers.

They set to work almost immediately and soon the
sight of FB5s, with a Lewis gun protruding from their
nascelles was sufficient cause for most enemy machines
that ventured across the lines to dive eastwards for safety.
Rees recalled:

"The Huns hated the type of machine I was flying at this time.
They hardly ever attacked us at odds of less than four to one. If there
were two of our machines together, we scarcely ever got attacked at

all."

Consequently, drawing the German pilots into combat became a matter of cunning as each pilot tried out different methods to ensnare his opponent. One particularly successful ploy was to turn away from any German machine which might cross the lines (the German pilots were under instruction not to cross over the front line) and attempt to lure him westwards. If he took the bait the FB5s would very gradually turn until they were facing east when, at the last moment, they would turn and attack, making the Germans the prey instead of the hunter. The enemy pilot could then either retreat (which meant flying further over the British lines) or accept combat in an attempt to return to his own side of the front. If the Vickers had the advantage of height, the chances of a successful outcome to the combat were greatly increased. On one occasion, the squadron decided to set a trap for the enemy deep behind the German front line:

"The machines found it so hard to catch the Huns that one day we arranged a Hun drive. Two of us went and sat over a Hun aerodrome while the rest of the squadron drove from the north and from the south. We did this towards evening, so that the Huns would be sure to go straight to the aerodrome, and not try to escape. My machine exchanged shots with three Huns but they were diving home so fast when they passed that we did not get them."

Dog-fights, as the swirling aerial combats of the latter part of the war came to be known, were rare events in 1915 and indeed, the name had yet to be coined. Most fights were short, sharp affairs but No.11 Squadron slowly began to build up its score of destroyed enemy machines and acquired a reputation as a highly aggressive unit.

" Far into 1916, German aviators shot down in our lines, when asked for their remarks on their capture, almost invariably replied that they had been brought down by a Vickers." [12]

Rees was constantly involved in the operations carried out by the squadron during the summer and early autumn of 1915 and his reputation continued to grow. These were not the days of high scoring 'aces' who became household names in 1917 and 1918. To achieve the aerial destruction of an enemy machine was exceptional due to the limitations of the aircraft in service at that time and, in terms of performance, the FB5 was outclassed by many aircraft, including some of the two-seaters which it was meant to protect. If however, an enemy machine could be drawn into combat, a skilled pilot could achieve success.

On 1 August, Rees, accompanied by Lieutenant Lane as his observer, encountered a hostile machine and twice attempted to attack it. On both occasions, the German refused to be drawn into a fight and eventually dived for the ground with the apparent intention of landing. Rees however, flew so close behind him that the pilot found himself flying too fast to be able to get into any of the fields and a low-level chase ensued, so low that they had to increase height to clear even the smallest of trees.

" This went on for some miles, and was quite one of the most amusing days I have had. We were low, and low flying was all new, that nobody shot at us for a long time. One could see all the sentries on the cross roads looking up and wondering who we were and what we were doing. By the time they had decided we were the enemy, we were out of range. One Archie battery opened fire on us, but the shells were set at 3,000 feet, so we did not worry much. Eventually, this Hun got away."

Rees' next combat took place on 31 August when flying at about 7,000 feet between Bucquoy and Bapaume and accompanied by Flight Sergeant Hargreaves, he came across a two-seater LVG, a much faster machine than the Vickers. The German pilot decided to stay and fight and throttled back to allow Rees to catch him. When the British plane had closed to about 200 yards the German observer opened fire with an automatic rifle. Hargreaves returned the fire but, before he could achieve any hits on the enemy, the pilot increased his speed and pulled away out of range. This cat and mouse game continued for about forty-five minutes and the two observers opened fire on each other about five or six times before Hargreaves discovered that he had fired off all four drums and was out of ammunition. Rees then broke away and headed back for Vert Galant. As he landed, despite the noise of his engine, he could be heard shouting for more ammunition. Without switching off his engine he took off again and began the slow climb back towards his patrol area. Near the same spot, he found the German machine flying about 1,000 feet below. Rees immediately dived and Hargreaves fired one drum of forty-seven rounds. The German reacted quickly and dived for the clouds. The steep angle of Rees' dive caused the petrol in the Vickers to run to the top of the tank and his engine stopped. Unable to follow the German machine, Rees then set a course for home. This second combat was witnesed by another machine from No. 11 Squadron, crewed by 2nd Lieutenant H A Cooper and A J Insall who were patrolling near Achiet-le-Petit. They saw the German break through the cloud and fall in spirals and irregular 'S' turns, apparently badly hit, before he again disappeared from view. Ground reports later stated that an enemy machine had been seen crashing.

During the summer of 1915, the British High Command had begun their preparations for a major assault on the enemy in an attempt to break the stalemate on the Western Front. The war was one year old and the casualty returns had long since assumed horrific proportions but there seemed to be no alternative to the slogging match which had typified the conflict since the advent of trench warfare. Marshal Joffre, the French Commander-in-Chief, was convinced that a combined assault by his forces in the region of Len-Arras and Champagne and by the British forces in the La Bassee-Loos area, could bring success because, once the front line had been broken, the Germans would be unable to halt the Allied advance.

On paper, the plan seemed highly feasible but in practice it was doomed to fail primarily because of the lack of artillery in the British sector and also because of the open nature of the landscape around Loos. The attack was scheduled to commence with a 96 hour bombardment of the German trenches and, in order to achieve the maximum effect with the limited reources available, the British preparations called for regular, detailed aerial photography of the German front and reserve lines to ensure that any changes to the defences were recorded and dealt with by the artillery. The battlefield covered an area of gentle chalk slopes which meant that any excavation, be it trenches or mines (of which there were a number in the area), was easily visible from the air and showed up clearly in a photograph. In addition to the main area of the battlefield, photographic missions were also mounted over other sections of the front in an effort to confuse the enemy. These missions also ensured that there were no significant changes which might indicate that the Allied plans had been discovered and that no German forces were moved in anticipation of the assault.

On the morning of 21 September, four days before the commencement of the battle, Rees, accompanied by Hargreaves, was ordered to fly a mission to photograph the German front line trenches between Peronne and Esterre [13]. The machine was fully prepared and Hargreaves carefully stowed away the camera and its eighteen glass plates. The FB5 then took off and made its way, without incident, to the Peronne end of the target area. Hargreaves later recorded his memories of the mission:

"I arranged with the pilot that we should patrol the lines twice to enable me to work out the central objectives of each succeeding photograph. Naturally for the first picture I was all ready and set, hanging over the front just waiting to reach the perpendicular line over the pre-arranged objective. This successfully accomplished, I quickly reloaded and just managed to get over in time to take the second objective.

By the time I had performed the changing of the plates etc., and got over the front again, I found that we had overshot our third objective. Without hesitation, I knelt up and swung my head round in a circular manner to indicate to my pilot that we had gone too far. To my great satisfaction he immediately heeled over and retraced our path, so that I had ample time to pick up my third objective. This operation had to be repeated several times but without any prearrangement my pilot grasped the situation perfectly.

Our third trip along the line brought us hundreds of greetings from our friends, the 'Archies' [14]. Their efforts were persistent and fairly accurate.

Much credit was due to the masterly art of piloting by Captain Rees, who performed all sorts of misleading evolutions to the watchful eyes of 'Archies' attendants.

Without hitch or hindrance, we shot every plate successfully. Before commencing operations each plate was numbered and arranged so that numbers 1,2,3 etc., should correspond exactly to that particular section on the country below, but in spite of the careful survey of equipment before leaving the aerodrome I found that after the first exposure, I had forgotten to hang up an empty bag to receive them when I had finished. Having no recepticle to receive them I was compelled to place them on the floor of the machine in front of me. This caused me considerable inconvenience when getting over the front again; I had to keep pushing them forward away from my knees. Just after completion and before I had time to collect the scattered plates from the floor of the nascelle, Captain Rees drew my attention to a machine coming up from the German lines with the obvious intention of pushing us off or at least shaking our morale. My pilot immediately switched his engine off and glided down towards the German machine. After dropping some 2,000 feet we were slightly above it and about 200 yards apart; we could clearly see that she was a new bus and vastly different from anything we had encountered before. The arrangement of the two fuselages with tractor screws and a nascelle with a propellor behind gave them an excellent distribution of gun power of which I believe they had three - one forward and two aft."

It is generally accepted that this machine was almost certainly an AGO, a two-seater, single-engined 'pusher' machine which made its first appearance during the summer of 1915. It is however, of interest to note that Rees in his combat report also declared that the machine which they encountered had at least two engines. From this date onwards, the type was regularly encountered by the machines of No. 11 Squadron and were always referred to as 'Two-Tails'; there is no record of any member of the squadron identifying them as AGOs either at that time or later.

Hargreaves held his fire until the enemy machine was well within range. The German machine had the advantage of speed and, as the two aircraft began to circle each other, he took the outer circular course. As Rees came alongside, the German observer fired bursts of about 50 rounds, reputedly from two guns, at a range of between 100 and 200 yards but failed to hit the Vickers. At a height of about 7,000 feet and with the range closing, Hargreaves fired off half a drum which seemed to have caused some vital damage as the enemy pilot immediately began to stall and spin before regaining control and putting the machine into a glide and heading back towards his base. He was later seen to crash whilst trying to make a forced landing near Herbecourt.

Climbing again, Rees continued to patrol the area, challenging any other enemy pilot who might wish to try and drive him down. The sky remained empty and eventually he headed for home where he safely delivered the photographic plates.

Later that same day, again accompanied by Hargreaves, Rees took off to patrol the area south-east of Albert. At about 5.30 pm, they spotted an Albatros two-seater flying at about 2,000 feet above Le Sars. Without hesitation, Rees made his attack. Bullets from Hargreaves' gun were seen to strike the German machine which immediately dived at a very steep angle with his engine on full power. Rees estimated that the German was flying at 150 mph and as he was unable to follow, he discontinued the action. As there were no reports received about the eventual fate of the Albatros, no claim was made.

When the photographic plates taken by Rees and Hargreaves that morning were developed, their accuracy and clarity led to high praise from 3rd Army Headquarters. They declared them to be "... the finest series of photographs ever taken in France to that date." This, coupled with the destruction of a more heavily armed opponent, led to the award of the Distinguished Conduct Medal to Flight Sergeant Hargreaves. For his actions on that day and for the aggressive nature of his activities since the arrival of No. 11 Squadron in France, Captain Lionel Rees was awarded the Military Cross.[17]

Nine days later, the successful partnership of Rees and Hargreaves attacked an Albatros near Gommecourt, emptying a full drum of ammunition at the enemy machine. The German pilot dived towards a cloud and Rees followed. Hargreaves fired off a second drum and the enemy machine began to spiral and nose dive. Anti-aircraft guns then began to fire and the Albatros received a hit in its starboard wing which was seen to break away at about a height of 5,000 feet. The fate of the two German airmen was sealed and the wreckage was seen to hit the ground on the British side of the front line. Upon investigation of the bodies, it was discovered that the pilot had been hit in the head by a machine-gun bullet and was therefore dead before the artillery fire destroyed his machine. The credit for bringing the Albatros down was therefore given to Rees and Hargreaves.

Not all combats were so clear-cut in their outcome and the phrase 'fog of war' was probably more applicable to aerial fighting than to any other form of warfare. Even at the comparatively slow speeds involved in 1915, the effects of an aerial combat were difficult to ascertain. On 22 October, Rees, accompanied by Lieutenant Skeate spotted an Albatros some 2,000 feet below then apparently unaware of their presence. As the Vickers

dived towards it, Skeate opened fire, emptying on
before the German realised what was happening. ...
enemy machine then turned, and commenced a dive
towards the relative safety of its own lines. Rees
followed and his observer fired a second drum at the
Albatros and both of them saw something break away
from the enemy aircraft but whether it was a piece of
fabric or simply a map falling from the cockpit, they were
unable to tell. They reported having seen the majority of
the bullets entering the enemy's nascelle but, due to the
superior speed of the Albatros, Rees was unable to keep
up with him and the German was last seen, under control,
heading eastwards.

Later the same day, accompanied by Lieutenant Slade,
Rees went in pursuit of an LVG which had flown over
their aerodrome. Climbing to 5,500 feet and about eight
miles behind the German lines, they lost their target, but a
second German machine, a 'Two-Tails', was flying about
2,000 feet above them. Unaware of their presence, the
enemy pilot continued on his course until anti-aircraft fire
made him realise that he was not alone and he began to
circle as Rees reduced the range. When the Vickers was
about 500 feet below him and still climbing, the German
observer opened fire. Slade however, did not return the
fire, preferring to wait until he was in a more favourable
position. The German had no intention of becoming
involved in a close combat and headed off deeper into his
side of the lines. Once again, the lack of speed of the
Vickers had prevented any decisive combat taking place
and had allowed another enemy machine to fight another
day. En route for his base at Villers Bretonneux [16]
Rees encountered another German aircraft which, as soon
as it spotted the Vickers, escaped eastwards. The enemy

pilots had not only learnt to respect the Vickers FB5 as a combat machine but also that discretion was the better part of valour and that if they decided to make a run for home, there was little chance of being caught.

On 31 October, Rees and Flight Sergeant Raymond were patrolling at 7,000 feet over Bapaume when they spotted an LVG approaching them with the obvious intention of catching them unawares. As soon as Rees turned to meet the attack, the hostile machine began to turn away and in desperation, at an extreme range of about 400 yards, Raymond opened fire and the LVG commenced a dive towards Pys with the Vickers in pursuit. For once, Rees saw the gap between the two machines beginning to close and continued the chase until both machines were at a height of 500 - 800 feet when the enemy pilot levelled off his descent. Both Rees and Raymond reported having seen what appeared to be fabric falling from the German aircraft. The Vickers was now at a dangerously low height, immediately above a German anti-aircraft battery and became the target for every machine-gun between Pys and Ivnes. In level flight, the enemy pilot began to widen the gap between himself and his pursuer and Rees was reluctantly compelled to abandon the chase. He landed at Villers Bretonneux without further incident only to discover that his machine had been peppered with small-arms fire from the ground.

This was to be Rees' last combat whilst serving with No. 11 Squadron for, a few days later, he received orders to return to England where he was to take up an appointment as an instructor at the Central Flying School. However, shortly before his departure, an event occurred which was to become famous in the history of the squadron and served to illustrate its highly aggressive nature.

Lieutenant Gilbert Insall [17] and Air Mechanic T H Donald were patrolling across the German lines at a height of 7,000 - 8,000 feet when they spotted an enemy kite balloon. Diving into the attack, Insall determined to drop an incendiary bomb in an effort to destroy it but misjudged his approach and was forced to break away amidst intensive anti-aircraft rocket fire. Noting the position of the enemy battery he began to climb away when he saw an Aviatik two-seater approaching from the north, some 2,000 feet higher. Turning towards the west, Insall got his machine into a position whereby Donald could open fire at long range with his Lee Enfield rifle. This action caused the German pilot to change course and head east out of harm's way. Insall continued to head towards the British lines hoping to lull the German into believing that he was heading for home. The ruse worked and the Aviatik again changed course and resumed his patrol of the line. Suddenly the Vickers changed direction and Donald opened fire with the Lewis gun and, once again, the enemy machine turned away in an effort to avoid combat or, perhaps, to lure Insall back over the anti-aircraft battery. Undaunted, the British machine gave chase and, as the Aviatik dived so did Insall who was determined to close the gap and bring the German within range. Again Donald opened fire and the enemy machine's engine was seen to stop just before he disappeared into a cloud. When the Vickers emerged from the other side its prey was down at ground level about to make a forced landing in a ploughed field.

Both the German pilot and his observer were seen climbing out of their machine once it had come to a halt and the latter was carrying his machine-gun. As Insall passed overhead, Donald fired again at the stationary machine and its retreating crew and, as they made a second pass they dropped an incendiary bomb, originally intended for the kite balloon, and whether by luck or good judgement, it hit the Aviatik and set it ablaze.

By this time, the Vickers was coming under an increasing amount of small arms fire from the ground and Insall commenced as rapid a climb as the Monosoupape was capable of. As they approached the front line he dropped towards the ground and Donald raked the German trenches as they passed. Hit in numerous places, the Vickers was on the verge of escaping when one bullet hit the fuel tank and, as the engine depended upon a pressure feed system for its fuel supply, it immediately stopped. There was very little time to think as they were so close to the ground and Insall just managed to clear a small wood near the village of Agny and make a safe landing a few hundred yards inside the French line and, despite heavy shelling, the Vickers survived without further damage until darkness fell.

Back at Villers Bretonneux, Lieutenant Hughes-Chamberlain was in the squadron office with the commanding officer:

"Dawes was cursing Insall up hill and down dale because he hadn't arrived back - "What the hell was the fellow doing now?", that sort of stuff and then the ... telephone rang and he picked it up and he started to blaspheme until Insall got it into his head to tell him "We've shot down a German aircraft." Dawes was highly excited. He yelled for Rees who came along and he said "Take a tender, put in a new tank, all the appliances, and petrol and everything else that you want and some mechanics to run the show." Rees was very good at anything of that kind; first-class man in fact." [18]

Rees and his small band of men drove down to the landing site which was some 15 miles away from the base, located the Vickers and, under masked lights, supervised the removal of the damaged fuel tank and the fitting of a replacement. They then made all the checks that were possible in the circumstances and, almost too late, they realised that the new tank was also leaking but managed to resolve the problem and declared the machine to be in flying condition. It was pointless risking two lives trying to bring the aircraft back so Donald returned with the mechanics and his place was taken by sand-bags which served as ballast in the front cockpit and, as the first light of dawn crept over the German trenches, Insall made a successful take-off and, a few minutes later, landed safely at his base. One week later both he and Donald were wounded and forced to land behind the German lines where they were taken prisoner and it was in these circumstances that Insall received the news that he had been awarded the Victoria Cross for his action on 7 November and that Donald had received the Distinguished Conduct Medal.[19]

There can be little doubt that No. 11 Squadron helped to create a tradition of highly skilled, aggressive aerial combatants upon which the reputation of Britain's fighter pilots in two world wars was built. They were worthy forerunners of men like Ball, McCudden, Mannock, Tuck, Malan and Johnson and no-one deserves more credit for helping to create this reputation than Lionel Rees, the very first of the original 'Few', who braved the skies in fragile machines of wood, fabric and wire to prove that aerial combat was possible as long as airmen were well-trained, well-led and fired with the belief that they were better than the enemy. This was the message which Rees took back with him to England on 21 November, 1915 and which, after one week's leave, he carried to Upavon. Shortly after his arrival he was commissioned to publish this philosophy in the form of a manual of aerial combat. This booklet, entitled 'Fighting in the Air', is of interest not only because it was the first of its kind, paving the way for others in later years, but also for its comparative brevity, simplicity and rather naive approach to the deadly business of aerial warfare. Based mainly upon Rees' own experience, it also drew upon the experiences of others and for that reason it can be said to representative of the views of front-line pilots and observers at that time. The selection of Rees to write the manual is an indicator of the regard with which he was held by those in high office and the fact that such a publication was being prepared showed clearly that there was a new attitude to military aviation by the end of 1915. On the outbreak of hostilities the previous year, supporters of military aviation had hoped that it would serve as the eyes of the army but many senior officers saw even that as too high an expectation of the new corps. Sir Douglas Haig had said in July 1914, "I hope none of you gentlemen is so foolish as to think that aeroplanes will be able to be usefully employed for reconnaissance in the air." By late 1915, the effectiveness of aerial reconnaissance had been proved and had led to the extension of the combatant nature of the war to the third element as armed machines set out to deliberately destroy the enemy's reconnaissance machines in order to prevent observations being carried back to the military planners. It has been argued that the efforts made by both sides during the four years of aerial warfare were to no avail as, if aeroplanes had not been used then both sides would have been at an equal disadvantage or, if aeroplanes had been used then there was little purpose in the great emphasis placed upon their mutual destruction as the intelligence which they carried was of little long term value; it did not take numerous reports from airmen to confirm to either side that an attack was about to be launched, the scale of the artillery barrage served as a more than adequate warning.

Fighter squadrons, such as No. 11, were organised primarily for the purpose of attacking and bringing down the enemy's machines and carried offensive armament whereas reconnaissance squadrons were equipped with machines that were, on the whole, heavier and less manoeuvreable and were intended to observe the enemy's movements, photograph his positions and, if necessary, bomb selected targets. These roles were not absolute and, very often, fighter pilots and observers carried out reconnaisance patrols while reconnaissance pilots often had to fight their way to and from a target and the heavier losses sustained by the RFC in 1915 required a new approach to military flying leading to the obvious conclusion that the more highly trained and better informed the novice airman was before he went to the front, the better were his chances of surviving once he was posted to a service squadron.

A former RFC officer, who served under Rees' command in 1916, recalled that the latter was a good pilot but probably not a great one. In terms of tactics, he held a very simple view, namely, attack the enemy whenever he was encountered and, in comparison to the great 'aces' he was a very long way behind tactically. If this opinion is an accurate assessment of Rees' talents then why was he selected to produce the first manual of aerial combat ? Looking back now, with the benefit of hindsight, it is possible to argue that Rees was perhaps a better pilot and tactician than might have been apparent at the time.

The period of Rees' actual combat flying was very short and, at the end of 1915 amounted to four months during a period when machines were underpowered and had very limited fighting capabilities. The relatively simple and lightly armed Vickers FB5 would have been no match for the later, much more powerful and sophisticated Sopwith Camel and SE5a which dominated aerial combats during the latter stages of the war. When the men who recognised as great tacticians, Ball and Mannock, made their names, aircraft design was very much more advanced. Ball began his flying career in the sluggish BE2c and later flew the Bristol Bullet but met with no success against an enemy who was armed with superior machines. It was not until he joined No.11 Squadron in May, 1916 and was given a Nieuport Scout that he was able to enter into combats of his own volition and, even then, he did not achieve any success in terms of enemy machines destroyed. Ball however, was lucky and managed to survive this danger period during which he evolved his own tactics whereby he stalked his opponent until he was in a position immediately below him at which point he would open fire with the Lewis gun which was fitted to the upper wing [20]. The Nieuport, although a fine aircraft had one very major weakness in that its wings tended to collapse if it was pushed too hard in a dive. Ball's 'modus operandi' eliminated this danger in combat. When, in 1917, the squadron in which he was serving was re-equipped with the SE5, Ball received special permission to continue flying the Nieuport in which he continued to achieve success.

That other great fighter pilot, 'Mick' Mannock, deemed by many to have been the greatest of them all, was viewed with some suspicion by his colleagues for a considerable time during the early part of his flying career. For him, the Nieuport Scout was a jinxed machine in which he initially found it almost impossible to obtain a confirmed 'kill'. Careful study of the problem and plenty of practice, coupled with the good luck to stay alive long enough, eventually paid off (he was airborne for over 40 hours during April, 1917, a period of intense German activity, before he managed to bring down an opponent). Once the skill had been mastered, he analysed the methodology, believing that there must be a formula for destroying an enemy machine just as he believed there was one for other problems. From this point his successes began to mount and he became almost unbeatable when flying the SE5a; if Mannock entered a combat he was expected to win. If the problem facing him did not conform to his formula for success, he would avoid action until it did. His motto, which he always passed on to young and inexperienced pilots was very simple: "Always above, seldom on the same level and never beneath". It was easy to abide by this ruling in 1917 - 18 when machines like the SE5a could climb to 19,000 feet and reach 10,000 feet in a little under 13 minutes. The Vickers fighter of 1915 had a ceiling of 9,000 feet and took 16 minutes to reach 5,000 feet. If one adds the ever increasing numbers of enemy machines which flew over the Allied lines to the mechanical advantages enjoyed by pilots during the latter part of the war then it is not surprising that personal 'scores' were higher. Very few of the pilots who flew in the opening rounds of the air war were still flying by 1917-18, many of those that had survived held command positions but, of those who did fly it is noticeable that it was during this latter period that they achieved most of their success in terms of the destruction of enemy machines.

By the last year of the war a number of squadrons were gaining reputations for the collective scores which their pilots were accumulating. This was as a result of the introduction of formation flying; no longer were individual machines venturing out alone or even in pairs. The usual patrol strength in 1918 was a flight or even a full squadron and this security in numbers paid dividends in terms of the numbers of enemy machines destroyed. In 1915 such tactics were beyond the capabilities of the aircraft as was clearly shown by No.11 Squadron during its attempt to escort the King on his visit to Netheravon. Given the advantages enjoyed by pilots in later years, there would seem to be little doubt that Rees and many others would have accumulated a substantial score and one cannot but ask the question what would the pilots of 1918 have managed to achieve had their combat service been restricted to the earlier part of the war ?

Rees was a member of that school of military gentlemen who saw their world vanish in August, 1914; a world where it was counted a blessing to have been born British, destined by divine authority to control the world. Today, patriotism, empire, even loyalty are words which have become viewed as objects of derision but to the generation that fought the First World War they were almost a religion, badges to be worn with pride. To serve King and Country was an obligation which they felt honoured to fulfil and, in the days before mass communication enlightened even the most basically educated, there is little wonder that the propaganda stories of atrocities in the early days of the war were accepted so readily when the entire nation had been indoctrinated with such opinions. Rees' attitudes are clearly evident in 'Fighting in the Air':

"The British pilot always likes the idea of fighting and is self reliant. He is a quick thinker compared with the enemy, so that he has the advantage in manoeuvre. He fights for the sport of the affair, if for no other reason. The Enemy Pilot on the other hand, is of a gregarious nature from long national training, and often seems bound by strict rules, which cramp his style to a great extent. The Enemy Pilots are often uneducated men, being looked upon simply as drivers of the machine, while the Gunner or Observer is considered a grade higher then the Pilot. This last gives a great advantage to us, as, whereas our Pilots act from a sense of 'Noblesse Oblige', the Enemy, when in a tight corner, often fails to seize and press an advantage."

Although this reads as naive propaganda, there is a great element of truth in it. Rees' opinion of the Germans as combatants is supported by many other Allied airmen who state that the enemy rarely flew missions over the British lines and, when they did, they were either in large numbers or very high up which made interception very difficult. The British airmen on the other hand, were actively encouraged (some might argue foolishly so) to cross the front line in pursuit of the enemy [21]. The Germans certainly, throughout the war, saw the observer as the senior member of the two man crew and he was therefore the commissioned officer whilst the pilot was often an NCO.

Rees saw the role of the fighter pilot as being very clear cut - to engage the enemy and destroy him. By the enemy he meant the machine and this would seem to hint at the chivalry which is believed to have existed during the early years of the war. The reality however, was very different. He saw the death of the enemy pilot as the only means of ensuring the destruction of the enemy machine.

"...it is not sufficient to make a machine land, as machines are comparatively easy to obtain. Every effort should be made to disable the Enemy Pilot, as this nearly always ensures the destruction of the machine as well."

If the pilot was to be hit then he had to be the main target, a comparatively small area which Rees estimated to be no larger than 2 feet by 1 foot 6 inches by 1 foot 6 inches. It should be the prime ambition of every British pilot or observer to be able to hit such a target consistently and, in order to achieve this, the attack had to be carefully studied and practised. A pilot must be constantly on the alert, always ready to make a surprise attack on the enemy by approaching the target unobserved and, at the same time, ensuring that he was not himself caught off guard by another enemy machine.

"If an unobserved machine opens fire it takes at least 2 seconds to pick him up and come into action. By that time the enemy has fired twelve rounds, which are quite enough to do serious damage."

There was little purpose in a fighting machine being in a position to destroy the enemy only to discover that he was out of ammunition. The most common cause of this embarassing and highly dangerous situation was that the pilot had opened fire too soon, expending his valuable ammunition to no other purpose than to make the enemy aware of his presence.

"There should be no long range shooting. One should try to close to within 50 yards in order to do any damage."

If a pilot had the advantage of surprise, range and reasonable skill at hitting the target, the final question which he had to consider was the angle of the attack. Traditionally, the image of a fighter attack during the First World War is that of two machines in line, the one at the rear being in close pursuit of the other, the pilot of which is weaving and turning as he desperately tries to throw off his pursuer. This was by no means always the case and was certainly not the approach advocated by Rees.

"If we attack a machine from directly in front or in rear the engine may cover the pilot's body or vice versa. This is the minimum target which the machine can present, and any shots hitting the target do damage, but there is a lot of room round the target in which shots which do not actually strike do no damage.

Now, if we imagine a machine being attacked from the side, or straight from above or below. The target which we must aim for [the pilot] still remains the same small one, but now the rounds, which before were non-effective, will hit the engine and Observer, and will become effective."

He summed up his ideas in a simple but rather lengthy list :

"Open fire before the enemy.
Open fire at the shortest possible range.
Open fire under the most favourable circumstances.
Try to disable the enemy at once.
Close as soon as you can, so as to prevent the enemy setting his sights and taking aim.
It is useless expecting to hit successfully at ranges over 400 yards.
Reserve your fire till within 100 yards of the enemy, but if discovered open fire before the Enemy.
At ranges of 50 yards and under, if attacking from the flank, aim at the enemy's leading edge as you see it (one or other wing top). This statement is only a guide.

If one must collide go straight up, as the enemy nearly always goes straight down. Then if one hits the enemy one hits him with one's undercarriage.

Do not collide unless by accident. If the enemy pilot is disabled the enemy machine may travel quite normally for a long time, so that one runs the risk of wrecking one's own machine uselessly.

If it is necessary to change drums, dive under a tractor[22] as that upsets his aim.

As a rule it does not pay to follow a machine below 3,000 feet. At that height the machine guns from the ground become dangerous, and if the enemy machine is not disabled before that it will probably not be disabled at all.

It is dangerous to cross the trenches at heights below 2,000 feet.

If no enemy is in sight never fly straight, even on our side of the lines. This prevents the enemy getting the size of the machine accurately. If the size is known it is very easy to get the range at short distances, as used in fighting in the air.

Do not take anything for granted. Work out all your own deflections, etc., for your machine. No two machines fly normally at the same speeds.

Do not get put out when you find that your pet theory does not work."

Almost obvious in its simplicity, Rees' manual also deals at some length with the actual mechanics of aerial combat; such items as the mathematics of deflection shooting, trajectory and sighting being dealt with in considerable detail and it is for this section in particular that 'Fighting in the Air' deserves to be remembered. A slightly amended edition was issued later in the war but the contents and the message were unaltered and it does not appear to have been superceded until 1918 when the manual 'Bring Down Your Hun' appeared [23].

Chapter IV
No. 32 Squadron, RFC
(1916 -17)

After a seven day leave Rees was posted as an instructor to the Central Flying School where newly trained pilots, after obtaining the Royal Aero Club Certificates at one of the numerous service and private flying schools, were taught to fly service machines. The CFS was not intended to teach men to fly but rather to take civilian pilots and turn them into military airmen. It had been established in 1912 on a 2,400 acre site, two miles from the village of Upavon in Wiltshire and the airfield, which soon came to be known as Siberia, was located on a rather bleak plateau and was a puzzle to many who saw it; the magazine 'Aeroplane' was unable to fathom the logic of its situation "...on top of a mountain where it is open to every wind that blows." Nevertheless, the CFS prospered and throughout the war and for many years afterwards, it turned out thousands of qualified airmen for the RFC and, after 1918, the RAF.

Due to the increasing numbers of aerial combats which were taking place on the Western front, the War Office decided to establish a number of single-seater squadrons early in 1916. Often referred to by the misnomer of 'Scout' squadrons, they were to set the pattern of future fighter development. The French airman Roland Garros had, the previous April, succeeded in shooting down a German machine using a machine-gun which could be fired through the arc of the propellor, damage being avoided by means of Sauliner deflector plates fitted to the rear of each blade. He went on to score a further two victories before being forced to land through engine failure behind enemy lines where his machine was captured intact. Within two days Anthony Fokker, a Dutch aero-engineer who was working for the Germans, had developed a synchronised machine-gun which fired forward without the need for deflector plates [1]. On 15 July 1915, the first Allied machine was shot down using this new method and the Germans appeared to have gained the upper hand in aerial combat. Although it is generally accepted that the advent of this device, fitted to the Fokker E1 (Eindecker), caused considerable problems to the Allied airmen, its effect has been exaggerated. As a flying machine the Fokker had a very limited performance and British pilots who flew a captured machine under test conditions in April, 1916, reported that despite a very well manufactured engine, the machine's "...speed is the same as that of a 80 hp Morane Scout but the climb is not nearly so fast. The lateral control is distinctly bad. The machine pulls up well in a very short distance after landing." It could be dived very steeply and, showing an air speed of 115 mph, it came out of a dive with complete ease. As a reconnaissance machine it was very poor and had no armour protection. Its average maximum speed at ground level was 86.4 mph. The Fokker's only advantage over comparable Allied machines was the forward firing gun which, coupled with the numerous British incursions over German territory, led to losses which would equally have affected the Germans had they crossed the lines in equal numbers. The enemy propaganda machine however, made the most of the opportunity and created a totally unwarranted reputation for the Fokker, turning it into something of a 'super' machine. Their despatches emphasised British losses whilst ignoring their own and bore no relationship to the real situation. British aircraft losses during four weeks in January 1916 totalled 13 whilst the Germans lost 9 with two others probably destroyed; hardly the 'scourge' which was reported in the press.

There were two distinct categories of fighting machine flown by pilots in the Great War. The first was an aircraft designed around the pilot's field of fire and the unobstructed view of the airspace around him. The second was the aircraft which was designed for performance in the air irrespective of its actual fighting capabilities. Amongst the former, the 'pusher' style of biplane was viewed as the ideal design with the engine out of the way behind the pilot who had a clear area of sky in front of him. In 1915, this type of machine was exemplified by the Vickers FB5. In the latter category, the 'tractor' machine was paramount with an engine fitted in front of the pilot, which was far superior to anything which could be fitted into a 'pusher'. Unable to develop their own forward firing gun system the RFC was forced to rely on 'pusher' designs to counter the threat of the Fokker and squadrons equipped with this type of aircraft, such as No.11, suffered fewer losses and were able to achieve a measure of success in destroying the enemy when he was willing to stand and fight it out. By mid-1915, Geoffrey de Havilland, a young engineer working at the Royal Aircraft Factory, had designed a single-seater 'pusher' machine, designated the DH2, which was the ultimate in design thinking for its type. It was a bold, ingenious and initially successful attempt to overcome the problems faced by those pilots who were confronted by the apparent menace of the Fokker.

As a flying machine, the DH2 had the typical characteristics of a 'pusher'. The 100 hp Gnome engine produced a great deal of torque which necessitated the pilot holding the stick hard over to counter its effects in order to fly straight and level. The aircraft's very high power-to-weight ratio meant that careless handling could easily result in a spin when the engine was switched off. The natural tendency to avert this action by raising the nose merely accentuated the effect which, if it occurred near the ground, could be disastrous. Instead of the normal fuel supply system, the aircraft had a hand-controlled needle valve which meant that there was no throttle and therefore no means of controlling the speed; the engine either ran at full power or was cut out by switching off the supply of petrol or cutting the ignition switch. According to the men who flew them, the DH2s had three speed settings: full speed, dud speed (when a fault occurred) and stop. This meant that the machine's landing speed had to be regulated by switching the engine on and off, or 'blipping' as it was called. This in turn caused the aeroplane to lurch to one side, an effect which the pilot had to be prepared for if he was to avoid a crash.

Although the pilot had excellent visibility and was positioned away from the engine fumes, his exposed situation at the front made him very cold indeed. James McCudden, the renowned fighter pilot, recorded that "I didn't care whether I was shot down or not, I was so utterly frozen. I liked this machine, but knew I should have to fly it for a long time before I became its master."

Whilst having an inferior performance to many other

types, the DH2 did have the ability to turn very sharply without losing height and, if it could close with an enemy machine, it could hold its own in combat. Armed with one forward-firing Lewis gun, with up to seven drums of ammunition (each containing 47 rounds) which could be changed in about five seconds by the pilot taking both hands off the controls, the aircraft was not the type of machine in which any pilot could be expected to build up a high score of enemy machines destroyed. Irrespective of the skill of an individual pilot the enemy could invariably escape by diving away as German machines were, almost without exception, faster in level flight and had a better rate of climb.

All these problems aside, the DH2 was still a great improvement on what had been available before and its only real rivals amongst Allied aircraft were the French Nieuport and the Sopwith Pup neither of which were available to RFC pilots until later in the year. The squadrons that were equipped with it were expected to achieve great deeds when they arrived in France and they did not disappoint their 'audience'.

The first squadron to receive the DH2 was No.24 which arrived on the Western front on 7 February, 1916, followed just over a month later by No.29. The third was No.32 which was to be formed at Netheravon ready for active service in the late spring. Command of these new units required a special type of officer with experience, a proven record of aggression in the air and a high level of leadership potential. No.24 was given to Major Lanoe Hawker, VC, formerly of No.6 Squadron. No.29 Squadron went to Major E L Conran [2] and, on 1 February, No.32 squadron was given to Lionel Rees who, since 28 November, 1915, had been a Temporary Major.

The selection of these three men is an interesting one and confirms their status in the RFC. Some years later, A J Insall (formerly of No.11 Squadron and a noted post-war writer on air matters) wrote:

"Hawker was a regular sapper, and he brought to the RFC all the calculating science of the engineer allied to the spirit of a gay cavalier [3]. It was the debonair spirit, more than anything else, that, in my opinion, marked the difference between Hawker and that other great DH2 fighter, Major L W B Rees, VC. Rees was a gunner, a great strategist and a great tactician. Speaking as an observer - and observers had opportunities not given to all to judge of a pilot's capabilities - there was no one in the RFC with whom I would sooner have shared the ups and downs of a close fight than Rees. It was always my regret that, although we were in the same squadron for many months, the chance never came my way. One felt in Hawker's case, on the other hand, that he had been born to fight single-handed, and it was hard to realise that he had once flown BEs with a passenger to do his fighting for him. I have often tried to make up my mind which of the two, Rees or Hawker was the greater; and I have never succeeded. Certain it is that both, given a machine of equal performance and neutral ground to fight over, would have made rings around any contemporary enemy pilot. Rees was the better shot - he could pick off a visiting card right or left handed with a service revolver at twenty-five yards; Hawker the more dashing pilot, the more capable of the unexpected manoeuvre that can decide an issue in a split second." [4]

As soon as he arrived at Netheravon, Rees commenced the selection and training of pilots and ground-crew for his new squadron. Essentially, the nucleus of No.32 was made up of surplus personnel from No.21 squadron which had already gone overseas. Three experienced men, Captains Gilmour, Hellyer and Allen were selected as Flight Commanders and the remaining places were filled by unattached pilots and newly qualified men from the CFS. One aspiring youngster was

2nd Lieutenant Gwilym Lewis, formerly of the Northamptonshire Regiment and newly qualified as a pilot [5], who thought that his chances of being selected by Rees were remote to say the least: "Most of my friends had gone to another squadron and I thought that I would go with them. Thankfully, I did not as they were all killed." In a letter to his parents written shortly after his arrival at Netheravon, Lewis recorded his opinion of his new commanding officer:

" Major L W B Rees is in command and it is he who makes the squadron mostly ideal. He has got permission to go out as a flying commander, and he can teach every member of the squadron how to fly [6]. He has published a booklet on how to rig the DH2 and was this evening giving a lecture on the Mono engine [7]. He knows the job thoroughly and, above all, is a perfect gentleman. I shouldn't be surprised if he comes home with a VC; he has already got an MC. Half the reason why I am so keen to go out is because I know several of the fellows well: however, I feel the chances are remote."

Seventy years later, Gwilym Lewis' boyish enthusiasm of 1916 had been tempered with the moderation of maturity but the pride of having been a member of No.32 squadron and serving under Rees still showed through:

" Rees was a very competent commanding officer and a very experienced aviator. He was very senior to the rest of us in the squadron (I was only eighteen and the baby of the unit, known to my colleagues as 'Cherub', and he was in his thirties) and full of guts. He was exciting to serve under, always very keen to have a go at the enemy and an expert at his job. Unusually for a commanding officer at that time he knew as much as anybody about engines and the rigging of aeroplanes, so it was no use anybody trying to pretend that there was anything wrong with their machine - he would have very quickly found them out.

He had a very quiet, pleasant personality and was always smiling. He never shouted at anyone and was always the perfect gentleman. It was he who developed the squadron's philosophy - always have a go at the enemy. One felt quite instinctively that he was a courageous man." [8]

Throughout the spring of 1916, the squadron developed its proficiency at handling the DH2 which had already begun to acquire a bad reputation with the two squadrons already on active service. A nickname, 'The Spinning Incinerator' had been given to it as a result of a number of machines in service with No.24 Squadron crashing with no apparent explanation; they were seen to enter a spin and one had caught fire as it came down. As a result of this, few held any real hope for the DH2 pilots against the Fokker until the source of the fire problem was pinpointed in March - the Gnome Monosaupape engine. Although a tried and tested design, the engine was very temperamental and required very careful balancing by the mechanics. The rough handling which was part and parcel of active service was diagnosed as the root cause of the DH2s problems as indeed it had been with the Vickers FB5 the previous year.

One of Rees' former colleagues in No.11 Squadron, Captain R Hughes-Chamberlain, serving as a Flight Commander in No.24 Squadron, was fortunate enough to survive the effects of an inbalanced engine:

"I had just been sent off on a stand-by patrol and had climbed to a height of some 4,000 feet by the time I was nine miles from Bertangles. Then, without any warning, one cylinder left the engine. It knocked off one propellor blade at the root and sailed through the top mainspar of the aircraft. You always had your ears pinned back for engine trouble in that squadron and I managed to switch off the petrol and ignition almost immediately.

The loss of the propellor blade was causing very serious vibration as the remaining blade (the DH2 had a two-bladed propellor) made the engine windmill in the slipstream. The aircraft appeared to be shaking to pieces. The damage to the mainspar dislodged one of the centre struts which carried the control lines to the ailerons and elevator. I looked round to see the mainspar sagging and, at the same time, noticed the ammunition drums, which were fixed to the side of the fuselage, flying away and bursting through the fabric of the wings.

I had little time to consider the damage caused by the drums because at this moment the mainspar gave way and dropped down some six inches. My control stick was almost useless. You usually manoeuvred by moving the stick only a few inches in any one direction but I found that I had to swing the stick round about two feet to get any response from the aircraft. The vibration was making the Lewis gun - which was mounted in front of me - hop around madly and I had little forward vision.

I realised that if I couldn't get the aeroplane to the ground soon, it would disintegrate in the air. In fact, it was disintegrating already. Luckily, I had not been very high and I managed to pull off a very good landing in a nearby field. I stood up in the cockpit and rested my head against the top wing for some time after I had landed, and then almost had a relapse when I realised that the tail booms, which carried the whole tail assembly, could be waved about quite easily with one hand. The aircraft was considered a complete write-off."

Hughes-Chamberlain had been lucky and, as the mechanics mastered the problems of servicing the Gnome engine, the reputation of the DH2 changed dramatically. The nickname 'Spinning Incinerator' was heard less often and Gwilym Lewis has no recollection of ever having heard it used in No.32 Squadron.

Throughout March and April, the new arrivals at Netheravon underwent intensive training as preparation for active service. According to Rees, the squadron had to train its own pilots and mechanics and even the Flight Commanders, with the exception of Captain Gilmour, had no previous knowledge of either the 100 hp Mono engine, or the DH2 machine. In all, between 20 and 30 pilots were trained to fly the new scout without a single crash but, no sooner were they proficient than they were posted to either No.24 or No. 29 Squadrons who had a priority call on pilots.

Being more manoeuvreable and agile than the Vickers FB5, the DH2 was capable of being flown in formation. Whilst serving with No.11 squadron, Rees had only experienced machines flying alone with patrols ending when a relief aircraft was sent up to assume the watch on the German lines. The greater flexibility and responsiveness of the DH2 led to the development of small combat formations and Rees very quickly developed his own theories:

"When machines fly in flights they can fly in a line, diamond formation or echelon. I rather prefer the echelon formation with the Flight Commander well out to the front.

X Flt Comdr

X

X

X

If this formation is used any disabled machine can easily turn out of the formation without interfering with the others.

The Flight Commander can be seen by every machine.

In attack, the Flight Commander can use his distance to the front in order to gain height, so that, if a single enemy machine is attacked, the Flight can bring a crossfire to bear from the sides and from the top.

If the enemy are also flying in formation, because the shooting is at present bad, I do not think there would be much extra danger if the enemy machines are singled out, and attacked one after the other."

In addition to inadequate flying training before being posted to a squadron, few of the pilots had ever fired a machine-gun in the air or, in some cases, on the ground and a great deal of time was expended enabling them to obtain as much practice at this as possible. Target practice took place over Salisbury Plain:

"Major Rees and all the other pilots would fly across the open Salisbury Plain to a special ground target and fire their Lewis Guns, they had a good view as the Gun was a fixture right in front of them. We were watching the practice taking place when we saw Major Rees' plane make a hurried landing. The propellor had been split apart by the bullet cases flying back when the guns were fired at a fast rate. So he gave orders for canvas bags to be made and placed where the cartridge cases fly out (no more broken propellors)." [9]

Range firing also resulted in modifications to the Lewis guns themselves and the DH2s of No.32 Squadron were fitted with a non-standard one and a half inch ring backsight and a Bowden cable which connected the trigger to the joystick, something which became a standard feature in later RFC machines.

Divisional manoeuvres on 28 April saw two of the squadron's machines taking part but with little success as one of them was forced to make two landings due to a plug cutting out and one of the ignition wires being broken by a small piece of rubber which had fallen from the pilot's pocket. At the end of the month the squadron took delivery of the first of the new machines which, as soon as they were up to full strength,they were to take with them to France. But, while the rest of the pilots flew the DH2, Rees and Hellyer spent most of their flying time at the controls of Vickers 'Bullet' Scouts which had entered service the previous autumn. Although powered by a 'tractor' engine and of an advanced design for that period, the 'Bullet' was handicapped by not being able to fire forwards through the arc of the propellor. In addition, the aeroplane's rather bulbous shape and the positioning of the wings greatly reduced the pilot's visibility and, apart from the few trial machines such as the two issued to No.32 Squadron, the design was not put into production. [10]

Although the war gave every impression of being fought a long way away, the introduction of aeroplanes had, as early as 1916, brought it much closer than the average civilian had realised. A perfect example of this occurred on 26 April when the squadron records show "Major L W B Rees left for overseas. Captain F E Hellyer took over temporary command of the squadron." The following day the Adjutant noted: "Major Rees returned this day, leaving later in De Havilland No. 5954" and, on 28 April, "Major Rees returned from overseas". Whether Rees made two visits to France during this three day period is unclear (it was probably only one) nor is the purpose behind the trip although one can speculate, with a degree of confidence, that it was for a dual purpose namely to ferry a new machine out to one of the squadrons already at the front and to prepare the way for No.32 Squadron's own overseas posting.

During the second week of May, Brigadier General H M Trenchard visited the squadron at Netheravon where he inspected the aircraft. [11] Two days later, as the date for their departure for France drew ever closer, the first members of the squadron went on pre-embarkation leave.

On 26 May, the squadron transport, under the command of Lieutenant Corbett, left for Avonmouth where they boarded the SS *Santa Isabel* the following morning. The remainder of the ground staff left Netheravon on the 27th, spent the night in a rest camp, and boarded the SS *Duchess of Argyle* at Southampton the following evening. After last minute engine testing, and a group photograph, the pilots of No.32 Squadron took off at 11 am on 28 May and flew a cross-country course to Folkestone. En route Lieutenant Hunt made a forced landing at Guildford, wrecking his machine and Lieutenant Henty made a safer descent after his engine had failed. The remainder of the squadron reached the coast without incident and, after lunch at the Metropole Hotel, they left for France.

Any aerial crossing of the Channel in 1916 involved an element of risk. Rees was the first into the air and made the crossing alone in order to make arrangements for the squadron's accommodation in France. As the remainder of the machines took off, two more were slightly damaged and had to be left behind whilst the others made a safe crossing in three formations, eventually landing at the RFC Depot at St Omer, some twenty miles behind the front line where they were complimented on their efficiency by Brigadier Trenchard.

The following day, one of the machines which had been left behind, flown by Lieutenant Henty, made the crossing to rejoin the squadron. Some distance out over the sea a tappet rod in his engine seized up but, fortunately, he had sufficient height to reach the French coast and attempt a landing on the cliff top. As he touched down on the grass he realised that he was moving too fast and, as the aircraft had no brakes, he ran over the edge of the cliff. Either by luck or judgement he managed to retain control of the DH2 and made a successful landing on the beach below. Unfortunately, despite this remarkable escape, the following day, whilst trying to take off, he ran into a concealed wire and the machine was written off although he himself appears to have escaped injury. [12]

The contingent aboard the SS *Duchess of Argyle* arrived at Le Havre in the early hours of the moring of 29 May and from there they made their way to a rest camp at Rouen to await transport. Two days later they were at the docks to supervise the unloading of the stores and left the following morning to rejoin the pilots at St Omer where they arrived at noon on 2 June.

The squadron was placed in the Tenth (Army) Wing of the 1 Brigade which flew in support of the First and Third Armies [13], and an advanced party was sent on ahead to prepare accommodation for the whole unit at the small mining village of Auchel. The airfield was already occupied by the FE2bs of No.25 Squadron under the command of Major Cherry and additional canvas hangers were erected for the DH2s and the remainder of the squadron arrived on 4 June after lunch at St Omer. Their stay at Auchel was intended to give the pilots an opportunity to become accustomed to the area and life on active service but, for two days the wet and windly weather prevented any flying and, on 6 June they were transfered to Treizennes near Aire where they were put to work almost immediately, replacing No.27 Squadron whose Martinsydes had that same day moved to St Andre-au-Bois. While the DH2s went on regular patrols over the lines, Rees, as squadron commander, continued to fly the Vickers in co-operation with the local anti-aircraft batteries trying to intercept any intruders over the British side of the front.

Each machine was allocated a specific area to patrol and "...hell was raised if a Hun gets through on your sector." They were now involved in the real war and, as if to remind them of this fact, they suffered their first fatality within twenty-four hours of their arrival when 2nd Lieutenant Stubbs took off in DH 6005 for his first patrol over the front lines. Observers on the ground noted that he was seen flying into a considerable concentration of anti-aircraft fire but appeared to have got through unscathed. Later, whilst returning to an aerodrome further south, flying at about 100 feet, his machine was seen to lurch upwards and crash. He was killed instantly and, when Rees arrived at the scene some time later, he was informed that despite two minor wounds, probably caused by the anti-aircraft fire, there was no apparent reason for the crash. The official opinion recorded in the squadron papers was that Stubbs had fainted at the controls of his machine. Far more likely however, is the possibility that some small but vital component was damaged by the anti-aircraft fire. [14]

On the same day 2nd Lieutenant Lewis had the squadron's first encounter with the enemy. On patrol at about 8.15 am, he spotted a machine flying towards him on the British side of the line. Unable to identify it as either friend or foe, he continued towards it trying to see its markings. Suddenly he spotted the black crosses and, as the two machines drew closer, he opened fire from a range which he insists, even today, was no more than 40 yards. The German broke to the left and Lewis gave chase, firing the occasional burst whenever the opportunity arose. He is certain that he hit the enemy observer who was seated in the rear cockpit as his last view of the German machine showed the gun to be pointing up into the air and no attempt was made to return his fire. The pilot, however, used his superior speed and safely recrossed the lines. On landing Lewis discovered that a report of his action had already been made and the official record stated that he had opened fire from a range of 300 - 400 yards.

"My CO wasn't at all pleased ... and told me I had lost a chance. He is such a fearful fighter himself, and a wonderful pilot. However, better luck next time, it was only my tactics which were wrong. It is a most extrordinary game. Better than football yet something of the same. It is the same feeling to charge a Hun who sees you as it is to collar one of the biggest chaps in the school scrum."

The squadron appeared to have made its mark on its sector of the front almost immediately and Lewis wrote in a letter to his father:

"But what would surprise you more is the respect we get out here as a DH squadron. We are absolutely 'the ones' here. The DH has practically scared the Huns off the front. Occasionally they manage to steal over at about 15,000 but even then they hesitate whether they dive on a DH or not, if he happens to be below them. The FEs complain that they can get no fights hardly now; it is awfully amusing. Of course, the DH's job is to attack and away he goes at any Hun he sees." [15]

Throughout this period of the squadron's baptism of fire, Rees flew regular patrols in his Vickers but, despite spotting enemy machines on several occasions, he was not involved in any combats. More often than not, the weather prevented any successful patrols with the cloud level regularly below 5,000 feet which meant that no enemy activity could be observed either in the air or on the ground. Duty pilots waited on stand-by for up to twelve hours each day, ready for take off at a moment's notice should the weather clear sufficiently for a patrol to be mounted.

The squadron's second casualty was Captain Hellyer, the senior Flight Commander. On 15 June, taking off in the machine normally used by 2nd Lieutenant Lewis, in order to carry out an engine test and patrol, his engine stalled whilst trying to clear some high trees, the machine side-slipped and crashed into a nearby field. The engine, mounted behind the pilot, broke loose from its mountings resulting in Hellyer sustaining several broken ribs and a broken ankle which meant that he was invalided home. Why he had decided to test Lewis' engine is not known, it was certainly not the normal procedure for a flight commander.

The 17 June was the first really fine day since the squadron's arrival and every possible patrol was mounted as the General Staff, in the midst of their preparations for the offensive which was to become known as the Battle of the Somme, demanded information about the enemy's positions opposite the Fourth Army's front. Nos. 25 and 32 Squadrons were to provide the protection for the reconnaissance machines which were sent over the lines in the area Laventie - Souchez and, at the same time, they were to prevent the Germans flying similar missions to observe the British build-up of men and equipment. Whenever possible, the two squadrons alternated their patrols to ensure maximum cover of the area and, during one of these, 2nd Lieutenant Owen Thomas caught up with a large formation of enemy aircraft and, although hopelessly outnumbered, closed with them and opened fire on a two-seater. The ensuing fight lasted for thirty minutes as both pilots tried desperately to get into a position whereby he could get a clear shot at his opponent and bring him down. It was not to be however, and the German pilot eventually broke away and headed back towards his own territory and Thomas made his way home.

During the afternoon, Lieutenant S P Simpson climbed to attack five Aviatiks which he spotted flying above him. Emerging from the middle of the enemy formation, he opened fire and the German observers quickly reciprocated. Simpson, however, used up all his ammunition and failed to achieve any noticeable success and was forced to break off the fight. Rees himself gave chase to two German machines in the 'Bullet' but both made a successful escape across the lines either because of their extreme range or possibly their superior speed.

In an effort to counter the effectiveness of the new scout squadrons, the Germans regularly sent over formations of between five and twelve machines. Consequently, contact became more frequent but still No.32 Squadron was unable to claim any confirmed destruction of a German machine. Spurred on by Rees' leadership and example, the young pilots ranged the skies over the Fourth Army front, rivalling each other in their efforts to be the first one to score a 'kill'. Their failure to do so was not through lack of effort or skill as they were successful in preventing any infiltration of their sector. Instead, their lack of score was caused by the enemy's refusal to fight, turning tail whenever they spotted a DH2. Always quick to adapt to changing circumstances, the Germans had soon learned that discretion was the better part of valour as far as the single-seater scouts were concerned; if a combat was to be entered into, then the reconnaissance machines which crossed over the German lines every day were very much easier targets.

The fact that No.32 Squadron was eager to fight and had absorbed Rees' principles of aerial combat, was clearly illustrated by Lieutenant Nixon who, on 18 June, ran into a formation of five Aviatiks at 11,500 feet over Lens:

"I closed with the rear one who opened fire at about 100 yards, and I commenced firing at about 50 yards. After firing my second drum I was hit in the arm. I then observed a De Havilland Scout about 100 feet below me attacking another Aviatik so went to help him, but he turned away as if his gun was jammed.

I attacked the hostile machine and fired my third drum at him from underneath. When my drum was finished I observed that the German's gun was jammed. I was unable to change my drum owing to the wound in my right arm, so I returned to the aerodrome."

Upon examination of his aeroplane, Nixon discovered that it had been hit in several places with damage recorded to spars, rudder, tail and several wires had been shot away, confirming that Rees' philosophy of aggressive action with the enemy was being taken to heart by the men under his command.

It began to appear that the squadron's pilots would be put out of action, one by one, without any apparent loss to the enemy. Three days after Nixon had been hospitalised, 2nd Lieutenant Simpson misjudged his landing and came down on the edge of a cornfield to the east of the airfield with the result that the machine overturned and he sustained a severe cut to the head and injured his right shoulder. His machine had two badly bowed centre struts, top main plane attachment plates broken, the front of the nascelle had been pushed right in, the rudder and the propellor were damaged, two bottom tail booms were bent and one cross bracing wire was broken.

The pace on the Western Front began to 'hot-up' as preparations for the forthcoming Allied offensive moved towards their final stages. On Thursday, 22 June, after several days of bad weather, the sun broke through and No.32 Squadron was able to mount twenty-six patrols. Several pilots reported enemy activity and it seemed that, at last, there was a strong possibility that a German machine had been destroyed but, as the action took place behind the enemy lines, no confirmation could be made. Captains Gilmour and Allen, accompanied by 2nd Lieutenant Coleman, had encountered eleven or twelve Albatros two-seaters over Lens and immediately went into the attack. Each officer fired two drums at different machines and Allen saw his tracers entering the fuselage of his opponent, just behind the observer. Coleman dived after a machine firing as he went and, when he pulled out at 4,000 feet he saw the enemy aircraft still falling until he lost sight of it at about 2,000 feet above Loos. Gilmour's Lewis gun jammed when he was in the midst of the German formation and he was forced to break away from the attack. Desperately trying to free the gun's mechanism, he released control of his aircraft and dismantled the gun but to no avail. When he landed, the bolt was found to be bent. None of the three machines were hit and all made a safe return to their aerodrome.

2nd Lieutenant Thomas was not so lucky when he suffered a broken gudgeon pin in his engine whilst on the evening patrol over Lens. The ensuing vibration forced him to switch off the engine and attempt to glide home. As he made his approach at 150 feet he tried a right turn but was unable to take the bank off afterwards with the result that the wing struck the ground causing the machine to crash. The DH2 was wrecked but, miraculously, Thomas was uninjured. [16]

On 23 June, the Allied guns opened the most intensive bombardment of the war with the intention of destroying the German defences before the infantry launched their assault one week later. For seven days and seven nights, without respite, the guns hammered out their message of destruction and the men of the RFC were given the dual tasks of ensuring that no enemy patrols crossed the lines to observe the preparations whilst also mounting patrols behind the German lines to check on the effectiveness of the bombardment and the state of readiness of the enemy's defences. Two days after the bombardment began, the 1st Brigade launched an assault on the German observation balloons in its sector. Five DH2s of No.32 Squadron, flown by Gilmour, Allen, Nicholas, Thomas and Corby, provided the escort for machines from Nos. 2 and 10 Squadrons which were to carry out the actual attacks. Rees accompanied them as far as the front line which he then patrolled to await their return.[17] Several times the escorts lost contact with the BEs due to cloud and, when they arrived over the target area, they discovered that the balloons had already been lowered and so the mission was aborted.

Despite the undoubted frustration felt by the pilots of No.32 Squadron as the days slipped by without a confirmed victory, their success in keeping their sector clear of the enemy was noted. On 27 June, Rees assumed temporary command of the Tenth (Army) Wing which covered No.25 Squadron as well as his own; a clear indication that a staff appointment could be expected in the near future.

The end of June brought several days of wind, rain and low clouds which severely hampered aerial operations and dulled the prospects for the opening of the British offensive. On the last day of the month, four machines piloted by Von Poellnitz, Nicholas, Hunt and Dobson mounted a patrol from Armentieres to Laventie in order to protect six REs of No.21 Squadron who were to bomb an ammunition depot and storehouses at the St Sauver Station at Lille. Again, no enemy machines intervened although the aircraft were submitted to a terrific anti-aircraft bombardment.

The following morning the pilots were up early as they, along with other RFC units, were scheduled to play their part in the opening round of the British assault timetabled for 7.30 am. The heavy concentration of German aircraft over the French sector further south meant that the pilots and observers of the RFC were fairly confident that they had control of the air over the Somme battlefield. German rail communications in their rear areas were to be carefully watched and, if any traffic was observed, attacked. The first machines, piloted by Thomas, Hunt and Henty, took off at 3.40 am, followed closely by Von Poellnitz, Allen and Bath, with orders to escort BEs of No.2 Squadron and FEs of No.25 Squadron on a bombing attack on the railway station at Don and REs of the 9th Wing in an attack on Lille. These machines were all still airborne when, at 5.55 am, Rees and Lieutenant J C Simpson took off, the latter to patrol the area around La Bassee - Loos - Souchez whilst Rees patrolled the front line and awaited the return of the bombers and their escorts. Both were flying DH2s and, shortly after leaving the ground they lost contact with each other.

It was not only the men of the RFC that were about that morning. Some time before Rees and Simpson had taken off, at an airfield near Valenciennes, a formation of about ten two-seater German fighter aircraft (mostly Rumpler C IIIs but with some Albatroses) of Kagohl 3 had also taken off to patrol the area over the town of Lens. They were commanded by Leutnant Erich Zimmermann, an observer. Lieutenant Simpson heading eastwards, alone, saw this formation and, undaunted by their superior numbers, went straight into the attack. Three of the German machines broke towards him and, in the ensuing combat, Simpson's machine was hit. Spectators on the ground saw the DH2 descending, apparently under control from about 8,000 feet to about 3,000 feet from which point it went out of control and crashed on the British side of the lines. When Simpson's body was recovered it was found to have eight bullet wounds in the head.[18]

Rees, meanwhile, was quite unaware of Simpson's fate and was patrolling over the famed coal-tip known as the 'Double Crassiers' near Loos when, at 6.15 am, he saw a large formation of aircraft flying above him in a westerly direction. Assuming them to be the British formation returning to their bases, he began to climb in order to escort them home. As he drew nearer, he took a look at the machines through his binoculars and spotted their German markings but, unconcerned by their numbers, he continued his climb and made his preparations to attack. It was the same German formation that had shot down Simpson and, when they saw a second DH2 climbing towards them they felt confident that he could be despatched in the same manner.

"As I got nearer, at about Annequin, the second machine turned out of the position and dived towards me firing his guns. I waited until he came within convenient range and fired one drum. This [sic] after about the 30th round I saw the top of his fuselage splinter between the pilot and the observer. The machine turned round and went home. This machine was marked with a big '3' and a small cross on the fuselage. I then went to attack a second machine. When he saw me he fired red Very's Lights, and three more joined him. They fired an immense amount of ammunition but were so far away that they had no effect. The escort machines swooped down onto their own machine instead of me, and so shot past him and went out of action. When I got to a convenient position, I fired one drum. After about 30 rounds a big cloud of blue haze came out of the nascelle in front of the pilot. The machine turned and wobbled, and I last saw him down over the lines under control. It looked either as if a cylinder was knocked off or else the petrol tank punctured. I then saw 5 close together. They opened fire at very long range. I closed, and fired one drum at very long range at the centre and the five dispersed in all directions. I then saw the leader and the two second machines going west. I overhauled them rapidly and, when I got near the lowest, he turned sharply to the left and dropped a bomb. He opened fire at long range. I closed, just as I was about to fire, a shot struck me in the leg putting the leg temporarily out of action. I fired another drum, but not having complete control of the rudder, I swept the machine backwards and forwards. I finished firing about 10 yards away, and saw the observer sitting back firing straight up into the air, instead of at me. I grabbed my pistol but dropped it on the floor of the nascelle and could not get it again. I then recovered the use of my leg and saw the leader going towards the lines. I got within long range of him. He was firing an immense amount of ammunition. Just before he reached the lines I gave him one more drum. Having finished my ammunition I came home.

I was using the Beliene sight fixed to the gun, but as the sun had only just risen it was not shining on the cross wires. Even without the cross wires the tracers appeared to be going very near the target simply through looking through the tube which is aligned on the axis of the gun. I met the enemy at 11,000 feet when I was at 9,000 feet. I had to raise the gun from its fixed mounting.

The Germans used their usual tactics of circling round and firing at an angle of 45 degrees between the tail and sideways. There were about ten machines flying in a ragged echelon - the leader well out to the front. The machines were of two types, probably LVGs and Albatrosses [sic]. The machine I got closest to had a fuselage very like a Nieuport. The pilot in front, observer close up behind, sitting back to back. The centre section, unlike a Nieuport, was solid and cut well away at the front. I did not recognise the observer's type of gun."

Rees, despite his leg wound, landed his machine without further incident at 6.50 am. After a near perfect touchdown he was assisted from the DH2 and immediately rushed to hospital for treatment to the wound which was in his left thigh.

The eventual outcome of this combat (other than that the entire German formation was turned back behind its own lines) has been unknown until now. Fortunately, the German records of Kagohl 3 have survived and confirm the account of the fight given by Rees. Two of the German machines were in fact brought down; the first was probably that which Rees records as having given off a "blue haze", the details of which are unrecorded but the second was that of the squadron commander, Leutnant Zimmermann who was killed and his pilot, Leutnant Wendler who was wounded. This was undoubtedly the machine which Rees noted as having an observer "firing straight up into the air". This latter machine crashed near Petit Hantay, a hamlet ENE of La Bassee.

The entire action had been seen from the ground and the men of the 22nd Anti-Aircraft Battery stated "...one machine must have crashed, as it was observed falling to the ground out of control, although not actually seen to crash." Gwilym Lewis, who watched Rees return to the airfield wrote to his parents the next day:

"I told you he was the bravest man in the world ... archies batteries say they have never seen anything so gallant or comic in their lives. The Huns were in a tight little bunch when he came along - after he had finished they were all scattered in twos and ones all over the sky, not knowing which way to go.

He landed in the usual manner - taxied in. They got the steps for him to get out of his machine. He got out and sat on the grass, and calmly told the fellows to bring him a tender to take him to hospital. I am afraid he has got a very bad wound, though he is lucky not to have had an artery in his leg shot, as I understand he would never have got back if he had.

Of course everyone knows the Major is mad. I don't think he was ever more happy in his life than attacking those Huns. He said he would have brought them all down one after the other if he could have used his leg. He swears they were youngsters on their first bombing lesson !! I don't know how he does it ! "

The following day Rees wrote a letter to his sister Muriel who was, at the time, living in Australia, in which he appeared to trivialise both the aerial combat and his injury.

"Dear Muriel,

Yesterday I had quite a good scrap. I met 10 Huns altogether. The first I sent home. The second I wrecked completely. The third put a bullet through my leg so that I could not manoeuvre quickly, but he was sorry he met me before I finished with him. All the others went back across the lines & as I am not allowed to go across I helped them home at long range.

I am now in No.2 Canadian Clearing Hospital. I am to go to the Base by the first train, stay there for a few days & then go to England. I should be alright again in a month."

Rees remained in France for a little over a week before being invalided back to Britain. The German bullet which had entered the lower part of his thigh had caused some damage to the knee and the wound was, consequently, more debilitating than had at first been assumed. Far from being "...alright again in a month" he had to resign himself to a long period in hospital followed by a lengthy convalescence. He was admitted to the Countess of Pembroke's Private Hospital at Wilton House near Salisbury on 10 July and there he remained until the latter part of the year. Initially he seemed to have accepted the situation and was optimistic about a rapid recovery:

> "I have got a lovely place. The view from the window is splendid, old trees, lawns, deer, trout streams, & the people are extremely nice. I have been here a week but have had rather a temperature & have not been sitting up till today ... I expect soon to be able to wheel myself about."

Whether this was a truthful letter or merely an attempt to reassure his sister we cannot tell but certainly, by the end of the month when he replied to a letter which he had received from his old comrade in arms from No.11 Squadron, Sergeant Batten, things did not look so promising:

> "Thank you very much for your letter. I have been unable to answer before as I had an operation and was not allowed to write. Even now I am tilted up, my feet above my head and a weight on my foot. I cannot imagine anything more uncomfortable."

Indeed, far from improving with time, his condition appears to have deteriorated so that, two months later, he was hardly any further along the road to recovery. In another letter to Muriel dated 29 October, he wrote:

" I have not written for ages but I have been in bed the whole time & it is very difficult to write in bed. Now I am beginning to get about again. I stood for the first time yesterday. Auntie Katie & Nora are still here & Auntie Katie pushes me about the grounds in a large perambulator [19]. The hospital is moving next Tuesday from here to Longford Castle which is about six miles away & just the other side of Salisbury.

There is absolutely no news to tell."

When the story of his gallantry on 1 July reached the hierarchy of the RFC, Lieutenant Colonel A G Board nominated him for the award of the Victoria Cross, Britain's highest decoration for bravery in the face of the enemy. The nomination was approved and the citation was published in the London Gazette on 5 August, 1916. Due to his injury however, Rees was unable to present himself at Buckingham Palace until 14 December when he was decorated by the King. By this time his story was well known and a large group of pressmen awaited him outside the Palace gates after the investiture in the hope that he might give them a brief interview or perhaps allow his picture to be taken. By arranging a taxi beforehand, Rees managed to escape their demands, shouting in reply to a request for a picture "Not if you were to give me a thousand pounds."

In France, his squadron went on to become a successful scout unit under the command of Major T A E Cairnes [20]. It seems that Rees' combat had acted as some form of catalyst; he had shown the pilots that he was only too willing to practice what he preached. When news of the VC award came through the whole squadron was delighted. Seventy years later Gwilym Lewis can still recall his feelings at that time:

"Rees' combat had a marked effect on the Germans on our front. That was symptomatic of 32 Squadron; they had better be careful of us. The Fokkers kept well away. The spirit of the squadron was very high indeed and the fact that Rees had been wounded did not affect our morale.

We were all very proud when we heard he had been awarded the VC - he was just the type of person who could wear it."

By the end of 1916, Rees was able to get about with the assistance of two walking sticks and was discharged from hospital and went to convalesce at his aunt's home, Greenhall, High Blantyre in Scotland. In February he reported his progress to Muriel:

"I am still existing & getting extremely bored with everything. My leg is gradually getting bent, but it is so slow that I am beginning to be afraid that we will push in France before I can get out again.

I can walk with one stick now & one day I could walk without any help."

Family and friends did all they could to keep him amused but, the feeling that events were passing him by continued to lower his morale. On 25 March he wrote:

"Things are going on much the same. Next Saturday I am due to attend another Medical Board, but whatever they say I am going to London to try and get a job of some kind. I am absolutely out of it here & am now simply wasting time.

I am told that I will be able in time to bend my leg to a right angle, at present it does half a right angle & about half as much again if it is forced, but I can walk for a short distance now without sticks

95

& for long distances with one stick only."

He need not have worried about his future employment. Events on the far side of the Atlantic were to bring his period of inactivity to an unexpected end much sooner than even he anticipated.

CHAPTER V
Washington DC
(1917)

On 6 April 1917, at a special session of the United States Congress, President Woodrow Wilson declared that a state of war existed between the United States and the German Empire. In Europe, the Allies rejoiced at the thought of the powerful addition of America to their cause. Now, at last, there might be some light at the end of the tunnel and victory seemed assured as long as America's resources could be brought to bear with the shortest delay possible. Time was running out for the Germans and the onus lay on them to launch an offensive which would win the war before the US forces arrived in Europe and tilted the balance away from them forever.

The Allied leaders had taken the greatest care not to be seen publicly encouraging America's entry into the conflict and, as late as 10 March, Wilson's advisor, Colonel House, a staunch supporter of the Allied cause had written to Lloyd George:

"Tell your people to take no steps to hasten matters directly or indirectly; it only hinders instead of helping us. Let us alone and we will go all the faster. The only thing I fear is you trying to push us - the strongest pro-Allies resent this.

Tell them we are with you to the finish of our resources in supplies money and men. We are prepared to go the whole hog. They have no idea how soon we can raise a big army; many thousands of young men already have the necessary training - cadets in our military schools and State institutions. Texas alone has 200,000 men who can ride and shoot, and other Western States are in proportion."

Despite such a proud claim, there were few on the eastern side of the Atlantic who did not regard the Americans with some scepticism - there had been little opportunity to take part in cavalry charges since the opening days of the war. Nevertheless the will was there and it was felt that the Allies should take the earliest opportunity to make the Americans fully aware of the true facts of life on the Western front. The British War Cabinet had already agreed, in principle, to send a military mission to Washington DC, and on 5 April, the Foreign Secretary, Arthur Balfour, was nominated as its leader, subject to agreement by the US Government. As a former Prime Minister, Balfour's name carried sufficient status for the mission to be accepted in the highest quarters.

Balfour was briefed to impress upon the Americans the need to send a small force of trained soldiers to Europe as soon as possible as an act of good faith and to commence the training of a large army which could, if necessary, complete its training in France. Any assistance which the US Government might need was to be given. Balfour was to be supported by a team of specialists to aid him in his task, who could advise both him and their American counterparts as required.

One of the main areas in which the US authorities lacked experience and knowledge was that of wartime flying. Although powered flight was developed initially at Kittyhawk, North Carolina in 1903, the US Army had proved to be as equally short-sighted with regard to aeronautics as their European counterparts; indeed it might be argued that they were even more conservative in their outlook. Before August 1914, such an oversight might have been forgiven when one considers America's very isolated position in relation to other major military powers. After 1914, however, to ignore the developments which were taking place over the battlefields of Europe was foolish in the extreme. The war in Europe had very clearly shown the potential of air power but, despite this, the War Department in Washington had learned nothing. A few stalwarts had been experimenting with military aviation since 1909 and in March 1916, the 1st Aero Squadron had been ordered to accompany a force of 15,000 men under the command of Brigadier John Pershing which was to enter Mexico and destroy the rebel forces under the command of Francisco 'Pancho' Villa. From their experience in this brief campaign, the airmen themselves learned a great deal but the General Staff appeared to have learned nothing. Perhaps the greatest lesson that should have been learnt was that the machines used by the army were quite unsuitable for military flying under the best of conditions, but certainly not for active service. Two years after the outbreak of hostilities in Europe, the Americans were still ignorant of the knowledge which was being gained daily in the skies above France and Belgium. In April 1917, when Wilson declared war on Germany, the US Army Signal Corps had about 100 trained pilots with 125 machines; the latter being totally unsuitable for combat service. The Balfour Mission hoped to be able to assist in this area of American military development and the man chosen as the military aviation advisor was Major Lionel Rees.

The mission assembled in London and left Euston Station under the greatest veil of secrecy possible, travelling by train to Dumfries in Scotland where they were delayed for 24 hours by the presence of a U-Boat off the coast of Northern Ireland [1]. The following day they embarked at Greenock and made an uneventful crossing to Halifax, Nova Scotia where they docked on 20 April, and boarded a train for New York. Arriving in the city they were driven through cheering crowds along streets decorated with the Stars and Stripes and the Union Flag to a house on 16th Street which had been put at their disposal by the owner. They eventually reached Washington DC on 22 April and commenced a hectic round of official and social functions.

With the exception of Balfour himself and Lieutenant General Bridges, it was Rees that seemed to capture the imagination of both the American public and the press, which referred to him in glowing terms whenever he appeared. In her memoirs written many years later, Mrs Wilson, the President's wife, recorded a dinner given to the principal members of the mission:

"...among the younger members of the party was an 'aviator' who has brought down seven [sic] German planes. Looks little more than a boy, and is very lame poor fellow."

Although the mission was primarily concerned with preparing the ground for the future and stimulating good-will, a great deal of useful work was achieved and in just over a week, a report was sent to the Chief of the Imperial General Staff in London which outlined the progress which they had made. With regard to the air service, the following decisions had been reached:

" a) Twelve picked American officers have been selected for an intensive course at Toronto. These officers will be trained as instructors but will not fly.

b) Fifty cadets of the US Army are proceeding immediately to Toronto with the rank of Sergeant to be trained with a view to obtaining commissions.

c) As soon as obtainable, up to 1,000 mechanics of proportionate trades will proceed to Toronto for training. In three months it is believed that units will be formed from the above personnel, provided with transport and tools, but with no machines. The US Government are desirous of buying aerodromes near ours. It will also be necessary for them to purchase machines from us.

In addition to the above, it is proposed to send to England complete personnel of squadrons with partially trained pilots to be trained and used by us until required by the US. These would be in US uniform and pay. The Air Service is very popular in this country, and the material is plentiful and good.

As to machines, Mr Layton has the subject under discussion. It would appear best for the US motor factories to make motors for us, and to relieve thereby some of our factories at home for the construction of aeroplane engines."

Strange as it may seem, the entry of the United States into the war did not ease the pressure on European industry which was working to meet the apparently insatiable demands of the armies at the front. In terms of aircraft production, the Americans were in no position to assist at all and in fact imposed an additional burden upon the British and French airframe manufacturers. Those, like Rees, who were fully aware of the conditions imposed by combat flying considered every existing American design to be obsolete. Even when European designs such as the DH4 were handed over to the

Americans to produce under licence, the manufacturers could not fulfil the demand and by the end of hostilities, only 417 American built DH4s had been used in combat operations in Europe.

As well as examining the situation regarding military aviation and reporting his findings to the British government, Rees was involved in a public relations exercise which was intended to win over the American public to the Allied cause. When one considers his natural modesty and reticence, his success was even more surprising and was given added weight by the appearance of his name in newspapers and magazines across America. Every effort was made to show the Allies in a good light whilst every opportunity was taken to destroy the image of the Germans. When one reads the propaganda which Rees released to the US press, it is important to note that April 1917 was to go down in the history of the RFC as 'Bloody April' when the Corps lost more men and machines than at any other time during the entire war. There was no hint of this in the report published in the New York Times on 1 May:

"Washington, April 30 - How the British and French are maintaining practical control of the air over the western battlefront was graphically described here today by Major L W B Rees ...

Whilst the Allies' operations are conducted almost entirely beyond the German lines, the Major said, the German machines now cross the Allied lines only rarely in raiding parties. The Germans have given up all attempts to guide their artillery by airplane and seek only to smash up the Allied reconnaissance over their lines... Major Rees gave it as his opinion that the British had defeated the Germans in every way in the air and deprived them of valuable reconnaissance power ... The Major stated that the purpose of his coming with the war mission was largely to tell American aviation experts the results of England's two and a half years of experience in flying. All the patents and designs used in British machines will be available for the Government with any other information in the possession of the British Flying Corps."

Where possible, Rees' own gallant service record was used to boost the image of the mission. Indeed, his decorations, personality and the limp which was visible evidence of his wound must have seemed a godsend to both the mission and the American press.

"   THE MODEST TALE OF REES VC - WHOSE MIDDLE NAME IS MODESTY. In the good old days when every press agent was a poet and every poet consequently had a chance to make a name for others whilst making a living for himself, wars bred heroes as thickly and inevitably as a compost-heap breeds flies. Without some such expert co-operation, it is extremely hard to make the bravest and most desperate of deeds seem as heroic as it really is. Take the sad case of Major L W B Rees ... to look at him you would never think he was a hero, for he is only twenty-eight years old [sic] and strikingly boyish and unwarlike in appearance. Yet he is one of the few living men who has the great distinction of wearing the Victoria Cross ... and the Military Cross... It was Major Rees who, single-handed and alone, performed what experts call " the best bit of air fighting" of the war, which means, of course, the most desperate and thrilling piece of fighting any human being ever took part in.
Would you like to hear him tell about it ? Very well, ask him and watch him turn red in the face, stutter, stammer and look furtively about him for some way of escape ... you will soon realise how much he needs a press agent." [2]

"The man said by many to be the greatest British airman living has steadfastly refused to have himself made much of. Now, however, he has put aside his dislike of personal publicity ... as a service to aviation and the cause of the Allies." [3]

Such adulation must have caused Rees to cringe with embarassment but it would have been just what the War Office and the British Government would have wanted in terms of propaganda and public relations. He had obviously made his mark with the American public and the military authorities in the capital and, when the Balfour Mission prepared to leave Washington in order to return to Britain, the US Army intervened:

"Please permit me to make this acknowledgement of the services rendered the United States by Major L Rees, RFC, in connection with the air service of the United States Army. Understanding that it is your intention to return Major Rees to England, I take this opportunity of expressing the hope that you will allow Major Rees to remain in the United States for duty in my office that he may continue to assist us with the development of the air service of our army." [4]

Squier's request was granted and Rees, who had been promoted to Temporary Lieutenant Colonel with effect from 1 May, was allocated an office in Washington DC and a car and ordered to give the Americans every assistance.

The remainder of the Balfour Mission left the US capital on 23 May and, the following day, Rees left for Dayton, Ohio where, two days later, after visiting a new aerodrome at Fairfield, he had lunch at Moraine Farm, the home of Orville Wright. This was followed by a four day tour of various cities in Michigan and New York State, the first of a series of similar tours which were to take him to every part of the USA and which turned him into a national celebrity. Much of the time he was accompanied by Major (later Lieutenant Colonel) Hiram Bingham [5] who had nothing but praise for his British associate both as a man and as an expert on military aviation.

"   The truth was, that the General Staff knew practically nothing about Military Aeronautics. We had to work out our own salvation - and keep going at the same time. Fortunately, we had the constant aid and assistance during those difficult six months, of Colonel L W B Rees, of the Royal Flying Corps. Colonel Rees had been used in England as an instructor, so his advice was particularly valuable. We learned to turn to him on all doubtful questions. That we did not make more mistakes was due chiefly to his long experience and good judgement. On my first tour of inspection of the cadets in the ground schools, I had the good fortune to be accompanied by Colonel Rees, and to witness the enthusiasm which his presence aroused among the cadets and the eagerness with which members of the various faculties plied him with questions both before and after his lecture. Merely to get a glimpse of him as he limped across the campus and to realise what he had done was enough to increase appreciably the zeal of the cadets.

It was only with the very greatest of difficulty that one could get Colonel Rees to speak of his great fight, even in private. His lectures were confined to discussion of recent developments in aerial tactics and amusing stories of mistakes that had been made by British pilots, due in some cases to inability to read maps, and in others to disobedience of specific instructions. His readiness to help us in the minutest details was particularly appreciated by Lieutenant John C Farrar whose duty it was to collect for the use of the schools all the latest information regarding military aeronautics. We continually received the very latest confidential information prepared by the Royal Flying Corps. Its use in the courses at the ground schools was of great psychological value. It raised the morale of the cadets and made them take pride and interest in the course of instruction. Unfortunately, it could not get them to the Front any sooner."

Most of June and July were spent on a tour of the USA during which Rees lectured on military aviation to cadets at military camps which had been established at unversities and other centres of learning throughout the country. Commencing at Columbus, Ohio, the tour included Urbana and Chicago in Illinois, Berkeley, San Francisco and San Diego in California, San Antonio and

Austen in Texas and Atlanta in Georgia. Mush of the subject matter included in his lectures appears to have been based upon the combat tactics outlined in 'Fighting in the Air' and the manual itself was serialised in the Air Service Journal during July 1917. The tour ended with Rees addressing the US Congress on 11 July when he described what he had seen at the various training camps. His report, in the best traditions of the diplomatic service, said very little and nothing which might offend. Undoubtedly, his discussions with Bingham and others were more frank as indeed was a letter which he sent to his aunt in Scotland:

" We went to San Diego ... right on the Mexican border. There was a fiesta going on when we arrived and a lot of Mexicans were in the town. There was a decorated parade of cars, and troops of all kinds were in the streets. I think they might have been better employed. The hotel we stayed in was not too dirty. I got a joy-ride around the aerodrome to see the size. I did not like to say I was not impressed, as Salisbury Plain was 20 miles across, and a good landing place all the way. We met a Swede at San Diego who built his own planes out of condemned Government parts and then flew the machines. I expect he will come to a bad end in the near future. He takes up people at ten dollars a time, and he has not killed many people yet.

At San Antonio ... I lectured the officers of the post and they all came except the old general who could not understand my English accent."

In August, he was off again to the West Coast in the company of the heads of the French and Italian Aviation Missions, Major Henri Dourif and Major Perfetti. Their task was to inspect the forests and timber yards of Washington and Oregon and encourage the men engaged in the timber industry to increase their output of spruce which was vital for the expansion of aeroplane manufacture. As usual, his personality endeared him to those that he met:

" That grin - the happiest, whole-heartedest most infectiously spontaneous one that hit Tacoma for a long time - it introduced Lieut. Col. L W B Rees ... this morning as he limped his long, slightly drooping person up the long slip from the Seattle boat."

Their arrival in Aberdeen co-incided with the calling off of the lumber strike in the area, and at the Grand Theatre in that city on 10 August, they were greeted by a standing ovation from a capacity audience. As was usual at each public meeting held on the tour, Rees addressed the audience "... in his deliciously broad English 'brogue' " then showed a number of motion pictures illustrating the work of the Allied air forces in Europe.

The autumn was spent back in Washington DC where he helped to prepare an instruction manual for the US airmen under training. When it was completed, Bingham summed up its value in a simple note of thanks which he sent to Rees:

" Permit me to congratulate you on the fine piece of work that you have turned out ... I shall make every effort to have this made up into a little book which can easily be carried in the pocket and shall try to see that every pilot in the American Army has one."

By this time, his task in the United States was almost over and US General 'Hap' Arnold expressed the official military view of his services as the time came for them to part company. [6]

" You must realise the very deep and sincere regret it occasions all of us that your duties here are finished. Every officer of this

Division shares with me the sentiment that it has been a privilege to have known and been associated with you. To see you later on the other side is something truely to be looked forward to.

On behalf of the Chief Signal Officer, I wish to express deep appreciation of the valuable service you have rendered here, and wish to thank you for your good cheer and extreme courtesy always."

On a less formal level, the views of the American officers who had served under Rees were best summed up in a Christmas card which he received from a junior officer, Lieutenant S Mervill Clement:

" I wanted to send this Christmas greeting to you, and to simply tell you how genuinely sorry I am that you are leaving us. May I also, Sir, thank you very appreciatively for the hospitality you have always extended me and the many many kindnesses you have shown me in the office. I shall never forget your patience at my constant interruptions in your work, and your generous spirit of helpfulness to us all in the Instruction Bureau - Good Luck always ! "

Rees spent the remaining days of 1917 and the first few days of the New Year staying with friends and, during the second week of January he embarked aboard the RMS *Carmania* along with a contingent of men for the American Expeditionary Force [7].

CHAPTER VI
No. 1 School of Aerial Fighting
(1918 - 19)

Due to the rapid expansion of the Royal Flying Corps during 1916 and the early months of 1917 and the changing nature of military flying, a number of flying schools were established throughout Great Britain where pupils could be trained in accordance with the principles laid down by Smith-Barry at Gosport. [1] The dramatic changes in aerial combat illustrated in previous chapters had resulted in a steep rise in the casualty rate, particularly amongst newly qualified pilots on the Western Front and losses in the air rose dramatically amongst the combatants of all nations from mid-1916 onwards. An estimated total of 165 aeroplanes of all nations were lost during July 1916, 189 were lost during August and 322 in September. During the Arras offensive of 1917, losses reached horrific proportions - 1430 machines being destroyed in April and May alone. [2] It very soon became apparent that, in addition to the normal flying instruction which was designed to produce a competent pilot, special schools were required where pilots and observers could be taught more advanced skills which would help them stay alive once they were in France.

One such centre was the No. 1 School of Aerial Fighting which was established at Ayr in Scotland. On 7 March 1918, Lionel Rees was appointed to command the school, a decision which was undoubtedly influenced not only by his abilities as an instructor and commanding officer but also by the fact that a sizable percentage of the airmen who would be passing through Ayr would be Americans. Rees' leg injury and his senior rank made it unlikely that he would obtain an active command in France and therefore this appointment, with its emphasis upon flying, greatly appealed to him.

The instructors at Ayr were all experienced airmen who had completed at least one period of duty with a front-line squadron. They had been recalled to Britain in order that they might pass on their accumulative knowledge to others and their decorations amply demonstrated their experience and success and greatly impressed their pupils.

The choice of Ayr as a training station may have appeared rather strange as, although situated on relatively flat land (the airfield was actually on Ayr Racecourse) [3] it was only a few miles from the mountains and this, coupled with the potential danger of sea mist, provided a perfect recipe for disaster should a pupil become lost or disorientated whilst in the air. However, due to its remoteness and coastal location, it was well suited for the practice of air-to-ground and air-to-air gunnery and its situation on a railway line made it easily accessible.

Each course lasted only a few days, up to a maximum of one week and in that short time, the school achieved a remarkable rate of success which can be measured in part by the decline in the casualty rate amongst new pilots in France. In addition to the obvious advantages to the pupils, there was an added benefit in that the instructors learned a great deal about the problems facing newly qualified pilots so that when they eventually resumed their duties with a service squadron they were far more sympathetic and therefore devoted more time to the induction of replacement pilots into their units.

The object of the school was quite simple; to teach pilots and their observers to fly and shoot in combat in such a way that their manoeuvres became reflex actions and thereby eliminating a delayed reaction which would have given the enemy precious seconds in which to destroy them. Once an individual had mastered the basic fighting skills, he was taught to use them in conjunction with other members of the same squadron. It was felt that pilot training at the Central Flying School and other similar establishments provided the novice with only the fundamentals of flying and that the much prized 'wings' awarded at the end of that course was only a qualification in the basic control of a flying machine. At Ayr, those same pilots would learn how to survive in the air and work as part of a team.

Upon their arrival at the school all pupils were given instruction in gunnery and pilots were tested to ensure that their flying skills were up to the minimum standards expected. Once this preliminary stage had been passed, all the pupils were taken up in a two-seater machine and, with the instructor at the controls, a mock combat was carried out against another aeroplane. Throughout the time in the air the instructor was meant to keep the pupil fully informed of everything that was happening and why. This stage was followed by the pupil flying a service machine in mock combat against the instructor, a procedure which was repeated until the pupil was able to demonstrate that he had mastered the technique. Instructors would then lead a number of pilots into the air in order to teach them the basics of formation flying and the various manoeuvres which they would be expected to be proficient in when joining the service squadrons. Pupils were also sent into mock combats against each other before being issued with fully armed machines which they used for firing practice against stationary and moving targets both on the ground and in the air.

Pupils were taught not only how to attack the enemy but also, most importantly, how to defend themselves against an attack. They were encouraged, within the limited time available, to put in as much practice as possible at any aspect of flying which they considered to be a weakness and straight forward flying was frowned upon as a waste of valuable air time. It was a firmly held belief at the school that a successful pilot required discipline and that without it, he would endanger not only himself but also his comrades. This discipline was not a passive, regimental obedience to orders but was something more akin to personal self-control. As an example of this pupils were actively encouraged to carry out stunt flying and to get as much practice at low flying as possible, both activities which were viewed with great disfavour at the CFS. It was however clearly pointed out to the pupils that any 'stunts' which they carried out should not cause any concern to others either on the ground or in the air. A pilot who was comfortable in his machine, who knew its characteristics and limitations in every possible situation was far more likely to make a good fighter pilot and, consequently, he was far more likely to survive those crucial first weeks at the front.

" All the flying here is stunting and we have service machines. Every time we go up, we are supposed to find another machine and have a dog-fight with it. The Colonel stays in the air a lot and is the best at scrapping - he and Foggin and Atkinson." [4]

In order that pupils would be familiar with the machines that they would fly on active service, the school was equipped with a wide variety of machines including Avro 504s, SE5s, Camels, SPADs, Bristol Fighters and Bristol MC1s and pupils only flew the type of machine with which their designated squadron was equipped.

Life at Ayr could prove to be as dangerous as that of a pilot with a service squadron as an anonymous American witness recorded in his diary [5]:

"March 20. Cush Nathan killed. He was flying an SE and the wings came off at five thousand feet. He went into the roof of a three-story house and they dug him out of the basement. A real fine fellow. I liked him. So did everybody."

March 26. George Vaughn cracked up an SE in splendid style. The engine concked with him over the town and he pancaked in a vacant lot and climbed up on top of a building. Later on, somebody wanted a picture of the crash and wanted him in it. He got back in the seat and the fuselage collapsed and the whole thing toppled over. Pansy run into a chimney with a Camel and scored one complete write-off."

The school's emphasis upon personal self-discipline applied equally to staff as well as pupils and, as many of the instructors were famous combat pilots , it was to be expected that the pupils would look up to them and try an emulate their behaviour. For this reason the instructors were expected to present a good example at all times. One breach of this discipline which might have had tragic consequences but was, fortunately only highly embarassing, concerned Captain James McCudden who had arrived at Ayr shortly after being decorated with the Victoria Cross in recognition of his combat record [6]. Instructors were permitted to make use of service machines for private flying in the belief that the pupils would gain confidence by seeing aeroplanes used as part of the day to day life of the senior pilots. McCudden was invited by Captain Latta, a fellow instructor, to visit his family at Failford House some six miles away and, after finishing work for the day, they both took off in an Avro 504, landing a few minutes later on the front lawn of Latta's home. During the course of the evening, Mary Latta, the sister of the pilot, managed to persuade McCudden to give her a short flight in the Avro, a practice which was strictly against the rules. After about ten minutes in the air the engine suddenly stopped and would not re-start and McCudden was forced to make an emergency landing in a field. All went well until the final moments when, after a safe touch-down, the Avro ran into a concealed depression in the ground which caused it to tip over onto its back. Fortunately, neither pilot nor passenger was injured but McCudden had the embarassing task of reporting the problem to Ayr so that some transport could be sent to pick him up and a guard provided for the aircraft until it could be recovered the following day.

There was no disguising the circumstances leading to the crash and the following morning the young 'ace' was summoned to appear before the Commanding Officer to face the consequences. All who knew about the incident waited to hear the outcome of the interview and wondered whether McCudden's status and image could protect him. Rees, however, was not amused and, as a fellow holder of the Victoria Cross, felt not in the least bit intimidated by the younger man and proceeded to give him what was described as a first-class dressing down, making it crystal clear that the rules of the school were to be obeyed by everyone, irrespective of rank, reputation or public esteem; there were too many casualties amongst the pupils and the instructors for any civilians to be added to their number.

Not all the pilots that passed through Ayr were novices. Many were highly experienced flyers who came there as members of a new squadron which was about to be posted to France. One such man was Captain Edward 'Mick' Mannock who comanded 'A' Flight of No.74 Squadron and who was already well on his way to becoming the top scoring British pilot of the war [7]. With him in No. 74 and himself a distinguished destroyer of German machines was Welshman Ira 'Taffy' Jones, who later recalled his short time at the school [8]:

"Most of the flyers chosen for 74 Squadron were sent to Ayr in Scotland for a course in aerial fighting. The school was commanded by the Welsh VC Colonel Rees, and amongst the instructors were the famous Major James McCudden, VC, Captain Gerald Maxwell, late of 56 Squadron, Captain Atkinson, late of 29 Squadron, and one-eyed Captain Foggin, who was tragically killed a few months later in an accident in France.

The course was simple. The instructor showed the pupil what to do and not to do during an air fight. Besides practising fighting, trainees were encouraged to throw their aircraft around with abandon, in order to gain the maximum confidence in the machines. It was an excellent course. Its teachings saved my life more than once in actual combat. At the end of it every pupil had to appear before Colonel Rees and explain not only what he had learned, but what stunting he had carried out. To the latter question one pupil replied: "I climbed up to 15,000 feet sir, and zoomed". No.74 Squadron was to be equipped with SE5 single-seater scouts. While at Ayr I did all my flying in this type of machine. Pupils who were to go to France with Sopwith Camels - rotary engined, single-seater scouts with exceptionally fast manoeuvreability - had to fly that type. The accidents were many. I remember seven funerals in one week as the result of the right hand turn close to the ground. Dozens of pilots were killed by the Camel."

As Jones pointed out, the most difficult of the new breed of fighters which the pupils had to master at Ayr was the Sopwith Camel which had developed a reputation as a difficult machine for the newly trained pilot to fly. One pilot H Harnet, described the machine as "... a buzzing hornet, a wild thing, burning the air like raw spirit in the throat." On the whole, casualties amongst the pilots at Ayr were rare with the exception of those who flew in 'C' Flight which was equipped with Camels. On the very day that Rees took command of the school two pilots were killed followed by a third on the next day. Two Americans were also killed, one of them an instructor of considerable experience [9]. The problems with instructing pupils to fly the Camel reached such a pitch at one stage that it was in danger of becoming destructive to the morale of the pilots who viewed the machine as something of a jinx. The cause of the difficulty was simple; the rotary engine which powered the aircraft meant that the engine cylinders rotated around the fixed camshaft creating a number of problems paramount of which was the torque which resulted from such a design. This, combined with the aeroplane's very forward centre of gravity, made it a "... one sided, feverish and vicious" machine until the pilot was taught to recognise the problem and counteract it. As he taxied for take-off the pilot had to ensure that he applied full right rudder in order to counter the aircraft's natural desire to attempt a loop whilst still on the ground. As soon as the tail lifted off the ground the rudder had to be straightened very quickly to prevent a sudden left turn which would inevitably result in the wing tip hitting the ground causing the machine to crash. Once airborne, the pilot had to remember to cut the choke immediately and then continually move the fine adjuster and throttle as he gained height. As the torque built up with the increasing engine revolutions, the nose would be forced down in a right hand turn. If, in order to counteract this, the pilot pulled back too far on the stick the nose would come up very quickly and the engine would stall. If he then tried to put the machine into a dive, the torque would try to set up an outward loop. Captain Norman Macmillan, MC, AFC, an experienced combat pilot, recorded his first, and very nearly his last, flight in a Camel.

" I thrust the control stick forward hard against the dash, exactly as we did in the old two-seaters. My little mount answered instantly, rose up under me, and plunged straight downwards towards the ground over the vertical and partly on her back. As she went she projected me outward and forward from the cockpit. My belt was an elastic-sided contraption and expanded so that I slid through. When I felt myself going I clutched downward to grab the seat. My fingers missed the seat but caught the petrol adjusting tap, which I had screwed off just before pushing the stick forward. My fingers closed around the tap, but the acceleration was too much for that flimsy resistance, and I shot out of the cockpit on to the guns along the top of the fuselage, where I lay for a moment with my nose feeling very much like being grazed by the propellor.

For an instant I lay while the acceleration died out and left only the terrific dive to earth with my plane partly on her back, and I literally standing on my head. Inch by inch I forced myself backwards and upwards towards the cockpit until, with my right hand, I found the ring at the top of the control column and pulled myself into the machine again. I got in, found the rudder bar with my feet, and gradually pulled the plane out of the headlong plunge. I levelled out at two thousand five hundred feet, having fallen head down for nearly a mile." [10]

As this account clearly shows, an experienced pilot

could easily find himself in very serious difficulties when flying the Camel and therefore a newly qualified pilot would have had very little chance of surviving in a similar situation. To resolve this growing fear Rees decided to take a Camel up himself. Without informing anyone of his intentions, he selected a machine and waited until there were sufficient pupils and staff around to see his performance and then took-off at full power, climbed to 500 feet and immediately commenced a flying display the like of which few of those on the ground had ever seen before. If anyone had harboured any doubts as to his skill as a pilot they were dispelled that day. He made the Camel do everything that she was capable of and deliberately put her into situations which brought out all her worst characteristics, handling them all with masterly skill. To the large numbers watching from below he demonstrated beyond any question that the machine could be mastered and turned into the most manoeuvreable fighter of the war. One of the Americans present said that it was "... a wonderful exhibition", never climbing above 500 feet, he "... certainly did fight the treetops and he wouldn't come out of a spin above fifty feet." On landing, he limped into his office and ordered all the instructors to repeat the performance, for that is what it had surely been and, from then onwards, although pupils still eyed the little fighter with wary concern, they were in no doubt that the instructions given by the staff of the school worked and that those who gave out the orders were also capable of carrying them out.

A sad post-script to this tale is that several of the pupils were so impressed that they took-off almost immediately to try and emulate the display. Within minutes the Camel had claimed another victim.

The American airmen at Ayr felt themselves privilaged to be there:

" Everybody here wants to get out of the US Army and join the RFC where they'll get a square deal. We certainly have gotten a rotten deal from the USA and the British couldn't have treated their own Field Marshals any better. We owe the British a lot and have a lot to get even with our own army for." [11]

Certainly Rees appears to have played a part in establishing these cordial relationships and was held in high regard by the 'Yanks'.

On 11 May, the No.1 School of Aerial Fighting was closed down at Ayr and the staff and equipment were moved to Turnberry some twenty miles further south where they were formed into the No.1 Fighter School, expanding their activities to incorporate those previously carried out by the No.2 Auxiliary School of Air Gunnery which had occupied the Turnberry aerodrome. In addition to the type of instruction which they had carried out at Ayr, the school now included instruction for two-seater fighter pilots, observers and the crews of bombers. The airfield was situated right on the coast and the weather made flying conditions equally as hazardous as they had been at Ayr. The staff however, were accomodated in the luxury of the Turnberry Hotel overlooking the golf-course.[12]

Divided up into four flights and equipped with Camels, SE5As, Bristol Fighters and DH9s, the school commenced work on 14 May. Pupils began each course with intensive instruction in ground gunnery (including firing at small model aircraft from a mock-up fuselage) which was followed by aerial combat exercises. A target was moored out at sea in order to provide air-to-ground

119

firing practice and camera guns were used to record the pupil's success, or lack of it, for examination at a later time. Air-to-air firing practice was provided by RE7s which cruised the skies towing large flags through the air. Twice weekly the pupils were pitched against the instructors in a dog-fight with camera guns recording the results. Also on the aircraft strength of the school were Bristol MC1s, Avro 504s, SPADs and Sopwith Pups as well as a captured Albatros Scout.

Although Rees appears to have run the school efficiently and with firm control he was not opposed to the staff and pupils letting off steam and a rivalry soon developed between his own command and the men of the North-Western Area Flying Instructors School [13] which had moved into the airfield at Ayr and there were regular raids which kept both stations on their toes. The instructors were also often involved in spectacular aerial stunts and a particular favourite was to fly past the Turnberry Hotel below roof level, in an inverted position. It was a practice which had to be discontinued after one pilot died whilst attempting it. The local residents, despite the obvious dangers and annoyances caused by the school, appear to have gone out of their way to make life as pleasant as possible for the airmen and several memoirs make reference to visiting private homes in the area whilst stationed at Ayr and Turnberry. Rees himself spent much of his free time at a house which he had rented near the airfield where his aunt Katie acted as hostess and to which he would often invite junior officers under his command.

There can be no doubt that the School of Aerial Fighting and the Fighter School were very successful and certainly played a significant part in the establishment of

Allied supremacy in the air over the Western front during the summer of 1918. Whilst little glamour was attached to the training of pilots, those who were involved were only too aware of the risks which the duties entailed both for instructors and pupils and no one would try to argue that the staff of training establishments played anything other than a vital role in the history of the air war. It could be argued that Rees' contribution as commandant of Ayr and Turnberry was of greater significance than anything else which he had done since 1914 and certainly, countless British and American airmen owed their lives to the skills which they learned in Scotland. So often one hears criticisms of courses of all kinds but there was never anything but praise for those run by Rees. Ira Jones noted, "It was an excellent course, and later its teaching saved the life of many a pilot on more than one occasion".

Rees remained at Turnberry right through to the end of the war and on into 1919. Much to his surprise, he had survived the first conflict to be fought in the air and ahead of him lay the peace which for many was a time of reconstruction and taking stock but for Rees and the others who were desirous of remaining in the fledgling Royal Air Force [14], it was a period of uncertainty that faced them. [15]

CHAPTER VII
RAF College, Cranwell
(1920 - 25)

The General Election of December 1918 brought Winston Churchill into the Cabinet with the dual portfolios of the War Office and the Air Ministry. It had been Lloyd George's original intention that the two ministries should be merged as the first step towards the disbanding of the Royal Air Force, a move which would have pleased both the Admiralty and the War Office. Other events took precedence however as the statesmen of the world met at Versailles to draw up the peace treaty with Germany, a matter which was to take until the summer of the following year to resolve. This delay was to prove the salvation of the RAF for, by December 1919, the government had reviewed the situation and had decided to maintain an independent air service. The position of Chief of the Air Staff had seemed to be destined for Sir Frederick Sykes who had held the post at the end of the war but internal manipulations led to it being offered to Hugh Trenchard with orders to drastically reduce the strength of the wartime RAF from 154 squadrons to a more financially realistic peacetime service. Amongst his proposals, Trenchard envisaged a new breed of officer who would hold a permanent commission in the RAF; who must either know how to fly or be willing to learn.

" Training would have to be specialised and I would recommend that one should, as far as one can see at present, train pilots as fighting pilots ... reconnaissance pilots ... bombing pilots.

It is important to keep training units distinct from service units."

Although the RAF was less than two years old, Trenchard saw the value of the traditions which had already been established:

" By changing the titles and making completely new squadrons, traditions, built up over four years of war, will be lost."

His plans were approved by the government and implemented almost immediately.

The restoration of peace found Rees still serving as Commandant of the No.1 Fighter School at Turnberry but it was obvious that the post would decline in importance as the need for new pilots decreased. Clearly, his expertise as a commander of a front-line squadron, trainer of airmen and administrator placed him in an advantageous position and, in April 1919, he was appointed Inspector of Recruiting as the service turned its attention to the selection of the right kind of man for the establishment of a peacetime airforce. Still officially a regular officer in the Royal Artillery, he was also promoted to Brevet Lieutenant Colonel and, on 25 July, was further promoted to Lieutenant Colonel (Aeroplanes) and given command of No. 2 Fighter School, South East Area. One week later, his application for a permanent commission in the Royal Air Force was accepted and he relinquished his army rank to become a Wing Commander. There had been no doubt in his mind where his future lay. Eleven years of peacetime soldiering in the artillery had brought him little advancement and to return after an absence of over four years, at a time when the services were contracting, would have been foolish in the extreme. On the other hand, his service in the RFC and the RAF had raised him to the position of a well known and highly respected officer with a proven record as a man who was willing to accept any challenge and who had the ability to carry it through to a successful conclusion. A future in the RAF seemed therefore to offer infinitely better prospects and he eagerly seized the opportunity.

Rees fulfilled all the criteria laid down by Trenchard for the new service in peacetime. His abilities as a pilot could not be questioned and the decorations which he wore placed him firmly in the category of a builder of tradition, a man to whom younger officers could look up to and respect. His natural shyness and modesty endeared him to all whom he met. RAF Cadet Wilfred Freebody recalled [1]:

" He never appeared to be career minded nor did he make capital out of his undoubted achievements. He was quite diffident about his decorations ... very polite and kindly and in this respect stood out in contrast against those of his contemporaries who thought themselves to be in the 'up and coming' category. He was modest and fun-loving and made jokes at his own expense."

On 18 September, Rees moved yet again and took over the command of RAF Eastchurch on the Isle of Sheppey. Established in 1912 as the Royal Naval Air Service flying instruction camp, Eastchurch had been that service's equivalent of the RFC's Central Flying School throughout the war until it became the RAF's Air Gunnery School. Amongst those stationed there in 1919 was Boy Mechanic Walter Dawson, who had enlisted for training as an aero engine fitter at Halton in February and, shortly afterwards, had been drafted to Eastchurch for technical training.

" Parts of it seemed strange to even RAF eyes. For example, the Station Warrant Officer was in the uniform of a naval CPO (old uniform could still be worn out) - that was a 'fore and aft' without crowns, anchors or stripes and he was a chap who threw his weight about considerably, so half a dozen of my draft were in the guardroom before we discovered the status of this unpopular type. The Station Adjutant wore the uniform of an RFC Captain. We lived 20 boys to a hut and each hut's occupants formed a class who moved together - marching to school or workshops or parades etc. and each hut was in the charge of a Boy Corporal who, to my surprise, wore full corporal's stripes under the Boy's 'cartwheel'. I became the Boy Corporal of A5 Class. Wing Commander L W B Rees was the Station Commander and the course was a 6 months 'cram', probably a hang over from the wartime need for quantity at the expense of quality."

It was at this time that Rees received an honour of which he was always particularly proud, the Freedom of the Borough of Caernarfon. His home town had suffered severe losses during the war and, in common with most communities in Britain, it felt that something should be done to commemorate the deeds of local men who had made a contribution to the final Allied victory. Most were agreed that little could be done to repay the debt owed by everyone to those who had made the supreme sacrifice, but it was a matter of some concern to many that those who had survived should not feel that their services were unrecognised. In Caernarfon, the Council decided to further honour those men who had received decorations for their gallantry and devotion to duty. A civic reception was to be held at which one man would be singled out as the focus of public attention and as a representative of all the men involved. In Caernarfon's case there was little difficulty in making the choice. A large number of individuals had received gallantry awards and several officers had been singled out for their administrative contribution, but only one man, Lionel Rees, had received Britain's highest military decoration as well as the Military Cross, the Air Force Cross and had been created an Officer of the Order of the British Empire. There seems to have been little debate as to how the town could recognise his achievements and he joined that short list of men who were created Freemen of Caernarfon [2]. The ceremony was held on 15 January 1920, at the Guildhall where Rees was also presented with a Sword of Honour in recognition of his gallant service. In a speech, one councillor reflected the town's pride in Rees' achievements as was reported in the Caernarvon & Denbigh Herald:

"Councillor Abbot, JP, said he had the greatest pleasure in seconding the resolution ... enhanced by reason of the fact that they were honouring a Carnarvonite, in other words a 'hogyn o'r dre'. Though they were a small community they had reared men who had become famous ... not least of these was Wing Commander Rees, the worthy son of a worthy sire. It was said that 'a prophet is not without honour in his own country' . But those proceedings that day belied that statement. They were honouring a prophet, not only in his own country, but in his own native town ... the youngest ever to be admitted to the Freedom of the Borough, the highest honour that the people of Carnarvon could confer upon anyone."

In his speech of acceptance, Rees was his usual modest self, reminding those present that " when he had won the Military Cross, he had with him ... one of the best observers in the Service" and again when he fought the action for which he was awarded the Victoria Cross "...he was lucky in the pilot who was with him." The first was obviously, and quite rightly, an acknowledgement of the role of Flight Sergeant Hargreaves but the second reference, presumably to Simpson, was clearly an attempt to play down the award as Rees' action had been single-handed. Finally, he showed another side of his personality when he announced that he had made arrangements for 2,000 local children to be entertained at local cinemas the following afternoon. In addition to the free admission, each child was to be presented with a packet of chocolate. A simple gesture but one that clearly showed his gentle nature and love of children and which seemed to contradict all the gallant platitudes expressed by the assembled councillors.

Such pleasant, but undoubtedly highly embarassing events soon gave way to the realities of service life when Rees returned to Eastchurch.

A major aspect of Trenchard's plan for the reformed RAF was the establishment of a cadet college which would be the main route into the service for permanently commissioned officers. There was considerable pressure for entry to be via the existing cadet colleges at Dartmouth, Woolwich and Sandhurst but the Chief of the Air Staff was adamant that flying instruction must be an integral part of all RAF cadet training and this could only be provided by a seperate establishment. The case was accepted and, on 1 November 1919, Air Commodore C A H Longcroft was appointed Commandant of the Royal Air Force Cadet College which was to be opened at Cranwell Air Station, Lincolnshire [3]. The nucleus of such a college had existed for some time in the form of Headquarters No. 12 Group, also based in the same county.

Cadets were to be taught general educational subjects such as mathematics and languages as well as receive professional training in such areas as flying instruction. The first senior flying instructor (the title Chief Flying Instructor was not introduced until 1930) was Squadron Leader 'Peter' Portal, DSO, MC who had commanded No.16 Squadron on the Western Front and, since 1918, No.24 Training Wing at Grantham [4].

By 5 February the following year, the preparations were complete and the first cadet intake comprising seventeen Royal Naval entrants and thirty-three direct entrants from schools, had arrived at the isolated and rather spartan college. The Naval intake were only required to serve one year at Cranwell after which, if their performance was satisfactory, they would be offered permanent commissions. The schools entry however, were to follow a two-year course and had been selected after sitting the same examination as candidates for Woolwich and Sandhurst. Unless a cadet expressed a preference for a particluar college, the first 40 or 50 in the rank order of examination passes would go to Woolwich and the remainder would be offered places at Sandhurst until that college had reached its required quota. Cranwell then took what was left over from the remaining successful candidates. Flying Cadet Mills, a member of that first schools entry recorded:

" At first our standard was low in comparison, for instance I was first for Cranwell but only forty-fourth for Woolwich. This changed very quickly. On the other hand, our medical standard was much higher and kept out several who would otherwise have qualified easily." [5]

The cadets for the new college came from similar social backgrounds as those who had traditionally entered the older military and naval establishments. Most young men were automatically excluded by the cost of the course which was £125 per annum but provision was made for a small number of cadets who were accepted on either reduced fees (usually the sons of deceased or serving officers) or free of charge (King's Cadets from the Boy Apprentice Schools). As official members of the armed forces all cadets were paid 5 shillings per day in their first year which rose to 10 shillings per day in the second year. Amongst those who aspired for entry in that first year was Boy Mechanic Dawson at Eastchurch.

" Early in '19, the Air Ministry announced that they would soon be opening a cadet college at Cranwell on a similar basis as Sandhurst and Woolwich and subject to the same competative exam, which included certain 'set' subjects and offered a choice of others - total marks to count so long as a qualifying standard was achieved in the 'set' subjects. I obtained entry forms and a couple of sets of past exam papers from the Civil Service Commissioners.

I had left school at 14 but fortunately had attended night classes. I decided that if I worked hard enough I stood a chance in the main subjects. But one of the 'set' subjects was French and I knew nothing of that. But, I bought 'Hugo's French Simplified' and set to work. A barrack block is not an ideal place in which to teach oneself French, but fortunately I made a very early application for leave to take the exam on the grounds that if I couldn't have leave it was no good working for it.

The Adjutant did his best to dissuade me, on the very understandable grounds that I would be in competition with Public School boys, many of whom would have been to a crammer, so I hadn't a hope and I would waste my entrance fee (£4 I think). Fortunately, the Squadron Commander came through the office, asked what was going on, said he would take over and took me into his office. He was Squadron Leader Chainey, an ex-Naval warrant officer, with a voice like a foghorn, apt to frighten the pants off Boys, until we found him a fine commander and good friend.

I doubt if he had ever sat an exam but he was no fool and I was closely examined as to how far I understood what I was taking on. He then gave me the sole use of an HQ office outside working hours and gave me valuable encouragement.

The great day arrived and I was dressed in my best uniform (still khaki in those days) an hour before I need leave, when a motor DR arrived to say the Station Commander wanted to see me immediately. So, a very worried Boy Corporal arrived at Station HQ. The Warrant Officer told me to report to the 'Adj' which I did and he said "Oh yes, the Old Man wants to see you" then he barged through the door to the CO's office and announced me - I heard a voice say "Send him in" and I was waved in. Startled at not being marched in. Still more startled when the CO said "Pull up that chair to the desk and sit down". I was fascinated by his top row of ribbons - the VC, the OBE , the MC and AFC.

He spoke to me quietly, asking about my home life, schooling, apprenticeships, night classes and specially about a scholarship to Sunderland Technical College. He soon had me completely at ease and said I had a better educational background than he expected but that I lacked experience of exams. "This is a big one" he said. "I took an earlier version before going to Woolwich". So he talked about exams, giving me practical and sensible tips and made notes as he talked. Then he said he would not expect me to remember more than half he had said so he gave me his notes, with an order to memorise them and follow them in the exam. Then he wished me luck. The result was as I had forecast - a failure to qualify in French but very satisfactory totals. I passed the second exam."

Dawson arrived at Cranwell with the College's second intake in September 1920. Lionel Rees was already there, having been appointed on 21 June to take command of the Flying Wing.

Trenchard had a crystal clear picture in his mind of what he wished Cranwell to become. Despite severe financial restrictions, the Cadet College was to provide a thorough all-round education for the future officers of the RAF. There was to be no place for anything other than excellence, particularly if such officers were to be accepted as the equals of their contemporaries in the Naval and Miliatry academies. Cranwell, located as it was in the heart of Lincolnshire was well away from any large centres of population and provided little which would distract the cadets from their studies. Divided into two squadrons, A and B, the cadets were housed in wooden or iron huts and exposed to the rain, snow and cold winds which blew from the North Sea across the camp's elevated position. Each day began at 6.45 am and cadets were expected on parade at 8.00 am. This was followed by drill and lectures which took them through to lunch at 12.30 pm. An hour and a half later, they were all expected to partake in various organised activities which lasted until 4.30 pm. Discipline was maintained, on the whole, by the cadets themselves although major incidents would be dealt with by the college staff. A clear divide seems to have existed between the cadets and their officers and instructors. Theodore McEvoy, a cadet of 1923 recalled [6] :

" I had the greatest admiration for Uncle Rees, but we, as humble flight cadets, had only limited contact with the great."

Dermot Boyle, a cadet of 1922 has similar memories [7]:

" We all held him [Rees] in high regard as a World War 1 ace, as the holder of the VC and as a courageous pilot. He was OC Flying Wing but in fact I never met him to talk to and only saw him on parades.

This was in no way unusual because of the great difference in rank and age and the fact that the cadets lived in a mess of their own. Had I broken flying regulations or become a doubtful pupil, I would very quickly have met OC Flying Wing."

It was not only the cadets who regarded Rees with some awe and respect, amongst the other ranks a former AC/2 Carpenter Rigger, Harold Jones, has fond recollections of him:

" A warm, outgoing personality showing the meaning of the saying an officer and a gentleman ... strict but fair, he would listen to reason and if he had occasion to punish, it was well deserved. One Sunday in the month he would have barrack room inspection and, on these occasions would often make critical remarks on items he had already passed, the people responsible would swear he had "eyes in the back of his head"

The cadets under his command were given extensive instruction in the theory and practice of mechanics. One must assume his rating in that direction must have been very high. I recall seeing the Wing Commander floating down by parachute from a Vickers biplane. He had been taken up standing on a small platform at the foot of the rear interplane strut. The Vickers biplane was on the station to give the pilots the experience of parachuting - they were actually tugged off the aircraft when they operated the parachute. Despite his gammy leg, the Wing Commander took his turn and showed the pilots how it was done.

The same way, most mornings he took off in his Sopwith Snipe to make a weather test before giving the OK for flying training to commence."

The enforced aloofness between staff and cadets did not, however, prevent the cadets forming an opinion of the character of Rees. Geoffrey Worthington, a cadet in the very early days of the college wrote [8]

"... he was a very senior officer at Cranwell and as Flight Cadet I saw very little of him except on parade and very occasionally to talk to. When flying I saw mostly my instructor and Squadron leader Portal ... My recollections are that we all loved Daddy Rees and thought him a splendid chap.

He tested me for the Fellows Memorial Prize (which I did not win !) but I thought him very brave to sit in the gunner's cockpit of a Bristol Fighter and urge me to throw him about the sky."

This reference to 'Daddy Rees' and the earlier description of him as 'Uncle Rees' appear in the recollections of many cadets from these early days. Air Vice Marshal Freebody [9] believes that this was because...

"... he appeared elderly partly because he was bald and also had a bit of a stutter which was inclined to give the impression that he was dithering. In fact he was far from being a ditherer and was constantly surprising us all with exploits which would put much younger men in the shade."

Different intakes appear to have bestowed upon him different 'relative' nicknames but always for the kindest of reasons:

" He was certainly much respected by the cadets. My recollection of him was that he was a man of high moral principle and that he adopted a somewhat grandmotherly attitude towards the cadets. Indeed, he was affectionately known as 'granny' Rees by the cadets at the College in my time." [10]

Cadets were, to all intents and purposes, confined to the camp and its immediate environs until they were in the Senior Term when they were allowed to visit Lincoln. This almost school-like atmosphere did not meet with the approval of all the staff. S P B Mais, Professor of English at Cranwell, whilst thoroughly approving of the nature of the college, felt strongly that the cadets were subjected to too much discipline and should be allowed the same sort of freedom granted to university

undergraduates. As part of their mechanical training, the cadets were provided with dismantled motorcycles which, when reconstructed, could be used for recreation and a free tankful of petrol was provided each week although few were able to find anywhere to go on the machine; they not being allowed beyond a ten mile radius from the college and Sleaford, the only town within that area, was out of bounds. Those that did venture out found that dare devil escapades were the only use for the motorcycles and accidents (for the most part minor ones) became a feature of Cranwell life and the local population became accustomed to the antics of the cadets on the country roads around the college. Officialdom, however, did not always smile on such events and Sir Theadore McEvoy recalls Rees giving the cadets a "stern harangue" during a Colour Hoisting parade about the evils of getting injured riding a motorcycle; he classed such injuries as
"unfair risks" as against accidents in the hunting field which were "fair risks".

In 1920, the Flying Wing was divided into A,B and C Flights with instruction being provided by battle seasoned veterans of the Western Front. The basic trainer was the Avro 504, a two-seater, tractor biplane powered by the ubiquitous 100 hp Monosaupape engine. In addition, instructors and senior cadets also had available the Bristol Fighter, the DH9a and the Sopwith Snipe (the latter being reserved for the personal use of the senior staff only). In the early days the actual flying training was limited and, even after graduation from the college, cadets were not awarded the coveted 'wings' of a pilot. The first trainees were the members of the Naval Entry of 1920 who had to complete the course in twelve months and consequently, the other members of the original intake did not commence flying training until February 1921, flying three or four times each week so that most had gone solo by the end of April. Others were not so lucky and, as late as the intake of 1924, there were problems ensuring that the cadets had sufficient flying experience. Former cadet E L S Ward recalled that "...our flying in those days was spasmodic - no more than once a week and sometimes we went as long as a month or so without flying at all " [11]. The training method used in those days was the 'Gosport System' introduced during the war and Sir George Mills has left a very clear account of his experiences as a member of the first intake.

" I got very impatient and rather frightened as I began to feel ready to go but felt quite calm when I was sent off alone. I lost my prop just before touching down but that was forgiveable on a first solo.

After this, apart from frequent short checks by our instructors, we always flew alone. We would be told what to practice and for how long; anyone who landed late when someone else was waiting was very unpopular. Very soon we added aerobatics on our own, often egged on by hearing that someone else had tried. Some were shown how by their instructors but I never was. This was in line with the Gosport doctrine that a pupil should be encouraged to find out for himself once he could fly reasonably safely. It could make you breathe a bit, making up your mind to do things, particularly for the first time! We never really spoke about being frightened even amongst ourselves, but no doubt most of us were from time to time. In fact it was this mixture of fright and enjoyment that made flying such fun and so fascinating."

All cadets were required to complete at least two cross-country flights, one to Lincoln and back and the second a triangular journey, usually Cranwell - Duxford - Bircham Newton and conducted in either a Bristol

Fighter or a DH9a. With little by way of navigational equipment and no means of communicating with the ground, it was vital that cadets recognised familiar landmarks from the air and sight of the 'Lighter than Air' sheds (which housed the airships) at Cranwell always brought a private sigh of relief to a pilot returning to the aerodrome.

The Commandant's Report for December 1921, gave details of the amount of flying carried out during the previous term when the cadets flew a total of 770 hours and 50 minutes of which 319 hours and 5 minutes were solo. The final term's cadets (who were also the first to complete the full Cranwell course) averaged 16 hours of solo flying each, having received an average of 8 hours dual instruction before being allowed to go up alone. During the term there had only been one accident in which the cadet concerned was slightly concussed.

In March 1923, Rees was appointed as the successor to Wing Commander Barratt [12] as Assistant Commandant of the Cadet College and, the following month, the Flying Wing and the Ground Wing were amalgamated under his command. With the added control that went with this new position Rees instituted a number of changes to the training procedures which he hoped would improve the quality of the trainees as well as increase the amount of flying available to them. Previously, the cadets had not been allowed near the aircraft during their first term and it was only at the commencement of their second year that they were permitted to touch the controls. Rees changed the format so that cadets were sent into the air as soon as possible after their arrival at Cranwell, followed by instruction on the Avro as soon as they had completed their observer's course. In future all cadets were to pass out on the Bristol Fighter and, if possible, the DH9a. This revised procedure was a success as can be seen from the statistics recorded in the Commandant's Report for August 1923 which shows that during the previous term, cadets had spent a total of 2,063 hours and 3 minutes in the air compared to 1,481 hours and 4 minutes the previous year - an equivalent gain of 15 months in flying training during the previous 6 months.

Remarkably, when one considers the novelty and precarious nature of flying in the 1920s, there were few serious accidents and most 'bad landings' resulted in the pilot and his instructor both walking away from the scene as in the case of Cadet Beaumont [13] who crashed and totally wrote-off a Bristol Fighter in July 1923 and was somewhat shaken but uninjured. During Rees' period at Cranwell only two cadets were killed in flying accidents [14]. This was not caused by good luck but rather by the high level of care taken by the instructors and staff. John Franks recalls Rees' concern for safety [15]:

"Occasionally he would decide to fly behind a Cadet, to give him confidence. I remember when I was in hospital after a minor flying accident, he came to see me & show me a photograph album full of pictures of fatal crashes at the School of Air Fighting which he had commanded during WW1. He was technically interested in the cause of aeroplane accidents."

Rees appears to have got on well with his colleagues at the college, perhaps life there brought back memories of his days at Eastbourne where he had been so happy nearly a quarter of a century earlier. The isolated location and comparatively small circle of officers and their families suited his personality. The Commandant was a man after his own heart, a native of Cardiganshire and a former officer in the Welch Regiment, Longcroft had been seconded to the RFC before the war and had quickly earned a reputation as an enthusiastic aviator. During the summer of 1912 he had established a number of endurance records for flights within Britain and he had commanded No. 4 Squadron on active service. Interested in all aspects of physical activity, he was particularly keen on riding to hounds and his love of the outdoors endeared him to Rees who, according to Lady Joan Portal, was "...deeply interested in country life" although there is no evidence that he ever took part in any form of equestrian sport himself.

As for his subordinate, Squadron Leader Portal, there can be little doubt that there was a common bond of respect and similar interests. A distinguished pilot, Portal was also keen on various field sports and it was he who first introduced Rees to the ancient sport of kings - falconry, which was to develop into something of a passion. Both men experimented with the use of birds of prey to remove other birds from the vicinity of the airfield at Cranwell as it was known that the mere presence of such a bird is sufficient to drive away most other species [16]. Wing Commander F C T Rowe, a cadet in 1920, recalled that Rees and Portal "... both kept hawks which were (when not hawking) tethered to posts outside their respective offices. Both in features resembled their falcons and when roused could behave like the same !" Lady Portal, often the general dogsbody of the two falconers when they required assistance with the birds wrote:

" I know he [Rees] and my husband had a great mutual interest in falconry. We kept peregrines and merlins & the airfield at Cranwell was full of partridges which flew in to feed on seeds in uncut grass. Rees amazed the married quarters by trying to persuade merlins to catch an outbreak of sparrows and pigeons which made their roofs a mess." [17]

Rees was also determined to master the sport of archery and the occupants of the married quarters were further harassed when, after the failure of the merlins to catch the unwanted sparrows, he tried to remove them by firing arrows at the roof.

The college authorities encouraged the cadets to become involved in physical activity of every kind. Either by inclination or as an example, Rees threw himself into the sporting life of the service, representing Cranwell at Pirbright in 1921 and 1922 where he fired the .303 rifle and, in the former year, became the RAF Revolver Champion. In 1923 he came first in the Foil and second in the Sabre competitions at the Royal Tournament as well as taking third place in the Officer's Bayonet Drill competition. In his free time he also took up skiing and went on an annual visit to Switzerland and, determined not to miss out on the limited time which he had on the actual slopes, he was regularly seen practicing on the hills around Cranwell, irrespective of whether there was any snow, in order to ensure that he was in good physical shape before leaving. That he was a man of action had been clearly demonstrated in the war and this almost excessive involvement in sport (he was by this time approaching his fortieth birthday) may have been a means of escaping from the comparative inactivity of his administrative post.

There can be little doubt that Rees enjoyed his time at

Cranwell and that he made a very significant contribution to the establishment of the Cadet College on a solid footing and generations of RAF officers who have passed through its doors owe him a great debt. Walter Dawson, the former Boy Corporal from Eastchurch, came across Rees again at Cranwell:

" He sent for me and asked who was paying my fees. I told him I was and he asked if I would object to the Air Ministry taking them over, since I had signed on for 8 years and he held that they were responsible. They did and refunded my first year's fees and waived the second - just as well because I had no means of paying the second year.

I always wished I had been able to thank Rees and tell him that I retired 41 years later as the senior officer employed by the RAF (there were no Marshals of the Royal Air Force employed at that time)."

This one cadet, plucked from the relative obscurity of an apprenticeship at Halton, one of Trenchard's so called 'Brats', retired from the RAF as Air Chief Marshal Sir Walter Dawson, KCB, CBE, DSO. There were many others who, like Air Marshal Sir Richard Jordan, have fond memories of Rees from their very early service days:

" He was a very shy man ... with very high standards of honour, efficiency and moral standards in life in general. I remember him damaging the undercarriage of a DH9a and writing out a report on himself in which he stated that he had been negligent & careless & should pay for the damage he had done out of his own pocket. This was typical of the way Rees expected the same standards for himself as he did from others. He was a very fine pilot & a great example to us cadets. Naturally as young men he was a hero to us, and has remained so all my life & I am now 85." [20]

With an almost obsessive fascination for gimmicks and gadgets there can be no doubt that Rees came to be regarded as something of an eccentric by some of those under his command as Sir Richard Jordan recalled:

" Two incidents ... have remained in my mind. Rees was the first and only officer that I remember who had a motor scooter to get around the camp. He was, of course, pretty lame from war wounds. The other was his originality. His hut at Cranwell had a lawn with flower beds at each end & it was a great sight to see Rees and his batman gardening. This consisted of mowing the lawn & weeding the flower beds at the same time and was done as follows: the little motor mower would be sent on its way by Rees who would then start weeding & the batman at the other end of the lawn would stop weeding, catch the motor mower & turn it back & Rees would do the same thing. This I consider was the first time & motion study ever done & showed how original some of Rees' thoughts were."

A mixture of admiration for Rees as a conventional RAF officer and his unusual approach to day-to-day problems is also illustrated by Air Vice Marshal John Franks in the following memoir:

" I have very vivid memories of him, especially in regard to his influence upon our flying training in those pioneering days. Rees insisted that cadet flying should include the Bristol Fighter & DH9a in addition to the Avro. His single interest was 'aeroplanes' and flying them. He was forever in the air and I can see him in his old overalls with leather helmet and goggles.

He was a bit of a crank - I remember he was reputed to have designed a bed for himself in which he lay inside a wooden framework, so that bed clothes didn't touch his body !! to ensure sound sleep for pilots. It was not adopted by the authorities!!"

That Rees had made an impression on the young men in his charge was proven when, in 1926, the Old Cranwellian Association was formed, he was invited to become one of its two Vice-Presidents, an honour which he enthusiastically accepted. It was not only the cadets who viewed him with affection, the college staff also appreciated his many gifts and his ability to see the humourous side of life, particularly if the joke was directed at himself. Amidst the numerous papers preserved at Cranwell is a short verse by one of the officers serving on the college staff:

"Uncle [Rees], whose inventive brains,
Kept evolving aeroplanes,
Fell from an enormous height
On our garden lawn last night.
Flying is a fatal sport -
Uncle's wrecked the tennis court ! "

Although the poetic style leaves much to be desired, this short verse illustrates the affection in which Rees was held and more than one person has claimed that he was "...the most popular officer in the RAF".

By the end of 1925, Rees was one of the most experienced training officers in the service, having served in various training capacities since his first appointment as an instructor at the Central Flying School nearly a decade earlier. He left Cranwell prior to his Christmas leave in 1924 and, on New Years Day was promoted to the rank of Group Captain and appointed Deputy Director of Training at the Air Ministry in London. Although it was a 'desk' appointment, it very clearly showed the way in which his career was developing and, coming only a few weeks after his appointment as Aide de Camp to HM King George V, it seemed that his future was secure and that he was destined to reach the very highest ranks.

CHAPTER VIII
Palestine and Transjordan
(1926 - 27)

Following the peace treaties which were signed between the Allies and the defeated Turkish Empire in 1919, the map of the Middle East had been dramatically transformed as various formerly Turkish territories were confiscated by the League of Nations and handed over to the victors as mandated territories, to be administered by them until such time as they were deemed to be capable of running their own affairs when they would be granted their independence. Great Britain was given Palestine, Transjordan and Iraq to supervise whilst France took control of Syria and Lebanon. To many, particularly the Arabs, the arrangement was seen as little more than a betrayal as the nationalist dreams of independent Arab states were, once again, frustrated. The change of control from the Turks to the British and the French was merely the the exchange of one weak colonial power for two who were much stronger.

As early as December 1919, the British Secretary of State for Air, Winston Churchill, had told the House of Commons, in a speech in which he was defending the future role of the RAF:

"I must remind Honourable Members that we still have an Empire to defend ... we have all those dependencies and possessions in our hands which existed before the war, and in addition we have large promises of new responsibilities to be placed upon us. The first

143

duty of the Royal Air Force is to garrison the British Empire."

Trenchard had argued, with some conviction, that the RAF was the most economical force to police the more remote regions of the Empire and he had been able to prove his point in 1920 when one squadron of bombers succeeded in destroying the power of the 'Mad Mullah' in Somaliland, something which the army had been trying to achieve, at great cost in both materials and men, since the beginning of the century. He had also argued that Egypt was a logical centre for a sizeable RAF establishment as the weather conditions made it ideal for flying training. Consequently, in October 1922, Air Vice-Marshal John Salmond was appointed as General Officer Commanding all military forces in the Middle East.

On 1 October 1926, Rees took over the command of the newly formed Headquarters RAF Palestine and Transjordan in Amman and, although under the overall jurisdiction of the Air Officer Commanding Middle East in Cairo, this appointment was, for all practical purposes, an independent command, the most important position which he had been given to that date. His responsibilities extended beyond the obvious control of all RAF units in the region to include all British forces for operational and training purposes as well as the Transjordan Frontier Force.

Initially the territories of Palestine and Transjordan were relatively quiet when compared to the constant unrest in the Iraq command and Rees' major cause for concern would seem to have been the increasing numbers of Jewish immigrants arriving in the region in pursuit of the Zionist dream of an independent Jewish state in Palestine. In 1926, the numbers involved had not yet reached the massive proportions of the 1930s and open conflict between Jews and Arabs could either be avoided altogether or, at worst, contained by the civil authorities.

The artificial boundaries of the mandated territories followed convenient political lines but, in many cases, they were historically and culturally meaningless, cutting across areas populated by one people and, in effect, making them citizens of two different countries. This problem was difficult enough within an area controlled by one foreign power such as the boundary between Palestine and Transjordan but, was very much more difficult when the boundary seperated territories controlled by different powers as was the case between Syria and Transjordan. The politics of the Middle East had always been a complex subject but these imposed frontiers only served to exacerbate the situation. One clearly identifiable group who felt themselves to be aggrieved by the arrangements were the Druze of southern Syria and it was from this quarter that Rees' major problem emerged very soon after his arrival in Amman.

A complicated and mysterious association, the Druze originated in Lebanon during the 12th century when Ismail al Darazi took refuge in the mountains there after fleeing from Egypt following the assasination of his insane master, Caliph Hakim, who had proclaimed himself a god some three years previously. As one of the Caliph's most fervent followers, Ismail al Darazi was in grave danger if he remained in Egypt and, once in Lebanon, he began to preach of the divinity of his former master. He managed to attract a sizeable following who formed themselves into a highly secretive community based upon a religious belief, the details of which were known only to the elders. This group, the Druze, came to play an increasingly important role in the life of the region and, as they were often compelled to defend themselves against religious persecution, they acquired a high reputation as warriors. After centuries of rebelling against any form of authority they were eventually forced, in 1861, to migrate to the mountains south-west of Damascus which became known as Jebel al Druze.

During the early years of the French mandate in Syria, many Arab nationalists were compelled to either go into hiding or exile but, despite these difficulties they managed to keep the flames of independence buring in Lebanon and Syria with the result that numerous local uprisings occurred. The appointment of a conscientious, hardworking but insensative officer by the name of Carbillet as governor of the Jebel al Druze in 1923 resulted in considerable unrest. He believed in improving the life of those under his control whether they desired it or not. His reforms in Syria were numerous and, on the whole, were of great benefit to the local population taking as they did the form of new roads, irrigation schemes, improved sanitation, new schools and courts, even a museum. To the Druze however, these changes seemed to threaten their traditional way of life. Worst of all, Carbillet managed, for the first time in Druze history, to collect the local taxes in full. Power seemed to be passing out of the hands of the local chieftains and into the hands of the mandatory power and their democratically elected representatives. When a Druze deputation was dismissed by the French High Commissioner in 1925, and Carbillet was replaced by Captain Raynaud (who could see no problem in the manner in which his predecessor had administered matters) tempers began to wear thin. Further delegations were either dismissed or totally ignored by the authorities in Beirut. Then, in early July, five Druze chieftains were summoned before the High Commissioner on the pretext that they could present their demands. Three arrived as requested and were promptly arrested on the orders of General Sarrail. Immediately, the most belligerent of the Druze leaders, Sultan Atrash, decided to come out in open rebellion against French rule. Within days, French aircraft had been fired upon, the town of Salkhad had been occupied and looted and, on 21 July, a column of about 200 French troops was cut to pieces at Kafr. The survivors of the column, some seventy in number, managed to reach Suwayda where they were besieged for two months.

The authorities still regarded the trouble as being of little major importance and virtually nothing was done for a few days. On 2 August, General Michaud left Azra at the head of a force of 3,000 men with the intention of relieving those men trapped at Suwayda. That night, they were attacked by a strong Druze force and defeated. Over 800 men were either killed, wounded, captured or deserted. One colonel committed suicide on the battlefield and Michaud was recalled to France. As a consequence of this action, the Druze took possession of 2,000 rifles, a battery of artillery and vast quantities of ammunition.

Overnight, the localised Druze rebellion was changed into a national revolt and Sultan Atrash was proclaimed President of the Provisional Syrian Government as many groups seized on the opportunity to rid their country of colonial control. In reality, however, the uprising was a shambles and, lacking any clear political leadership or support amongst those members of Syrian society whose opinions carried the most weight, it was doomed to failure.

France placed General Gamelin in command of the forces in the region and, by the use of airpower and tanks, he was able to relieve Suwayda by 24 September but was unable to regain control of the Jebel al Druze. There then followed many months of guerilla fighting with Druze attacks upon roads, railways, police stations and settlements that were believed to be pro-French. In October, fighting broke out in Damascus itself resulting in the use of artillery against areas of the city where rebels were believed to be active. By November the High Commissioner had been recalled to Paris but there was no indication of any solution to the situation which was to witness acts of great brutality from both sides. By early 1926, the rebels had failed to make any real gains and a new High Commissioner, de Jouvenal, visited London where he sought, and received, the support of the British government in bringing the conflict to an end. In the spring, the government forces in Syria went onto the offensive and the Druze began to lose ground. Repeated attempts were made to try and persuade the tribesmen to surrender but they invariably chose to continue the fight and by April a new French governor was in the Jebel al Druze. Sultan Atrash, however, managed to evade the net that was closing in around him and continued to roam the region at the head of a substantial force of armed men, crossing over into Transjordan as the need arose, in order to evade capture. This action contravened the agreement reached between the British and French governments who had decided that any Druze warriors that crossed into British territory would be compelled to

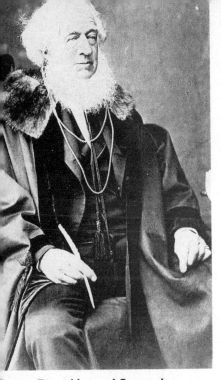

James Rees, Mayor of Caernarfon.

2. Lt Col Charles H Rees, VD

Caernarfon Castle and the Slate Quay at the end of the 19th Century. The Rees home was inside the town walls to the left of this picture.

4. "A strong, intelligent, good looking but rather shy boy." Lionel Rees aged about ten years.

5. 2nd Lt L W B Rees, Royal Garrison Artillery c. 1903.

6. A Vickers FB5 (Gun-Bus) two-seater fighter similar to those flown by Rees with Nos 7 and 11 Squadrons. This example has a modified nose section. The positions of the engine and the Lewis gun can be clearly seen.

**7. Fokker E.1.
(Eindecker)
[Michael Schneelke]**

Ago C.1.
robably the type of
eroplane which No.11
quadron nicknamed
'wo-tails'.
mperial War Museum]

9 Albatros C.1.

10. No. 32 Squadron at Netheravon shortly before take-off for France, 28 May 1916. Bac[k] row L-R: Charles Bath, Herman von Poellnitz, E Henty, Gwilym Lewis, John C Simpson, Nicholas. Second row: William Nixon, S P Simpson, Owen V Thomas. Third row: Regina[ld] Stubbs, Gerald Allen, S G Gilmour, LIONEL REES, Hellyer. Front row: F H Coleman, Co[...] P B G Hunt.

[Gwilym H Le[...]

11. Airco D.H.2. single-seater scout as flown by No.32 Squadron in 1916. The position o[f] the engine can be clearly seen. The box beneath the centre of the upper wing was the fu[el] tank.

[Imperial War Muse[um]

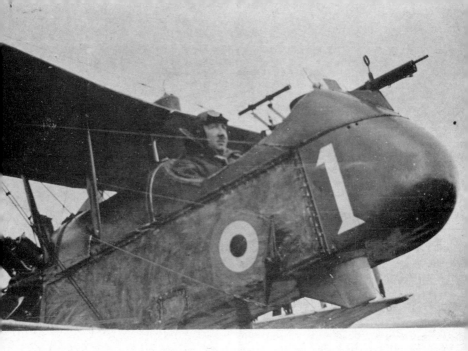

A DH 2 of No. 32 Squadron with its pilot, Lieutenant Herman W von Poellnitz (later a ptain and an MC whilst serving with the squadron), at the controls. This view clearly ws the pilot's exposed position, the Vickers machine-gun and the sight which was fitted his type of machine.　　　　　　　　　　　　　　　　　[J M Bruce & G S Leslie Collection]

The Vickers E.S.1. 'Bullet' aeroplane which was flown by Rees when No.32 Squadron t went to France.　　　　　　　　　　　　　　　　[J M Bruce & G S Leslie Collection]

14. 2nd Lieutenant Gilbert Insall, VC, MC.

15. 2nd Lieutenant Algernon Insall

16. Major Lanoe Hawker, VC, DSO.

17. Flight Sergeant Hargreaves, DCM.

2nd Lieutenant Gwilym H Lewis (left) with Lieutenant Owen V Thomas. [Gwilym Lewis]

"Auntie Katie pushes me about the grounds in a large perambulator." Rees, recovering m his wound at Wilton House, autumn 1916.

20. A captured L
biplane showing
French markings

21. Aviatik C III

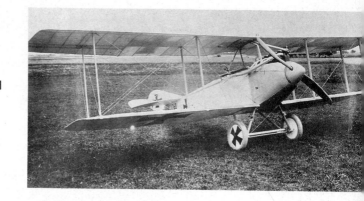

22. Sopwith Camel

3. Major Lionel Wilmot Brabazon Rees, VC, MC. The official studio portrait used for publicity during his stay in the USA during 1917.

24. Lionel Rees (centre) with other members of Allied war missions to the USA at the Detroit Athletic Club, July 1917.

25. Cranwell Celebrities 1921 - 22. Caricatures of senior members of the college staff (wi' their later ranks added). L - R: Sqd Ldr England, Grp Cpt Rees, Grp Cpt Godman, AVM Longcroft, Wng Cmdr Barratt, Grp Cpt Kilner, Flt Lt Rhodes. [RAF Cranwell Library]

26. Staff Officers, No. 1 School of Aerial Fighting, Ayr, April 1918. Front row (L - R): Cpt G C Maxwell MC, Cpt W D South, Cpt S W Taylor MC, Cpt K H Marshall, Lt Col L W B Rees VC MC, Cpt J W Woodhouse DSO MC, Cpt F Paterson, Cpt J B McCudden VC DSO MC MM CdeG, Lt F M Thomas.

Second row: 2 Lt R J Sladden DCM, Cpt A D C Browne, Cpt J D Atkinson, Lt J R Bost, Cpt L A F Foers MC, Lt H A D Edwards, Lt D J Rollo CdeG, Cpt J M Burd MC, Lt I M Harris. Third row: Lt R M Makepeace MC, Lt E L Zink, Lt J R G Rowden, 2 Lt R W Farquhar, 2 Lt H W Elliott, Lt D Sutherland, Lt H L McNaughton, 2 Lt R W Weatherby, Lt H B Redler MC. Fourth row: Lt D H de Burgh, Lt W A G Young, Lt F M Howard, Lt H Jones, Lt A Armstrong.

[Alex Revell]

27. "He was forever in the air I can see him in his old overal with leather helmet and goggl Rees next to a Bristol Fighter Cranwell, c. 1924.

28. Lionel Rees receiving the Sword of Honour presented to him by the town of Caernarfon, January 1920.

29. A DH9a after one of Rees' infamous crash-landings, Palestine c. 1927.

30. Grp Cpt Rees (front left) with some of his staff, RAF Headquarters, Amman, c. 1928.

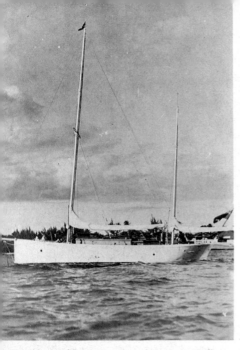

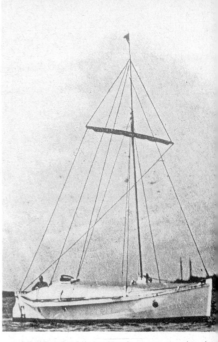

31. Ketch *May* at anchor, Nassau, 1933.
The ensign on the stern is that of the
Royal Welsh Yacht Club.

[Stanley Toogood]

32. Ketch *Aline* after her conversion by
Rees, 1937.

33. Interior of the cabin of the ketch *May*. Note the large radio receiver on the right and t
patent bottle rack in the far cabin (the design of the latter was detailed in *Yachting World*,
November 25 1932).

[Stanley Toog

34. Wing Commander Lionel Rees VC, OBE, MC, AFC, Officer Commanding RAF Helwan, Egypt, 1942.

[Via Chaz Bowyer]

35. Mrs Sylvia Rees and Aline (Eileen) at Mangrove Cay, Andros, April 1952.
[Cyrus Sharer]

36. Lionel Rees at the tiller of the *Aline*, c. 1950.

return to Syria. If necessary, military force would be used to make the Druze comply.

A substantial number of dependents of Druze tribesmen arrived in British territory during April and their leaders, remaining in Syria, contacted the authorities in Amman to request permission for these refugees to remain, under British protection and jurisdiction, in a camp which they hoped to establish near the old fortress at Qasr el Asraq. Permission was granted on condition that no Druze warriors were to enter Transjordan, that tribal chieftains would accept the responsibility for the good conduct of the non-combatant refugees and that they, the chiefs, remained in Syria. As a concession to the rugged and unpredictable nature of life in the region, the authorities granted the refugees the right to have a limited number of armed men in the camp by way of protection.

In Syria, however, events did not progress so peacefully. On 18 July, the French forces launched an attack against the area where the rebels were still harassing the authorities. Six columns, totalling 8,500 men supported by artillery, tanks and armoured cars moved into an area only 14 miles long and 11 miles wide. They then commenced to drive the rebels (and anyone else who happened to be in the area) towards Damascus. There were acts of great barbarity, particularly by Senegalese troops who, in one village, killed every Syrian that they came across irrespective of their involvement in the rebellion. French troops entered and searched abandoned villages and shot, without any pretence of a trial, dozens of the inhabitants whom they believed to be either rebels or harbourers of rebels. The Druze, in return, ambushed French forces wherever they could and took their revenge. This period of terror continued into October 1926 and, as a consequence of it, the British authorities realised that the agreed conditions concerning the refugee camps in Transjordan were not being adhered to and that substantial numbers of warriors were sheltering there along with several chieftains, including possibly Sultan Atrash and other leading figures in the revolt. Despite protests from Amman and demands that the agreement should be complied with there was no satisfactory response from the Druze camp. As the situation in Syria showed no sign of being resolved before the onset of winter it was decided that a show of strength on the part of the mandatory power would be necessary the following spring.

As the senior military official in the region, responsibility for the organisation and execution of this operation lay with Lionel Rees. Although the 'demonstration of military strength' would involve significant numbers of RAF personnel, it was to be mainly a ground force exercise and he gathered together a column consisting of three sections of No. 2 Armoured Car Campany, RAF, three companies of the Transjordan Frontier Force and the DH9a machines of No.14 Squadron. One of the officers serving with the column, Stanley Vincent, who had served under Rees at Cranwell, had fond memories of the armoured cars which were to prove particularly effective in the months ahead [1] :

"I had many interesting experiences with the good old Rolls-Royce armoured cars. It was then 1926 and most of the chassis were 1912, and one 1910. These had been private cars for some years, then bought during the war and had four and a half tons of armour and extra leaves to the springs put on them. They would still do their 60 mph over a mud flat."

Although the distance from Amman to the camp at Qasr el Azraq was not great (50 miles by air or 75 miles by the 'Desert Track') the expedition had to be planned with great care as the availability of water was always a matter of some concern. The usual watering place was El Durmi near Qasr Qaraneh where, by digging into the bed of the dried up river, supplies could be obtained in great quanitity, albeit slowly. This possibility was eliminated when reconnaissance patrols reported that the wadi was occupied by the Beni Sakhr and "...it would not be politic to drink their water at the beginning of the year." An alternative route had therefore to be found and consequently numerous air and armoured car patrols were sent out and which discovered a route that was considerably shorter with a good surface, something which could not be said of the traditional road.

On 12 April, Rees, accompanied by Lieutenant Colonel Bewsher [3] made a personal reconnaissance of the proposed route and decided that one five mile section was unsuited to the weight of transport which they intended to use and further flights were ordered to discover yet another way of reaching Azraq. Fortunately, this revealed an excellent flat track along the Wadi Hoopoe which, despite the absence of water along the way, was selected as the route for the expedition.

On 13 April, the advanced party, comprising one armoured car section, seven lorries and seven tenders, covered the 54 miles and established camp at Qasr el Asraq without incident. Two days later a water convoy transported 3,300 gallons to a 'dump' some 15 miles west of Zerqa where the Transjordan Frontier Force was to water the following day. Leaving their headquarters the

Transjordan Frontier Force, accompanied by one section of armed tenders and escorted by one flight from No.14 squadron, reached the water safely having covered a distance of 24 miles. This force comprising 450 mounted men are recorded to have consumed 1,400 gallons of water at the halt, which clearly illustrates the logistical problems involved in desert operations. The following day, after a further stop (when 2,000 gallons of water were consumed) the column arrived at its destination at 2 pm without any undue fatigue or injury to either the men or the horses. The heavy Leyland lorries however, proved quite unsatisfactory for the transportation of supplies and the RAF transport drivers reported that they "...were unable to carry the weight, and the solid tyres cut up the track in the three days so greatly that a new track had to be made. They were much too slow getting over bad places, even those places which armoured cars would consider normal, and could not make up time when the going was good." In addition to the ground transport, two Vickers Victoria aircraft were used to convey supplies to the column by air using a hastily prepared landing strip at Azraq.

In his report on the opening stages of this operation, Rees commented that the 'Heath Robinson' system which he had adopted for supplying water was quite unsatisfactory and had only just managed to provide the desired quantities; had the column encountered any real difficulties then they might have been in very serious trouble due to the lack of adequate water supplies. In his opinion, any future operations of a similar nature should be supported by purpose built water tanker lorries which should preferably be six-wheelers or tracked in order to negotiate the difficult terrain without any major problems arising.

On 18 April, an initial examination was made of the Druze camp and evidence was found of the recent movement of mechanised vehicles in the area which confirmed the belief that the Druze leadership had been seeking sanctuary at Azraq. A few chiefs actually called to see Rees and assured him that they were only too willing to comply with any request or order which he might make and, as a consequence, he issued a proclamation demanding that the terms of the Anglo-Druze agreement be complied with and nearly all the leaders and about 300 men were seen to leave the camp heading for Syria.

The next step was to try to ascertain the numbers of people left in the camp and the mounted troops and one flight of aircraft carried out a detailed reconnaissance of the area as a result of which it was estimated that there were approximately 2,462 persons in the Druze camp, mostly women, old men and children but that there were also about 300 men, either traders or guards, still there. When questioned, these men openly admitted that the agreement had not been adhered to but that most of the 'illegal' refugees had now left: 650 men under Sultan Atrash himself had gone on 26 March and 800 men under the command of Emir Adil Aslan on 15 April. These figures apparently supplied quite freely, showed that the authorities had been quite justified in their concern as together these two Druze forces made up the majority of their fighting strength and had therefore posed a serious threat to the region. Their continued presence in Transjordan would, at best, have caused mistrust between the British and the French. It was also discovered that there were a number of non-Druze refugees from Syria or

Palestine living in the camp. The use of aircraft to help estimate the numbers and location of the refugees had not only announced to the tribesmen that there were military aircraft readily available should any trouble break out but also they were able to make an accurate calculation of numbers without the refugees being aware what was happening as they would otherwise have almost certainly have hidden many of their warriors to prevent their detection by ground units.

Concerned about the whereabouts of the departed tribesmen, Rees ordered that the area to be patrolled should be expanded for the next few days to ensure that the prohibited warriors were indeed back in Syria. Little of interest was discovered but the patrols, by both land and air, made detailed reports of the terrain and its suitability for future operations should the need arise. Those Druze remaining within the camp were then issued with passes if they were to carry arms for defensive purposes and a number of 'illegal' refugees were ordered to leave and return to the mountains, being watched from the air until they were at least 18 miles away. It was probably hoped that these men would, when they rejoined the main Druze force in Syria, report the situation in Transjordan and clearly point out the determination of the British forces to see that the agreement was complied with in future. Remarkably, Rees received a most unusual letter from Sultan Atrash who thanked him for his assistance in persuading the Druze to return to the field. He, their Sultan, had failed to convince some of his men that they should return to Syria and recommence their offensive against the French but the arrival of Rees' column at Qasr el Asraq had caused them to change their minds and they had gladly agreed to return to Jebel al

Druze !

The problem of identifying those who were entitled to be in the camp and those who were not was a difficult one and, whenever a head count was taken and passes checked, a different total was reached. Determined not to be made to look foolish and to establish the rule of law, Rees set up a series of courts martial which tried those found without a pass and sentenced them accordingly. On the whole, the sentences were light and consisted of short periods of imprisonment followed by deportation back to Syria but, occasionally, the offence was of a more serious nature and carried a heavier sentence. Rees was not afraid to use his power when necessary and, when Hayle El Atrash, a nephew of the Sultan, was found without a pass he was sentenced to be deported. Unfortunately, en route to Syria he assaulted his guards and was brought before a second court martial which sentenced him to twelve months imprisonment. Despite the fact that all the Druze regarded the members of the Atrash clan as being privileged persons, and therefore above the common law, Rees confirmed the court's sentence regardless of any possible backlash from the angered tribesmen.

Life in the camp, although undoubtedly more interesting than that in Amman, was basically a matter of administration and it quickly settled into a routine as long periods of boredom were broken up by short periods of activity and 'home-made' entertainment. In his autobiography, Vincent recalled how the men of the armoured car unit relaxed:

" At Azrak were two 'lakes' in which it was nearly pleasant to bathe at the end of a hot, sticky and dusty day - the qualification 'nearly' being caused by the mosquitos ! We had our camp about half a mile away for this reason; to bathe we would put on our trunks in our tents, get into a Rolls tender and drive to the water's edge - run and dive in. Even then much splashing was necessary before putting one's head out ! After ten minutes or so of good cooling, one of us would say "All out - Go !" Whereupon a rush would be made to the bank and so to the Rolls tender and away as quickly as possible, in a heap, without pausing to dry!"

Regular patrols were mounted by the men under Rees' command during which a number of arrests were made. Usually this was carried out by small numbers of soldiers who intercepted larger numbers of tribesmen who had been spotted from the air and, generally, such events passed without difficulty. The Druze treated these incidents as something of a joke and returned to their rightful location without comment. One cannot help but wonder, however, what their reaction might have been had the armoured cars and aircraft not been so readily available. As Vincent noted, "...four armoured cars with Vickers guns trained on them are not things with which to trifle." On 30 April, Major J W Smith of the Transjordan Frontier Force, totally unarmed and accompanied by only one trooper and one horseholder, intercepted a party of eight armed men and arrested them all, later handing them over to the police at Asraq. After interrogation they revealed the location of a further eight tribesmen who were also taken into custody without any problem.

Despite rumours that the Druze leaders were preparing to return to Qasr el Asraq with their armed followers as the tide of war continued to flow against them in Syria, the early days of May passed without incident and Rees kept his men employed preparing the area for any future operations which might be required:

"The chief duty of No.2 Armoured Car Company was the making of roads, in the first instance in order to deliver to a forced landed machine a new engine [4], and later on in order to allow cars and soldiers to arrive at tactical positions behind the inhabited area, should the necessity arise.

Reconnaissances were made to find out the extent of the basalt area, and it is established that no forces except those in the area could operate south of the Syrian 'Border actual' inside the area Umm a Jemmal, Hamman es Sara, Azrak, Jebel Kurma, and to the east without overcoming difficulties which with the means at their disposal, are practically insurmountable.

Air reconnaisance was useful in checking information as to the movement of herds, and as to the location of Abdul Ghaffer's Camp.

A daily Air Mail service was organised at Amman and many officers were transported.

The situation at Azrak is now completely under control, and is such that the 'Druze Committees' are asking for our help in order to keep affairs going on as they should.

Should trouble arise in the future the road Zerka - Azrak will provide a ready means of approach for some time to come, and tactical roads are constructed which will allow vehicles and soldiers to approach the inhabited area unexpectedly and will make it comparatively easy to occupy tactical positions of vantage in the basalt which surrounds Azrak Castle." [5]

Upon receipt of this report, the British High Commissioner, no doubt wishing to economise wherever possible, issued instructions that the forces at Qasr el Azraq were to be reduced by the 25 May. No sooner had Rees received this order than reports reached him of disturbances elsewhere in the territory. The Druze, natural rivals of the Rualla tribe, complained that the French authorities in Syria had given the latter a number of villages situated on the main route north of the basalt and Asraq. They saw this as an act intended to provoke emnity between the two tribes as it would make communications between the Druze in Syria and those in Transjordan very difficult. They also claimed that the Rualla, acting upon instructions received from the French, had attacked a camp west of Asraq, just outside the area covered by martial law. The camp, which belonged to Abdul Ghaffer Pasha, had lost all its tents, stores, cattle, guns and clothes. In addition, the attackers had killed a shepherd and a cousin of Sultan Atrash and taken the Sultan's brother and several others away as prisoners. Fearful of further attacks, Abdul Ghaffer had moved his people into the area over which Rees had jurisdiction and surrendered on 16 May. As the attack had taken place outside his administration, Rees could do nothing other than offer the Druze his protection and ensure, by means of aerial patrols, that the Ruella remained in French territory. Once they had been located they were carefully observed, Rees himself going up on one patrol to see them:

"The Ruella on the march were a fine sight, when halted they had 1,072 tents and camels without number. They occupied a grazing area of about 15 miles by 6."

The situation, although still relatively calm, was deteriorating and it appeared to Rees that the root cause of all the problems that were building up in Transjordan was the activities of the French forces near the border. His operational diary entry for 23 May showed the changing situation:

"On the 15th an incident occurred for which I can see no justification. A French column with an escort came to the ruined viallage of Semme inside our border near Nasib on the railway. Although our police asked them to refrain the French galloped into

Semme. Naturally the Beni Sakhr who were grazing in and around the ruins opened fire and this gave the French an excuse for machine-gunning the tents, quite at random, and killing some five men, a woman and a child. Not only this but the French have, apparently wounded and carried off one of our Arab Legion Policemen."

These disturbances and the reduction in the garrison at Qasr el Asraq combined to cause a marked change in the attitude of the local Druze. On 26 May, Major Smith ordered eight men to halt in order that their passes might be inspected. They disregarded his orders completely and went back into the Basalt area from where they had appeared. Later it was discovered that a much larger group, numbering about 60 men, was gathering in the Bassalt and, a troop of soldiers was fired upon when they attempted to arrest a small group of mounted men east of Airi Beida. In addition, a permanent camp was discovered in Wadi Hassan and large numbers of armed men were observed near a camp at Jebel Hassan. Major Smith led a force into the camp at Wadi Hassan only to find it deserted and, when the Druze returned in the evening, they behaved aggressively but were persuaded to move off south without causing any real incident. About an hour later, Smith heard the sound of gunfire coming from the direction in which the Druze had travelled and a restless night was spent before the small force moved off the following morning after destroying the tents, stores and ammunition that the Druze had left behind.

At the same time, a troop which had been sent to patrol the northern watering holes in the area of Ain Ankiyeh was fired upon by a band of armed men. This was repeated during the evening and Rees, who was with the unit, gave the order that warning shots were to be fired in the air. When this failed to have the desired effect, he ordered one of the attacking tribesmen to be shot and, as a consequence, one of the Druze had his leg broken and his horse killed. In addition a second horse was wounded. This demonstration of intent succeeded in persuading the other tribesmen to cease fire and move away.

Rees now had no alternative but to issue a proclamation by way of warning the Druze that the situation which appeared to be developing would not be tolerated by the authorities.

"Proclamation under Martial Law, No. 10.

Yesterday at 9.30 hours a band of Armed men opened fire on my troops east of Ain Beida. My troops fired into the air in order to make the band come in and surrender. In the evening my troops were again fired on at Ain Ankiyeh and it was not until dusk that direct fire was ordered. Numerous instances occurred during the day of armed bands moving in the Military Area refusing to obey orders to halt and adopting a threatening attitude.

I hereby give warning that orders have been issued to my troops to open fire on anybody:-

a) who refuses to halt when called upon to do so.

b) who endeavours to avoid capture after being challenged.

c) who opens fire on my troops."

Realising that the situation could very easily get out of hand and that his force of one company of the Transjordan Frontier Force and one section of armoured cars was not sufficient to control any possible trouble, Rees sent a radio message to Amman at 3 am on 27 May requesting reinforcements. An additional company and two more sections were able to cover the 62 miles, some of it in darkness, and reach his camp by 7.30 am thereby proving the wisdom of constructing new roads.

To secure the area and to make the Druze fully aware that the British force at Azraq had been reinforced, Rees ordered his men to occupy every known water hole and thereby make it difficult, if not impossible, for anyone else to operate in the area. He also ordered that no more passes were to be issued and that any unregistered horses found in the area under martial law would be shot.

The situation could have easily erupted and Rees, with the relatively small force which he had at his disposal, would have been unable to do anything about it. Each of the warring factions, the Druze, the Ruella, the French, the British or even the bands of uncommitted brigands who roamed the region, could spark off trouble. The only hope was to prevent that trouble breaking out which would be a very difficult task requiring a great deal of tact and diplomacy.

The root cause of the difficulties was clearly the hostility which existed between the Druze and the French authorities in Syria and, although the former had already been militarily defeated, the latter were refusing to allow the situation to stabilise until they had accounted for all the Druze warriors and their leaders. Towards the end of May, Rees contacted Colonel Arnaud of the French army and set about trying to find a peaceful solution to the problem. He felt great sympathy for the Druze and believed that they had just cause for complaint but he also realised that they would have to enter into negotiations with the French if they were ever to leave British territory and return to Syria. He asked Arnaud to allow them to return to Jebel el Druze without fear of French reprisals and, in return, he would arrange for the construction of a good quality road along the northern edge of the Bassalt or, if that should prove to be too expensive, an armoured car road along the same route. This would act as a deterent to future incursions by the Druze into Transjordan and, indirectly, the French would also find it difficult to explain their wanderings into British territory. Arnuad agreed in principle but asked Rees to delay his plans as it would cause the French grave embarassment because they already had a column operating in the Basalt area. Rees accepted the delay and the French, in return, promised to provide him with any intelligence which their column might gather during this operation. A second meeting was arranged at Umm el Jemmal when the French informed him that Sultan Atrash was back at Wadi Hassan with a sizeable force of armed men.

Rees and Arnaud then agreed to leave the northern border of Transjordan open and the British forces then began a drive with the intention of forcing Atrash and his men back into Syria. Arnaud, accompanied by other senior French officials, arrived at Qasr el Azraq on 14 June to commence discussions with the Druze leaders, the Chief British Representative and Group Captain Rees. From the start, the meeting seemed to be doomed to failure as the Sultan made a speech which was clearly intended to inflame the French. Before Arnaud could break up the meeting however, the Chief British Representative was able to calm the situation and the Druze appeared to divide into two groups; those who wanted to continue with the negotiations and those who wished to continue fighting. When it became apparent that the latter could not be moved from their belligerent position they were asked to leave and the remaining Druze negotiators were given assurances about their safety and treatment should they decide to return to Syria. The offer was accepted and, two days later, the British authorities gave them a deadline of 1 July, by which date they were to have left the area under martial law.

Those Druze who had rejected the French safeguards then began a propaganda campaign to try to disuade their comrades from leaving. Fearing that if this was successful then the whole negotiations might be endangered, Rees ordered all refugees who did not hold passes or who were not members of the group returning to Syria, to leave the camp immediately. This seemed to achieve the required effect and, when Colonel Henry, Governor of the Jebel al Druze, arrived at Asraq on 21 June, most of the tribesmen present in the camp accepted the terms for their return to Syria and, four days later, there were only three tents remaining.

The dissidents, however, had not mellowed and, fully aware that Rees had every intention of using military force to ensure that his orders were carried out, they had moved out of the Military Area and were forming a new camp at Umari Wells some 15 miles further south. Atrash declared that he and his followers (who numbered about 1,300 men) had every intention of attacking the French at the first opportunity and would remain at Umari Wells unless ordered to move on despite the fact that there was a grave shortage of grazing for their animals. He had selected the spot very carefully and, by using the tribe's considereable wealth, he was able to transport food by road from Amman. He was also able to launch raids into Syria without hinderance from Rees' force as the water holes on the route were too scattered for him to be intercepted.

Such a situation was in open defiance of Rees' orders and could not be tolerated. If he allowed Atrash and his men to remain at Umari Wells then all the agreements with the French might be endangered and, not only would the British be accused of harbouring rebels but also those Druze who had been promised a safe return to Syria might find that the authorities had changed their minds in view of the continuing attacks. If however he moved a British force against the new camp, he might rekindle many of the troubles of the previous month. In order to try and preserve the peace, Rees decided to give the Druze the option of leaving without the obvious threat of military force. This would enable Sultan Atrash to preserve his dignity whilst maintaining cordial relations between the British and French authorities.

On 3 July, Rees issued a proclamation stating that the boundaries of the Military Area had been extended:

"...to include the area within a line drawn from Kasr Amru to Kasr Kharanah to Ruba Wells, thence due East to the Nejdian frontier to a point South East of Jebel Kurma and from this point to Jebel Kurma. Both Amari and Hazim are included within this area. Any person who within this area contravenes the orders of the Military Authorities will be liable to be tried by a Military Court and to suffer the penalties prescribed by the Military Authority."

Sultan Atrash and his followers were informed of these new boundaries by means of leaflets dropped by British aircraft flying over their camp. Having allowed the Druze two days to consider their changed circumstances, Rees then issued a further proclamation:

"Whereas it has come to my knowledge that there is an assembly, including a number of Druze Combatants, at Amri in the area under Martial Law, I hereby order that all persons there assembled who are not habitual residents of Transjordan shall leave Transjordan territory on or before the 16th instant, after which date I shall take measures as appear to me to be necessary to enforce compliance with my order."

This, whilst clearly stating the position of the Druze at Umari Wells, gave them sufficient time to move out of British territory without fear of attack from the authorities and the result was more than satisfactory. RAF air and ground reconnaissance reported that the Druze had immediately begun to search for a new location for their camp, deciding to settle in Nejid territory, outside of the expanded military area. A column of cars was seen to travel from Amman carying food for the move and 200 camels from Umari carried their possessions towards the new location. In order to speed up the evacuation and to guarantee that all the tribesmen left, Rees ordered that all food convoys were to be prevented from entering the camp at Umari and diverted to the new site at Hassiedat. As it was estimated that there was only sufficient food at Umari Wells to last a month, the tribesmen would be compelled to leave by 25 July and the deadline for their departure was extended to that date in order to avoid any possible cause for confrontation.

Patrols kept a watchful eye on progress throughout the month and the reports they made indicated that the Druze were making every effort to comply with Rees' orders. Two days before the deadline expired, Umari Wells was reported to be clear and an armoured car sent to the new camp as Hassiedat stated that all the Druze were there, a fact which was confirmed by aerial reconnaissance on 25 July. On that date Rees ordered all forces to withdraw from Qasr el Asraq and return to their normal stations. As a gesture of goodwill and by way of recognising the Druze compliance with the authorities, all prisoners confined in British prisons by the military courts were released. Each week, to ensure that the rebel tribesmen remained in the Nejid territory, an armoured car was sent through the Military Area and aerial patrols checked the roads. Any raiding parties that were observed were then reported to the French authorities.

The British forces in Transjordan, and Rees in particular, had handled the situation with diplomacy and tact. The excesses which had taken place in Syria could very easily have overflowed across the border but Rees' policy had been to avoid confrontation whenever possible in the belief that open fighting solved nothing and only created further problems for the future. Throughout the entire disturbance no member of the British forces was injured or killed (one local policeman was wounded by the French) and the Druze only suffered one man wounded; a remarkable achievement when one compares it with the large casualties sustained by both sides in Syria. The authorities faith in giving Rees his own semi-independent command had been more than justified and he had shown his ability in yet another area of military activity.

CHAPTER IX
Archaeology
(1926 - 29)

Innumerable travellers who have visited Qasr el Azraq, the centre of activity of the Druze incidents of 1926-27, have been struck by its unexpected beauty, an oasis of loveliness amidst a barren desert. The renowned archaeologist, O G S Crawford, who visited the site, described it in his memoirs:

"...one of the most romantic sites I have ever seen. For some sixty miles one motors over rolling desert, which is covered by a brown carpets of flints that chinkle under the wheels. There were mirages everywhere looking exactly like lakes, but at last we came to a real lake, with bright green reeds growing on the margin. It was a strange sight in such a desert. The scenery was most beautiful; at the back of the lake were some purple covered mountains that looked exactly like the heather covered hills of Killarney, and in a clump of palms at the north end of the lake were the blue towers of a Roman [sic] fort."

Located at the northern end of the ancient caravan route through Wadi Sirhan, on the western edge of the Arabian Desert, the oasis had long been of strategic importance. The fortress, once an imposing structure of black basalt was, by the 1920s, only an empty shell. Inscriptions on the stones date the building to the 13th century but other inscriptions would indicate that its origins may have been much earlier, either Roman or Byzantine; some even argue that the site was used by the

167

Nabatheans in the 2nd century BC. That it had been in constant use through the centuries was the result of its location next to the plentiful supply of water in the form of large pools and marshes, fed by a freshwater spring. T E Lawrence, who had used it as his headquarters during the final assault on the Turks, had described it as a " ...luminous, silky Eden " and, as the only permanent source of water in 12,000 square miles, it attracted a great deal of both human and animal attention.

Azraq seemed to captivate all who visited the region and Rees was no exception. In quiet moments during his occupation of the oasis, he wandered amongst the ruins of the old fort and his mind must have drifted to that other great castle on the banks of the Menai Straits in whose shadow he had spent so much of his childhood. The inscriptions at Azraq fascinated him and he wondered as to their origins. On long walks alone in the surrounding desert he collected flints and other small rock fragments which clearly indicated, even to his untrained mind, that the area had, at some point in the distant past, been inhabited by more than just a small garrison at the fort. Like a fish drawn to some irresistible bait he was hooked and commenced a fascination with the ancient history of the Middle East which was to remain with him for the remainder of his life.

Whenever possible, Rees endeavoured to combine military patrols with his new found interest and tried to enthuse others who accompanied him - not always successfully, as a young pilot of No.14 Squadron, John Franks, recalled [1]:

"His hobby was flying & motoring about the Sinai & Transjordan deserts by day & by night with a large scale map & a Bible finding places of biblical interest. An ADC sitting in the back of a motor car in which he was taking round a rather bored French colonel from Damascus, told me of an amusing incident, when he was pointing out the spot on a steep mountain track where it was mentioned in the Old Testament that Jacob had wrestled with the Angel who had put his thigh out of joint. His pidgin French confused the colonel whose reply was "Ah, Je comprende, accidente automobile." Nobody even smiled!"

The introduction of aircraft into the Middle East, primarily for military purposes, had a profound effect upon the archaeological understanding of the region for, not only could great distances over inhospitable terrain be covered very quickly but also details of the landscape, invisible from the ground, could be seen from the air; a feature which had previously been only visible in small sections, if at all, could now be viewed in its entirety and, above all, photographed.

The pioneering work of tying together aerial photography and archaeology had commenced almost as soon as the First World War had ended when Colonel Beazeley published some views on the subject in the 1919 and 1920 issues of the Geographical Journal but few saw the possibilities which this new facility offered and aerial photographs were, on the whole, only used to provide a new perspective of already identified and studied sites. In 1925, one of Rees' former subordinates in No.11 Squadron, Gilbert Insall,VC, whilst flying over Salisbury Plain, took a photograph which he realised showed a feature which was unnoticeable from ground level. Archaeological investigation led to the discovery of what came to be known as Woodhenge, a major early Neolithic site [2]. The potential for archaeological aerial photography was then realised by a small group of scholars who saw tremendous scope for its use in the relatively unknown deserts of Mesopotamia and Transjordan, regions which had only recently come under British control. The fact that the RAF was charged with the supervision of these regions led O G S Crawford approaching the Air Ministry in an endeavour to enlist their help in conducting an archaeological survey of the region.

"The result was very gratifying. An undertaking was given that, subject to certain obvious limitations, ancient sites might be included in the normal routine of practice photography. Further, it was agreed that these, and many existing but obsolete negatives of sites abroad, should be handed over to the Director of the British Museum, to form a nucleus of a national collection. In order to set the scheme in motion, I decided to visit the countries concerned, and collect and bring back with me the first instalment of obsolete negatives."

The RAF instructed its officers to assist in any way that they could as long as no additional burden was placed upon the Service's already stretched budget. Rees' position as OC Palestine and Transjordan, his proven talents as a diplomatic representative of the Service, his interest in archaeology and the fact that he was already photographing archaeological sites on his own initiative, made him an ideal candidate to assist in this programme. Crawford arrived in Amman in 1928 and was immediately impressed by Rees' personality:

"We landed at Amman at three o'clock and were met by Group Captain Rees. He was an enthusiastic amateur archaeologist and had collected a large group of wasms - small boulders with names chipped on them. He knew Transjordan thoroughly and used to patrol the tracks in six-wheeler Morris trucks, to keep them usable - a defence precaution that was then necessary.

I stayed with Rees at Amman for three weeks that were crowded with interest. The day after my arrival he had to accompany the Acting High Commissioner for Palestine, Sir Harry Luke, on a tour of the frontier; though primarily intended to be administrative, the tour became in fact almost exclusively archaeological, for we were three enthusiasts."

In addition to arranging field visits to notable sites, Rees allowed Crawford access to the sizeable collection of photographic negatives which he had already collected since the establishment of the command two years previously. He knew that the archaeologist would be pleased with the plates as many of them had been taken with the purpose of recording interesting ground features in mind and anything which had caught Rees' eye became a target for further photographic missions.

"The photographs were taken, mostly, as a matter of training. They are extraordinarily useful in showing new pilots the landmarks of the country, because in the desert there are often no landmarks except some of the old ruins. It is thus important that pilots should know them." [3]

Rees was already making considerable use of the photographs to assist him with his own researches into the archaeology of the region and little did he realise how valuable they were to become years later. Dr David Kennedy, head of the Aerial Photographic Archive for Archaeology in the Middle East, makes the point that if one were to examine the photographs of Qasr el Azraq as a single example, they clearly indicate the enormous changes which have occurred during the past sixty years even in such a remote and barren landscape. When Rees had his headquarters there the area was much as it had been for hundreds of years and both the Druze and

171

military camps were only temporary affairs. Today, however, there is a sizeable town of some 3,000 people on the site and the ground features have changed almost beyond recognition. For this reason alone, Rees' work in photographing the area under his command is of immeasurable value to modern archaeologists.

Rees' position as 'guide' to Crawford was one that he was already accustomed to, having the previous year undertaken a similar role when the RAF had been hosts to the American archaeological expedition sponsored by the Field Museum of Natural History. Mounting such an expedition into the desert was frought with dangers far beyond those posed by the hostile environment and arrangements had to be made for the archaeologists to accompany RAF armoured car patrols wherever possible or, at the very least, be escorted by experienced military personnel to ensure that they were not attacked by one of the numerous bands of marauding Bedouin in the region. They had to maintain regular radio contact with RAF Headquarters in Amman so that should they encounter any difficulties, assistance could be swiftly rendered in the form of aircraft from No.14 Squadron. The leader of the expedition, Henry Field, was very impressed with the arrangements and the co-operation which he received:

"Group Captain Rees guided me to many sites, including most of those published by him ... he assisted the expedition in every posible manner and was able to make valuable suggestions as to the probable localities where prehistoric man may have lived. Owing to the kindness of the British Air Force, the expedition was allowed to visit places which otherwise would have been totally inaccessible." [4]

East of Qasr el Azraq lay the region known as the Basalt (or Harra) so called because of the large areas of basalt boulders which covered the surface. Rees spent a considerable length of time studying the numerous cairn groups and stone circles which were located there and discovered that they were not only evidence of ancient man's use of what is now a barren region but that they also contained evidence of their use, at some period of their history, by a literate race of people. Inscriptions and/or drawings were to be found on or near to nearly every large cairn that he examined but were rarely found on the medium sized cairns and never on the smaller ones. He also noted that similar inscriptions were to be found on rocks that were remote from any cairns. As all these inscriptions were similar to those which had previously been discovered in the area of the Safa Depression he was able to date them to the period known as the Safaitic Period which extended from about the first century BC to the fourth century AD. The inscriptions are believed to have been carved by the ancient Bedouin and other semi-nomadic tribes and are very similar in style to those found in Southern Arabia and the language is closely related to Arabic, making them very distinct from the inscriptions of the settled peoples of the region who, at that period, were writing in either Arameic or Greek.

Rees labelled the stone circles 'villages' and believed that cattle could have been penned inside them. As they were located many miles from known sources of water he concluded that there must have been a dramatic change in the water supply of the region and that once that valuable commodity had ceased to be available then the 'villages' had ceased to be inhabited. He speculated that the cairns had also served as a form of defensive feature or guard houses for the Roman roads which, at that time crossed the region. The larger cairns were all about the same size and contained a single chamber some 8 feet by 3 feet in which it was possible to sit upright. They were circular in shape, built on a stone plinth and roofed over with six or seven flat stones on which were piled a heap of small stones. Some had a proper doorway and each had a line of smaller cairns, forming what Rees described as a tail, which were in no way linked and had no means of access. They served no obvious residential purpose and he concluded that they were a flexible defensive feature, allowing the guard protection from whichever direction he might be attacked.

"The guard attacked in the rear could quickly slip round or between the small cairns ... On a small hill - west of Kasr el Hallabat, the large cairn and part of the tail have been replaced by a Roman dressed stone breastwork wall."[5]

He went to great lengths to record the inscriptions and drawings which he saw and made some interesting observations regarding the variations between those located in the north of the region and those found in the south, stating that the latter resembled very strongly similar drawings found in Africa thereby suggesting that some form of ancient cultural or even racial link may have existed with that continent.. He even went so far as to attempt to read the inscriptions but, as he used a publication which had an incomplete script table for Safaitic, these are now viewed as having little value. M C A Macdonald, a leading authority in this field sums up this aspect of Rees' archaeological work thus:

"His 'translations' of some of the names, though obviously 'jeux d'esprit', are pleasingly ingenious, thus the name Asad (the common

Arabic word for lion) is rendered 'Lionel', and so on. His contribution to Saphaitic epigraphy lay in his discovery of the texts and his making them available to the scholarly world... His copies, though far from exact, are not at all bad, considering that he could not read the inscriptions at the time he was copying them. They certainly compare favourably with those of several other travellers and explorers." [6]

Before this time, archaeologists of the Middle East had devoted most of their attention to the regions around Transjordan where there were obvious sites of great interest; to the west lay the numerous biblical sites of Palestine and to the east the remains of the ancient civilisations of Mesopotamia. Little in the way of study had been made of the Transjordanian desert as it was generally believed that such an inhospitable region could hardly have supported much in the way of human settlement. The generally accepted view was that the only people who could have survived in such a region were nomadic tribesmen who would have left behind little of interest to archaeologists. It was the enthusiasm and work of amateurs like Rees that led to a change in this view and caused the region to become one of major interest by the mid-twentieth century.

Certain sites were already renowned and were receiving attention but it was not these that caught the eye of the amateurs. Petra, the great Roman city was certainly magnificent but on a scale which was far too grand for men like Rees to become involved with. Instead, they turned their attention to the small items that others had ignored or failed to notice before the days of the aeroplane. When Crawford visited Amman he noted obvious sites in his records but he also mentions, albeit only in passing, the lesser discoveries made by Rees :

"...we proceeded to the ruined but well preserved Roman town of Umm el Jemal; the doors of some of the houses were formed of a solid slab of stone that could still be moved on its pivot. All around were the stone walls of the town's deserted fields. From there we went to Umm Keiss, an extinct volcano ... from the top of which was a splendid view over the Roman town of Bosrah, whose field-walls are perfectly preserved, row upon row ... All around were remains of the habitations of unknown ages ... we could see Kasr Amr, a group of baths built in the desert by Ommayad sultans early in the eighth century AD.

Our next excursion was in the desert. It was an ideal camping trip, for all the chores were done for us by our escort and we had nothing to do but enjoy ourselves. The tracks were fairly good ... the weather was perfect and the desert air marvelously clear and sparkling, especially at dawn. We visited the remains of a fishing village beside a dried up lake, and some flint-sites of a much earlier date where flint implements and flakes were abundant."

Rees' activities appear to have been mainly concerned with establishing that the region had, at one time, supported a substantial permanently settled population. He was convinced that there was ample evidence to support this hypothesis and that the region had only become an empty wilderness as a result of a dramatic change in the climate during the period of recorded history.

In 1927, one of the RAF officers serving in the Middle East, Flight Lieutenant Maitland [7] published an article in the very first issue of the archaeological journal 'Antiquity'. Entitled 'The Works of the Old Men in Arabia', this was the first attempt to describe and explain some of the archaeological features which were to be found in the desert east of Amman. In particular, Maitland was interested in the numerous walls and enclosures which could be clearly seen from aircraft flying over the Bassalt. Rees was also interested in the same area of study and attempted to explain what was visible from the air and in the aerial photographs of the region. He made numerous flights over the areas which were clearly divided by the walls and also visited them on foot. His findings were published in 'Antiquity' in 1929 and caused a minor sensation in the world of Transjordanian archaeology and were translated and published in the French learned journal 'Syria' in the same year. Unfortunately, today, Rees' theories are discounted by experts in this field who have a great many more facts available as well as the technology of the 1980s. Dr Alison Betts [8] however does not dismiss Rees' contribution out of hand:

"As to Rees' contribution to scholarship, I should not dismiss his work as naive or old hat. To do so would be to do him a grave disservice. He went to an area about which very little was known (as is still the case to a great extent) and where no one else wanted to go anyway. For a long time there had been a general feeling that nothing went on in the desert areas ... Rees showed that these areas had much potential for study. He reported his findings conscientiously. he also made special efforts to bring his findings to the attention of people who could comment on them with more authority - notably O G S Crawford and Henry Field, and helped them to examine the area for themselves. It is true that the interpretations in his publication are based upon a layman's background, but the information itself is of great value. I have certainly made use of the photographs for much of my work and it is un likely that these features would have come to light until much later if it was not for Rees and Maitland."

Rees had found the study of the ancient history of Transjordan totally absorbing, particularly his attempts at translating the pictographic languages of the Safaitic period. Recognising the problems which he faced in this

177

field, he began a study of the more 'standardised' languages of the region such as Greek, Hebrew and Arabic and he became, with practice, something of an expert on the oral and written tradition of the area.

Originating as he did from Wales, it is not surprising that, when he was appointed to the military command of Palestine, he began to feel a great awareness of the religious and cultural background which was common to both societies. He cannot have been unaffected by the close proximity of historical sites such as those in Jerusalem and the Jordan Valley which were as much a part of his own Welsh heritage as the castles of the old Welsh princes in Caernarfonshire. It was almost inevitable that the two interests should blend together and develop into a fascination with the history of the Israelites as laid down in the Old Testament, a field of study which was to become something of an overiding passion to him and which he was to remain involved with for the remainder of his life.

Unlike his study of the stone remains in Transjordan, where he published his theories very quickly, he kept his biblical research very much to himself, only occasionally giving a lecture to small groups of interested listeners. It was not until 1948 that he gave his theories their first general airing with an article on the exodus of the Israelites out of Egypt [9]. It would appear that this was intended to be the first of a series of such articles but nothing further appeared and, sadly, the bulk of his papers have long since vanished. From what little that has survived however, it is possible to build up part of the picture which he was trying to create.

When Rees had faced the problem of the Druze tribesmen seeking sanctuary in the territory under his command, pleading that they were escaping from the tyranny of the French authorities in Syria, he found that the situation equated in some ways with that faced by the kings of Bashan and the Amorites as related in the Book of Numbers [20: 14-21 and 21: 31-33]:

"And Moses sent messengers from Ka-desh unto the king of Edom. Thus saith thy brother Israel, Thou knowest all the travail that hath befallen us. How our fathers went down to Egypt, and we have dwelt in Egypt a long time; and the Egyptians vexed us and our fathers: and when we cried unto the Lord, he heard our voice, and sent an angel, and hath brought us forth out of Egypt: and behold, we are in Kadesh, a city in the uttermost of thy border. Let us pass, I pray thee through thy country: we will not pass through the fields, or through the vineyards, neither will we drink of the water of the wells: we will go by the king's highway, we will not turn to the right hand nor to the left, until we have passed thy borders. And Edom said unto him, Thou shall not pass by me, lest I come out against thee with a sword."

"Thus Israel dwelt in the land of the Amorites. And Moses sent to spy out Ja-a-zer, and they took the villages thereof, and drove out the Amorites that were there. And they turned and went up by way of Ba-shan; and Og the king of Ba-shan went out against them, he and all his people, to the battle at Ed-re-i."

Rees saw himself as the 'ruler' of the desert region of Transjordan and felt that the request made to him by the Druze was similar to that made by the Israelites. Rather than face unnecessary conflict with them he, unlike the kings of the Old Testament, allowed them restricted passage through his land, indeed the kingdom of the Amorites covered much of Transjordan and the king's highway of biblical times was still in use in the twentieth century and was the major routeway between Syria in the north and the Gulf of Aqaba in the south. The fort at

Azraq was situated on this ancient route and it was not therefore surprising that Rees was drawn to the biblical precedent for the situation in which he found himself:

> "I was faced with the problem that defeated Og, King of Bashan and Sihon, King of the Amorites; and in order to find out where they failed I read up about the Exodus."

This piece of historical background reading to a modern problem stirred his methodical and military mind. The more he studied the story as related in the Old Testament, the less satisfied he became with the traditional interpretation. There is no evidence which would suggest that he had ever been an avid student of theology or that he was a great believer in the spiritual aspects of the christian faith. Instead, being by nature a practical man, he found the miraculous events of the Exodus somewhat far-fetched and began to seek for more logical, scientific explanations. At no time, however, do his theories contravene the essential facts or beliefs as laid down in the Bible; far from it, they explain the previously inexplicable and, it might be argued that in doing so, they strengthen the story.

Historically, most scholars accept that the Israelites left Egypt sometime between 1300 BC and 1200 BC. Moses is supposed to have kept a careful record of their journey but this was very soon lost so that the details of the events which befell them only survived as part of an oral tradition which was not written down, in the form of the early books of the Old Testament, until some six hundred years later. This led to a vagueness and a lack of accuracy in the recording of the locations of certain events and, whilst the point of departure, Egypt, and the point of arrival, Caanan, are undisputed, the other places mentioned in the history are almost all open to question.

Rees found that one location above all was of the utmost importance if the route of the Exodus was to be understood with any degree of accuracy:

"As regards the route, the incidents on the march are clear only if Mount Sinai is put in its proper place; and ... I intend to disagree with everybody as to its exact position." [10]

He argued that at the time of the Exodus, and for many years afterwards, the location of Mount Sinai was of little significance to the Israelites. Although, as the place where God gave the ten commandments to man, it was a place of utmost importance to Moses, it was a place of shame to others who had reverted to their pagan rituals whilst awaiting the return of their leader. The traditional location for the mountain, at the southern end of the Sinai peninsula, is rejected totally by Rees who brings evidence to support his theory:

"About the year 400 AD, there was growing unrest in the Transjordan desert which culminated over 100 years later in the birth of Mahommed. This unrest caused certain holy men in Jerusalem to feel that life in that town was not worth living, so they decided to go away into the desert. They apparently turned up Deuteronomy XXXIII. 2, which said that the Eternal had appeared on Sinai in the south; quite forgetting that when Moses sang that song he was well over to the east of the Jordan.

Whatever was the reason, they travelled south and came in due course to the end of the Sinai peninsula. When they arrived, even if they had not known it before, they found that the place was called Sinai and that it was a very holy place. There were the Turquoise mines that had been presided over by the Egyptian Goddess Hat-Hor, the mother of Turquoise; and a very ancient site where the Semitic people had worshipped Sin, the Moon Goddess.

The name [Sinai] means very little as on modern maps one

frequently finds the same name in the forms Sinan and Snainerat. It merely means jagged or toothlike.

That it was always a holy site seems to me to make it impossible for it to be the Sinai of the Exodus. If Moses had wanted to worship the Moon Goddess, Pharoh would never have let the Israelites depart because everybody knew that for at least 400 years the Egyptians had oppressed the Israelites and the Moon Goddess had done nothing about it.

Even at the Burning Bush, Moses did not know to whom he was speaking and had to ask his name and the name was quite a new one. Nevertheless, the Holy Men settled down there and a Monastery was built in 500 AD."

Rees then went on to argue that when the Israelites reached Mount Sinai, the Lord appeared to them as detailed in the book of Exodus [19:16 & 18]:

"And it came to pass on the third day in the morning, that there were thunders and lightnings, and a thick cloud upon the mount, and the voice of the trumpet exceedingly loud; so that all the people in the camp trembled.

And Mount Sinai was altogether on a smoke, because the Lord descended upon it in fire: and the smoke thereof ascended as the smoke of a furnace, and the whole mount quaked greatly."

Rees saw this as being a clear description of a volcanic eruption and the only volcanic region to the east of Egypt, within a range that the Israelites might have reached, was located in Transjordan and it was here that he located Mount Sinai, in the mountain range east of Aqaba.

Having accepted in his own mind that Sinai was here, he then commenced to place the other events of the Exodus in what he believed to be their correct geographical perspective. The crossing of the Red Sea he placed in the marshy area around Lake Timsah, near the northern end of the Gulf of Suez. The word Red was a mistranslation and should have been Reed. Unfortunately, the water features of that region had been altered out of all recognition by the construction of the Suez Canal during the 19th century and, consequently, he was unable to pin-point the exact location which he was seeking.

"They crossed the Reed Sea in April on a night when a very cold and strong east wind was meeting the water laden air of the Delta. Such conditions at this time of the year make for an exceptionally heavy thunderstorm, and the storm actually did arrive ... storms may be quite local but the rain sometimes comes down so heavy and with such a definite edge that one can well describe it as a wall of water.

Although the prevailing wind is North-West, at the beginning and end of the winter the wind sometimes switches over to an easterly direction and blows with gale force.

After such a storm, the whole country becomes waterlogged and quite impassable to wheeled transport and animals. So the story of the crossing is literally true. The walls of rain water, not sea water, held the chariots till the sea swept back."

Having crossed the Reed Sea, the Israelites marched for three days in the desert of Shur, in the midst of which they found bitter water.

"In this dune country, all water, if any, is bitter. The sun sucks up the moisture and the salt dries out. Besides turning the water sweet by throwing in a tree, Moses ordered the well to be drained three times. This is still the way to find sweet water. You get down under the top crust of salt, drain away the salt water and eventually, if you are lucky, reach fresh water."

Had the Israelites then travelled south as was suggested by the traditionally accepted route, then there surely would have been some mention of the sea which lay parallel to their route. There was no such mention and, Rees argued, this was because they were in fact heading east, across the Sinai peninsula. It has been argued that it would have been the height of foolishness for them to have selected such a course as it would have grave consequences should they have encountered any of the settled races who populated that area. This was not the case said Rees as, following on from their apparently miraculous escape from Egypt, Moses had told the Israelites that they had nothing to fear as the Lord was protecting them [Exodus 16:23-27].

If one can accept Rees' theory that the Children of Israel headed out of Egypt by this easterly route then many other mysterious facts in the story, such as that described in Exodus 14: 21-22, suddenly become explicable.

> "And the Lord went before them by day in a pillar of cloud, to lead them the way; and by night in a pillar of fire, to give them light; to go by day and by night.
> He took not away the pillar of cloud by day, nor the pillar of fire by night, from before the people."

Here we have the suggestion that there was a great deal of urgency in their journey; that they were moving day and night as indeed they would be not only to escape from the Egyptians but also to get across the wilderness as quickly as possible. The whole of the eastern seaboard of the Red Sea, their traditional route, was under Egyptian control, including the traditional location of Mount Sinai. Had they followed this route there would have been no special need for speed before reaching the mountain (where they then remained for a lengthy period of time) as they would have been in danger for the entire journey.

If Rees' assumption that Sinai was in fact an active volcano is accepted then the above verses make perfect sense. By day a distant volcanic eruption would appear clearly, over a very great distance, as a tall column of smoke and, in the darkness of the night, that same eruption would be visible as a glow of light. He argued that this is therefore solid evidence that the Israelites followed the easterly rather than the southerly route and that they were heading towards modern day Jordan. He also stated that if his route was to be followed carefully on a modern day map of the region then, not only can most of the names mentioned in the Old Testament story be discovered (by going back to their original meanings) but that they will also be found in their correct sequence. The student has simply to rid his mind of the prejudice caused by the centuries old belief in the southerly route. By way of example, the Old Testament references to the Wilderness of Sin (located in the south-west of the Sinai peninsula) helps to pin-point the traditional location of Mount Sinai. Instead, might the true location not have been the Wilderness of Zin, which name comes from the same linguistic root, which is in the south of modern day Israel, directly on the route suggested by Rees.

When the Israelites reached this barren region, Moses would have known that there was a strong possibility that they would find water due to the recent heavy rainfall. Travelling ever eastwards they kept the 'Eternal' before them until they reached Mount Sinai. Somewhere in this region, perhaps at Kadesh-Barnea, they halted having found a plentiful supply of fresh water.

The organisation of the Exodus and the problems facing Moses were similar to those faced by any military commander at the head of an army. Despite having initially been allowed to leave Egypt with the Pharoh's agreement, the Israelites had clearly seen their former masters change their minds and one attempt to recapture them had already been thwarted. It would have been obvious to Moses that his first priority was to put as much distance between his people and any renewed Egyptian pursuit. To do this they had to head east, far beyond the frontiers of Egypt. To have followed the coastline south, through areas under Egyptian control, to a mountain which was an Egyptian shrine, would simply having given publicity to their progress and invite the Pharoh to give chase. It is therefore logical that Moses would have decided to lead his people directly eastwards, away from Egyptian territory, even if it did mean crossing the inhospitable wilderness which we today call the Sinai Desert. Moses was an educated man and would have realised that it would be impossible to expect such a large group of people to navigate any form of accurate route across an often featureless region. Indeed, so great are the numbers of Israelites believed to have been that it is unlikely that they could have travelled in one mass. Some scholars of the Exodus story have estimated that they may have numbered as many as 2,000,000 although such a high figure is highly improbable. Rees believed that their number was very much lower although still large enough to make their movement a major problem. The existence of an active volcano beyond the horizon would have provided a constant, or eternal, point of reference which even the most simple minded or uneducated people could follow. Moses is recorded as having spent some time away from Egypt before the start of the Exodus and this must surely have been what we would now describe as a reconnaissance mission when he plotted out a route through the desert.

Rees believed that his theory was, if not perfect, then more acceptable than that which had hitherto been accepted as true. He had, however, one further 'pet' theory for which, unfortunately, none of his evidence has survived but which would appear to have been the key to the whole story. To the east of his Mount Sinai location, there existed marks in the desert which, when he saw them from the air, he thought to be unique. Just below the mountain there was some form of evidence which suggested that a large number of people had stayed there for some considerable time. Using a system of dating rocks by their colour (which has since been shown to be partially inaccurate due to the movement of rocks over the years) he concluded that the site was so old as to be invisible from the ground as the rocks blended into their natural surroundings. Even he had failed to find the exact site on foot.

"I like to think that this was the position of the camp at Sinai. It allows an excellent site for the Dwelling, which could be seen for miles, and would give all the necessary conditions for the incidents that happened at Sinai."

Unlike his other archaeological theories, this location of the route of the Exodus was not without a good background of scholarly research. For many years he made a careful study of the texts of the Old Testament, wherever possible going back to as near the original texts as practicable. He did not make use of the English, or any other modern translation, preferring to study the Greek account and then compare the placenames which he came across with those shown on both modern and ancient maps of the region and their traditional Arab spelling and pronunciation. Unfortunately, as has already been pointed out, most of his papers have not survived and therefore it is not possible to check out his sources and the 'route' which he took to his conclusions. Today, a sizeable body of learned opinion would seem to agree with his location of Mount Sinai and would regard this theory as somewhat routine. It must be remembered however, that when he first began to work on these ideas, they were revolutionary and it is unfortunate that nowhere does there appear to be any acknowlegement of his pioneering work in this field.

CHAPTER X
Retirement
(1929 -31)

Those individuals who knew Rees and came into daily contact with him knew that his duties were unaffected by his new found passion for the past, describing him as an enthusiastic and untiringly energetic officer. They all seem to have fond memories of him as a senior officer, colleague and, in a few cases, friend. He does however, appear to have gone out of his way to further cultivate his image as something of an eccentric although it was probably more akin to what might today be described as a rather 'zany' sense of humour. The Assistant British Resident in Transjordan, Alec Kirkbride [1], had very warm memories of Rees and his cheery disposition:

"He and I spent several months reconnoitring and making out motor-tracks through the desert in Jordan which lay to the east of the Hajez Railway. We used to go out with a couple of Royal Air Force armoured cars and some tenders; when we got lost, which was not infrequent, Rees used to infuriate the station at Amman by sending out a message such as this, "We are lost somewhere within fifty miles of the Wells of Bair. Send an aircraft to find us and tell us where we are." The column then just sat and sent wireless reminders until an aircraft did find us.

He loved to try his hand at making our position in the desert by means of observations of the sun and stars with navigational instruments. he would make long and complicated calculations with the oddest of results. One night he fixed our position to his entire satisfaction by the stars, and the next day, as we did not move on for some reason or another, he decided to check the result by solar observation. When he had finished, he looked across and said, with his cheerful smile that never failed, "It is most extraordinary, I could have sworn that we had not moved, but, according to my results, we dropped three hundred feet in altitude during the night and went twenty miles further east!"

During one of our waits for an aircraft to tell us where we were, he announced his intention of getting up before dawn the next day and seeing what lay beyond a range of hills some miles away. He wanted me to go, but I refused, saying that there were more ranges of hills beyond, looking exactly alike for miles and miles; much further, in fact, than either of us could walk. He would not be deterred and was gone when I woke up. When breakfast was ready, I looked across towards the hills to see if he was visible. I could see him running towards us, in his halting gait, clad in a pair of shoes and a pair of stockings; his shirt was in one hand and his shorts in the other. His explanation when he arrived was to the effect that it was much cooler that way."

His skills as a pilot certainly appear to have diminished whilst in the Middle East and he acquired a reputation as an habitual 'crash-lander'of aircraft. He was fully aware of the problem himself and, as a consequence, would refuse to carry any passengers in any machine flown by himself on the grounds that the risk was too great. Despite this problem which was probably caused by his old war injury (and undoubtedly by the poor quality of the landings strips in the area) he was regularly airborne and appeared to be under some form of divine protection. On one occasion, whilst attempting to land at Ramleh in Palestine, he was involved in a spectacular crash. Those who say the machine come to a halt in the middle of the runway were convinced that he could not have survived and, when the crash tender and ambulance reached the machine, they were amazed to find him sitting in the cockpit, with no visible evidence of any injury, studying his wristwatch. His only comment before climbing out of the aircraft was to criticise his would-be rescuers for their delay in reaching him, "You should have been here two minutes ago!" On another occasion he was not quite so fortunate as he struck his face on the aircraft's instrument panel and broke his nose thereby earning the local nickname of 'Bootnose'.

Being the senior officer in the region, Rees was not always obliged to pilot himself and often another officer would be detailed to play the part of an aerial chauffeur. Several times whilst flying the Group Captain over the desert, these junior officers were horrified to hear him announce that they passing over some feature of possible archaeological interest and that he was going down to take a look. Ordering the pilot to, "Cut the engine", and with the parting instruction,"Send transport", Rees would clutch a spade (which he always carried with him on any journey) and leave the aeroplane, making the descent by parachute. He assumed that the young pilot knew his position and, fortunately for him - and the pilot, such faith appears to have been justified and, every time it happened, a vehicle turned up a few hours later.

His amiability and total lack of pretentiousness endeared him to everybody and a favourite anecdote from this period tells of his having wandered off alone into the desert when, far from any possible assistance, he met with two armed bedouin who demanded his money. Assuring them that he had nothing in his pockets other than a handkerchief he managed to turn their aggression into interest and then into sympathy. Before they parted company the two arabs had given him, in the best traditions of Islam, a shilling to help him on his way !

That he had made a marked impression on the NCOs and other ranks at Amman cannot be denied and, when, in 1926, the Royal Antediluvian Order of Buffaloes established a lodge in the city, it was named after him [2]. To those nearer his own status he was a constant source of amazement as Alec Kirkbride recalled in his memoirs:

"If anyone had doubted his fearlessness, they had only to see his automatic shotgun in action. It was a weapon of which the bolt action came to pieces in about one in every ten shots. Rees said that he had bought it to encourage the makers, but I felt that they wanted discouraging from launching such a dangerous weapon on the world.

He was a non-smoker and a fanatical tee-totaller. He was delighted when I opened my valise one evening to be greeted by a cloud of fumes from the whisky which had emptied itself on to the blankets from my last bottle. He enquired anxiously every night until we got back to civilisation, as to whether I could still smell the whisky and, when I answered in the affirmative, said "Good, it should teach you to give up drinking the horrid stuff."

Sir Harry Luke, Acting British High Commissioner for Transjordan in 1928-29 became a close friend and wrote to the Times shortly after Rees had died:

"Your notice of Group Captain Rees fails - I think inevitably - to shed light on the character of a rare and strange personality. I say inevitably because Rees was a 'solitary' and hence not easy to know. I was fortunate in having been able to penetrate beneath the reserve of this unusual man whose highly original characteristics failed to endear him to his immediate superior in Egypt at the time.

I got to know Rees fairly well, partly through a shared love for the Syrian desert although I never approached his uncanny knowledge of that fascinating region, which he came to know as the palm of his hand. Rees, a batchelor, possessed of private means, was a man whose unselfish and generous instincts were matched by the monastic austerity of his personal life. Few, I fancy, of his brother - officers knew that at the time of which I write (and possibly also at others) he declined to touch his pay, preferring to divert it into various charities of the RAF."

Luke appears to have touched upon one very important point in this letter when he mentions the attitude of Rees immediate superior, the Air Officer Commanding the Middle East. It would appear that it was his involvement in the archaeology of the region which was the root cause of the friction between them and, when Rees made a request for an extended leave period in order to continue his research, it was refused and the situation appears to have become intolerable. It does not, however, appear to have affected his relationship with senior officers of the service back in London and, when his period of command in Amman came to an end in December 1928, he was granted leave before taking up his new appointment in April 1929 as the Officer Commanding the Inland Area Depot, back in Britain [3]. The following January he was given command of No.21 Group Headquarters at Uxbridge.

The life of a 'chairborne' officer did not suit his personality; there was little opportunity to fly and the thought of a future as a paper administrator did not appeal to him at all. His next promotion, if it came, would be to Air Commodore and would mean the abandonment of the 'active' type of commands in which he seemed to flourish. One of his former Cranwell cadets, A D Gillmore, found nothing unusual in the fact that Rees went no further in the career structure of the Royal Air Force:

"I am not really surprised that he left the Service before reaching Air Rank. He seemed to me to be essentially a practical man, and the sort of high level Staff jobs he would have had to take on with further promotion were not really his 'cup-of-tea' at all. I think he would have found them very irksome."

Another Old Cranwellian felt much the same :

"...studying Biblical archaeology was entirely in keeping with his character. I am sure he found more satisfaction in that pursuit than he would in reaching Air Rank. I suspect the one contributory factor in him not reaching Air Rank was that he did not positively aspire to the role."

Rees' father had died in 1930 and, although he did not leave a will, one can assume that he made some financial provision for his children. Indeed, it may have been such an inheritance that prompted Lionel Rees to make the break from the RAF, believing that he was financially independent. Certainly, the fact that neither he nor his sister Muriel had married meant that he had nothing to prevent him pursuing a totally selfish life in the years to come. There seemed little prospect that the RAF might be involved in any major conflict for the foreseeable future and therefore remaining in uniform would merely serve to ruin memories of many happy and fascinating years. On 31 July, 1931, after nearly thirty years of service to the Crown, he retired to live at 3 Upper Hale Lane, Edgware although it was obvious to all who knew him that a sedentary life in suburbia could not possibly last.

CHAPTER XI
The *May*
(1932 - 35)

When Lionel Rees acquired more than just a casual interest in sailing is unrecorded but, having spent his formative years in Caernarfon, there was undoubtedly an element of salt water in his blood from birth. Both his father and grandfather had been members of the Royal Welsh Yacht Club at Porth-yr-Aur in the town, although there is no evidence to suggest that they were anything more than what would now be termed social members. Following his retirement from the RAF, Rees went on an extended holiday to Scotland where, in years gone by, he had spent so many happy days in the company of his mother's family. It was during this visit that he was able to reassess his life and, having put the Service behind him, he purchased the *May* a boat which was to cause such a dramatic change to his life.

The *May* had been built in 1902 by Alexander Robertson at Sandbank, Scotland as a Loch Fyne class of ketch. With an overall length of 34 feet 6 inches, a 9 foot 3 inch beam and a fully laden weight of just over 12 tons she was a sizeable vessel which, despite her age, could instill great pride in her owner. Although basically a sailing boat, she was equipped with a 2-cylinder Kelvin paraffin engine which could be utilised to take her in and out of her moorings. Rees spent the summer of 1932 "...playing about the Clyde" where he learned how to handle his new boat before sailing down the Irish Sea to Caernarfon where he moored alongside the Promenade and raised the ensign of the Royal Welsh Yacht Club.

His stay in the town of his birth was, however, short lived as his family ties were long since severed. His natural wanderlust led him to prepare for a journey further south so that the boat could spend the winter in the English Channel whilst he lived at the house in Edgware. When he set sail is not actually recorded but it was almost certainly during September, 1932. With a small group of friends to see him off he slipped out into the Menai Straits and, in a letter to one of those friends, Major Lloyd-Jones, he later recalled the event:

"As I crossed the Bar on that lovely evening, I looked back for the last time. The setting sun was lighting up the castle and the old walls with Twthill and the distant hills all bathed in a roseate hue. I shall carry this picture with me to the day of my death."

This romantic picture was indeed his last view of Caernarfon for he was destined never to return.

Reaching the Channel without any mishaps, the winter months passed with the *May* safely moored in the Beaulieu River on the Solent whilst Rees spent his time in London lecturing to various learned societies about his research into the archaeology of the Old Testament. Then, the arrival of a postcard changed the whole course of his life. Written by an old friend from Transjordan who was serving as the Chief Justice of the Bahamas, the message on the card suggested that Rees should call to see him at some future date "...if he were ever in the area". Thoughts of that far-away tropical island colony set his mind to thinking about the possibility of making a crossing of the Atlantic in the *May*. It was the British climate that finally convinced him:

"One winter, *May* and I, finding it a little cold in the Solent, had sought shelter up the Beaulieu River (a beautiful place, worthy of its name). Whilst the thermometer stood below freezing, conditions were good; but one day the sun came out. A loud crash against the ship's side made me leap on deck; and the next moment I was rigging an ice-breaker as protection against the ice which was floating down from the duck pond further up the river.

I said to *May* - "What do you know about that ? " and as she only groaned when a particularly large piece of ice hit her, I suspected that she thought just as I did about it."

The more he thought about it, the more the idea appealed to his natural sense of adventure. He had no ties or responsibilities and nothing else with which to fill his time. His lack of sailing experience does not seem to have worried him at all. His mind was made up and, as winter passed into spring and spring into summer he made his preparations. What his sister Muriel thought of the idea of him sailing single-handed across the Atlantic is unrecorded but it can safely be assumed that she was becoming rather immune to shocks brought on by Lionel's unusual schemes. Taking aboard the *May* only those few items which he regarded as essential, he disposed of all his remaining property, what little there was. Seeing no further use for his decorations and awards and perhaps feeling that they might be lost on the voyage, he presented them to the two institutions which had meant the most to him in his life; the military awards went ot his old school and the Sword of Honour was presented to the RAF College at Cranwell [1].

During the summer, he sailed westwards along the Channel coast to Falmouth and from there, on 2 July, 1933, with sufficient supplies aboard to last for three months, he set sail towards the south-west. He kept a detailed diary of the voyage and the reader will forgive me if I quote extensively from it for it not only tells the story of the crossing but also provides an insight into Rees' personality.

"A good north-easterly breeze took me well out of the Channel, past Ushant in two days. Having obtained a sufficient offing, I set squaresail and raffee; but no sooner was everything coiled down than a line squall, extending from horizon to horizon, came up from dead ahead. This was the first of many surprises, as hitherto I had always associated a line squall with the change from bad weather to good weather with a north-westerly wind.

There was nothing for it but to hand the squaresail and change over to fore-and-aft rig. Soon I was sailing close-hauled and reefed against an increasing south-westerly breeze. The sea had not risen very much, and progress was good, when suddenly the ship was lifted on to the top of a conical wave of the kind against which the Channel Pilot issues a special warning. Having no visible means of support, the little ship simply collapsed on to her beam ends in the succeeding trough. There was a loud crack as the starboard main shrouds chain plate gave way. It was a bad fitting anyway, and luckily there was no further damage, except that all the starboard rigging was strained - but not, apparently seriously. Most of the remainder of the day was spent in repairing the damage, and by the time the job was completed I was cold, wet and very miserable (a condition for which there should be some special yachting word)."

It was not an auspicious start to the voyage but Rees was undaunted. Men with less confidence in their own abilities would have headed for the safety of a harbour where the boat could be thoroughly checked but Rees decided to continue.

"On account of the ship's rig and the scend of the sea ... it was necessary to lay a course much further into the Bay [of Biscay] than was desirable. For nearly the whole of the next fortnight a series of small depressions passed at about a day's interval. In the mornings the course was no better than south (Mag.), but in the afternoons it was posible to point towards the south-west.

Gradually the general direction of the wind veered, so that the track on the chart shows a curve. During the whole of this period only one day was fine; and then there was so little wind progress was only 5 miles in the 24 hours. Even oilskins and sea-boots failed to keep out the weather, and the cabin was getting wetter and wetter. Usually, as a compensation, the wind moderated in the evenings, so that it was nearly always possible to enjoy a good hot supper and a good night's rest."

Alone with the *May* (with which he conducted regular conversations) his only first-hand contact with the outside world were the small fishing fleets which plied their trade in the area. Occasionally one would come alongside and a shouted conversation would ensue but usually it was only a distant wave.

His first sight of land was Cape Ortegal in north-western Spain but he was unable to get out of the wind and seek the shelter of its leeward side before nightfall and, the following morning, four exhausting hours were spent trying to beat to windward but it was to no avail and he was forced to heave-to about 30 miles off the coast and await a change in the conditions which would enable him to get out of the Bay of Biscay and into the Atlantic Ocean.

At last, after several days delay, the wind changed to an easterly breeze and, with the sun shining, the *May* escaped her prison and, with her squaresail set, began to head south down the coast of Spain. The good weather, however, did not last and by the afternoon Rees again had to heave-to as the wind gusted to gale force. The following morning he discovered that the leech (or edge) of his sail had been split in several places and he decided to steer a course for Corunna where he could carry out effective repairs and obtain a well earned rest.

"In the morning the sound of a cock crowing awakened me to a glorious sunny morning. Through dreamy consciousness filtered the realisation that usually seagulls do not crow, so I hurried on deck to find myself very close to a small Portugese fishing steamer ... The morning was so fine I reconsidered my intention of putting in to Corunna and decided to make for the Azores. For the first time since leaving England it was possible to get out of oilskins and sea-boots and to open up and dry the cabin.

Soon the steamer track was left far behind, and for the first time in my life I could sleep on in the mornings as long as I liked. There was no more crowing, no bells, no striking clocks and nobody to interfere with me. On board I had food and water for three months. I was free - entirely free."

This expression of delight at his isolation and the evident satisfaction at having survived the trials of crossing the infamous Bay of Biscay is totally in character. Rees was always happiest when facing, and overcoming, adversity by using his own resources. Major Lloyd-Jones wrote of him some twenty years later, "He found it difficult to make friends and was always happiest on his own, flying high over the deserts of Arabia or sailing the seas." Life aboard the *May* gave him the adventure and isolation which he had always sought. His survival depended upon his own wits and he owed nothing to any outsider. Social contact would be at his own discretion and when he felt the need to escape, he could simply weigh anchor, hoist the sail and be gone.

The Azores were ahead and a northerly wind carried the *May* towards them without incident. Conditions had improved so much that he was able to set a course, lash the wheel and relax or do the chores unhindered whilst the boat steered herself. About half-way between the mainland and the islands, as he approached the more tropical latitudes, the temperature began to rise and the miles slipped by more pleasurably. At 5 pm each day he would heave-to and then go below to listen to the events of the day on the BBC news broadcasts from Daventry on the massive radio receiver which he had on board. Although he had no facility for transmitting, the radio was no mere luxury as he was able to use the Greenwich time signal to plot his position. Indeed, all his navigational instruments were somewhat unusual as he had decided to base his navigation upon the methods which he had become accustomed to in the air. An RAF 'bubble' sextant was used to take a reading directly from the sun instead of the constantly moving horizon and, with an RAF slide-rule, the necessary calculations were speedily completed. Evidently he had become more adept at the art of navigation than he had been when wandering the deserts of Transjordan.

"One need only look up the correction for height once when the voyage starts as it is quite easy to remember it. I used tables only for amusement or for working out great circle courses, which were also amusement, as the wind would never allow me even to approximate to a great circle course. My wireless never failed to give the Greenwich time-signal but, as a matter of interest, I worked lunars for GMT, and found that I could get the time correct to within about 5 minutes.

I used the sextant the way we do when flying by night. That is to say, I bring the bubble in my level up to the sun or the star but the 'May' was jumping about too much for that, so I reversed the process and brought the level up to the sun."

As the boat ploughed her way south-westwards, Rees recorded the beauty of the sights which he saw under differing conditions. His fascination with and desire to understand everything that he experienced is evident in his record of the voyage.

"My day commenced before sunrise, and one was always repaid for the early rising. One morning was especially beautiful, about a third of the way across [from the Spanish coast to the Azores] when the whole seascape was covered with little detached rainstorms. There might have been about a dozen or more. As the sun rose, each seperate rainstorm formed its own semi-circular rainbow, some having more than one.

After that swarms of di-atoms [microscopic algae]. For several days the sea was full of them. There were long ones and round ones, pearl necklaces and balls filled with diamonds, and all the rest of the little fellows.

A small fish appeared which for two days continued to rub his nose up and down the curve of the rudder with apparent enjoyment; and one evening two squid jumped aboard, leaving, much to my annoyance, great pools of ink on the deck. As the islands were approached, flying fish appeared, and turtles; even a whale showed itself for a short time one evening.

These days were nearly calm, and that made navigation very difficult. On one day the error was excessively great, and I found that it was due to a kind of double swell that was running. The swells were of two slightly different wave-lengths, which 'beat' at every fifteenth wave. The ship was therefore for several seconds above and then for several seconds below her normal level; and this was in addition to the level caused by the obvious waves which were passing. A few days later the same difficulty arose again."

His supplies of fresh 'greens' were, by this time, dwindling and, in order to compensate for this and maintain his balenced diet, Rees put some sprouting onions into a jar and used the green shoots which they produced in a salad.

His confidence in his navigation was rewarded as he approached the Azores. After 31 days at sea he estimated that he should soon sight the island of Terceira, the most north-easterly of the group. In the late afternoon, the island appeared in exactly the right position and he sailed passed it before heaving-to for the night within sight of Topo lighthouse on the island of Sao Jorge. The following morning he set a course westwards, between the islands, and using the engine arrived off the harbour at Horta two hours later at sunset on 9 August. A pilot came out and guided the *May* to her berth and by midnight, 33 days out of Falmouth, he was safely moored and went below to sleep for the remainder of the night.

His stay in the Azores was a prolonged one as, in addition to replenishing his supplies, a number of repairs had to be carried out to the boat. For nearly two weeks he worked on her daily, assisted by a gang of small boys in return for a few cigarettes and some sweets. In the evenings he was feted by the British residents, an experience which he appears to have thoroughly enjoyed and news of his arrival on the island was even reported in the British press via the Reuter's correspondent.

At last, he was ready and, with the intention of following the route of Christopher Columbus who had sailed from the Azores in 1492, he prepared to set a course for the Bahamas. He awoke on the morning of 25 August to discover a gale blowing and was forced to remain in the harbour to ride out the storm. Whilst there, *May* dragged her anchors and fouled the moorings of a large buoy and, as soon as the wind had abated, a diver came out who cleared the anchors in return for a bottle of beer. On Sunday, 27 August, with a light, favourable wind, the *May* sailed out of Horta harbour steering a course due west.

Almost as soon as Rees was out of sight of land, the

weather deteriorated and by afternoon a cold rain was falling steadily, made worse by a contrary wind but, by the following morning the unpredictable weather had changed yet again and the ketch was speeding across the surface of the ocean.

"Things were going so well that I worked out a great circle distance to the Bahamas. This was a fatal step to take, as the wind immediately changed and I was virtually unable to make any westing for exactly one calendar month.

Making the best of a bad job, I sailed southward as speedily as possible, so as to get into the Trade winds. My problem was to get sufficiently far south to miss the equinoctial gales, and yet not to run into the hurricane belt before the hurricane season was over. The problem was complicated by the fact that the Trades are very uncertain during the hurricane season. In an endeavour to make the journey as short as possible I cut too closely to the edge of the Sargasso Sea, with the result that a lot of too calm weather was encountered."

Throughout September, the light southwesterly winds impeded his progress. Squalls were followed by periods of extreme calm but, the falling rain reduced the threat of a shortage of fresh water and, in fact, there was sufficient for freshwater baths on board. In the area of the Sargasso Sea, large quantities of seaweed floated by, sometimes in sufficient quantity to enable small striped crabs to crawl about on the surface. At night, Rees kept a light burning (to avoid collision with any other vessel which might be in the area) and this fascinated the flying fish which appeared to aim for it and, consequently, landed on the deck where, in the morning, they were collected and cooked for breakfast. "They are perfect little gentlemen. They taste excellent and they have no bones or nasty insides worth considering."

The marine life which he encountered, although not
plentiful, was fascinating to observe and he displayed an
almost child-like interest in it.

"On calm days the eddies under the stern would be full of
'goggle-eyes', the food of the dolphin. They have a dreadful life.
Every dolphin is full of as many of them as he is able to hold. Their
little black eyeballs stick out as hemispheres; but even that,
apparently, does not help them. The dolphin is a course fish to look
at and to eat, and appears at his best on a coat-of-arms.

For about a fortnight three shark pilot fish travelled a few inches
in front of my bow. Every few moments they would shoot off to
catch some food, and they increased in size visibly. One day they
disappeared, but the next morning the largest of them came back
leading a shark. The shark stayed a few hours, but as he got nothing
to eat from me he soon got tired of staying around.

One or two types of seagulls were at times visible, but the most
common bird was the bo'sun bird. He is most beautifully
streamlined, like a marlin-spike, hence his name. He has a double
tail; a small one of normal size, which he seldom spreads, and
another consisting of a few long tapered feathers. When he wants to
hover these feathers stick straight up, and give him stability, when by
all the rules of flying, he should be stalled and out of control."

The *May* did not reach the trade winds until she had
passed through latitude 19 degrees North. In one month
Rees had sailed 1,000 miles but was only 500 miles west
of the Azores. Towards the end of September the winds
increased and, as he entered the hurricane belt, he logged
distances of over 100 miles each day. His wireless
informed him that there were gales over England and that
a hurricane was heading for Cuba and it seemed that,
before long, the weather in mid-Atlantic was about to
follow suit. Concern about this made him set a new
course which would take him some two hundred miles
further north and, for two weeks, he was compelled to

steer the boat manually as the wind's direction made it impossible for him to lash the wheel so that the *May* could steer herself. By the end of October he was being carried along by the Caribbean Current and, hearing a hurricane warning on the radio, he decided to abandon his plan to make landfall, like Columbus, at San Salvador and, as he approached the Bahamas, he headed straight for the capital, Nassau, on the island of New Providence.

His new course meant that he would approach Nassau from the north-east and he found himself too close to the shore of some of the more remote of the islands as light began to fall. Still worrying about the hurricane, he decided to spend the hours of darkness well out to sea and it was not until noon the next day that he sighted the Hole in the Wall lighthouse. With a recorded speed of 8 knots (the fastest of the whole voyage) he crossed the last stretch of open water and sighted the lights of Nassau at 10 pm. One hour later he was approaching the harbour and, despite some confusion over the harbour and buoy lights, he crossed the bar safely and entered the calm water beyond. At 2 am on 21 October, sixty-five days out of Horta, Rees dropped anchor near the harbour offices at Nassau.

His arrival caused considerable interest in the town and news of his journey was flashed to news agancy offices throughout the world and newspapers as far apart as London and Brisbane carried short articles giving brief details of his voyage. Today, when solo trans-Atlantic crossings are commonplace, it is difficult to appreciate what Rees had achieved. He was not the first Briton to make the solo voyage on an east-west direction; on 17 June, the same year, Commander R D Graham,RN, had arrived in St John's, Newfoundland in the cutter

Emanuel after a 24 day crossing from Bantry in Ireland. Rees' voyage, although in an area of the ocean which was generally considered to be calmer, had covered more than twice the distance travelled by Graham and he had been at sea, alone, for a total of 96 days. In the pre-radar and pre-computer assisted steering days of the 1930s, the crossing was a major achievement for any seaman, let alone an amateur and there is little doubt that Rees regarded this calculated adventure as his greatest achievement, something which far exceeded anything which he had done previously.

A reporter was one of the first to board the *May* after she had been given a clean bill of health and allowed to tie up at the eastern end of Prince George's Wharf:

"As far as we could see everything was spick and span in the roomy cabin. For a man who likes his own company, Captain Rees [sic] has a comfortable craft ... when you get on deck and see everything so small you wonder how any man had the vitality to face such a venture as a lone crossing of the Atlantic, but when you study the gadgets that are fitted up and hear the Captain's explanations you begin to realise how these things are done - if you like doing them."

Chief Justice Tute, the inspiration for the voyage, was aboard the *May* for two hours before leaving with Rees for lunch at his home, Breezy Ridge. As he left, Rees was asked about the crossing and why he had done it. He replied, "Mr Tute asked me to come to tea, so I've come."

By the end of the month, *May* was in Symonettes's Shipyard in Nassau undergoing an overhaul. The blistering Atlantic sun had taken its toll on the paintwork but, otherwise, she was in remarkably good condition. On Wednesday, 8 November, she was back in the water and moored in the harbour, east of Fowler Street. Rees, however, was not yet satisfied and felt that having come so far it would be foolish not to complete the crossing of the Atlantic by sailing to mainland America, something which Columbus had failed to do. He spent the next few days making his preparations for this final stage, taking a break on Armistice Day when he was the Guest of Honour at the capital's Service of Rememberance.

At 7 am, on 21 November, Rees slipped quietly out of Nassau harbour bound for Miami, Florida. For two days the conditions were perfect as he steered the *May* through the Berry Islands westwards across the famed Tongue of the Ocean, over 2,000 metres deep. On the third day the weather deteriorated and he had to spend a worrying night amongst the shipping in the middle of the Providence Channel, landing, a little before dawn, on Great Isaac lighthouse where he spent a pleasant day with the keepers. Preparing to set sail in the evening he encountered some difficulty with his anchor which had become jammed under some coral and the moon was well up before he was en route for the Bimini Islands. As dawn broke he was horrified to discover that he was in the middle of what appeared to be uncharted mudbanks and was compelled to retrace his steps in an effort to get around them. It was some time before he realised that he was mistaken and that the 'mudbanks' were in fact areas of deep water on the edge of the bank. Sailing along this edge he passed the entrance to Bimini Harbour and dropped anchor at Gun Cay a few miles further south where he spent the night. The following morning he entered the Gulf Stream and, during the afternoon sighted the skyscrapers of Miami on the port bow. Using his engine, he entered the harbour at sunset but, as he moved towards the dock to enquire as to where he should berth, the *May* ran aground. It was ironic that his voyage should have ended with such an elementary error.

Once again, the local population expressed its admiration of his achievement and there was a seemingly endless stream of vistors to the *May*.

"I met several very charming people, who showed me all the sights of the district. As far as possible I welcomed all visitors, and kept on board for them drinks and candies. One visitor, I think, really did enjoy his visit, as he stayed for 24 hours, going ashore only to sleep and bring off a friend. Towards the end of my few days stay, being so busy visiting and being visited, there was no time to buy even a fesh supply of sea stores! I left Miami at midnight without being able to bid adieu to those who had been so good to me." [2]

Rees does not explain his apparently hasty departure from Miami but it was almost certainly brought about by his rather introverted personality; whilst it was delightful to be a celebrity, there was a limit to the amount of attention which he could tolerate. By quietly slipping away in the middle of the night he could return to the isolation which he had always welcomed and which, since the start of his voyage, he had become accustomed to. He enjoyed his own company and, if he wished for conversation, then *May* was a more than adequate companion as every movement and creak spoke volumes to him. His life had changed - gone was the discipline and order of military life; from the day he had sailed from Falmouth he had become master of his own destiny. From now on he would do what he liked when he liked. He could follow his many interests to his heart's content without a care or responsibility in the world. As he sailed back to the Bahamas he had made up his mind about where he was going to start this new life which was to be as different from the old one as it was possible to be.

CHAPTER XII
Cruising
(1933 -35)

Rees spent the winter of 1933-34 cruising amongst the myriad of islands which make up the Bahamas group. With Nassau as his base, he sailed on a number of short voyages gaining experience of the waters in the area and visiting the different settlements on neighbouring islands. His interest in everything around him is again evident in his writing from this period and, in a very short space of time, he acquired an immense knowledge of the area.

"Exploration [of the islands] is a little difficult, as the bush is so full of thorny creepers; and there are at least two kinds of poison wood that raises blisters whenever they touch the skin. Investigation is, however, well repaid as the whole colony is full of the remains of the pirates, buccaneers, early colonists and the old Lucayans. These latter came from Mexico way, and are especially distinguished by the fact that they bound the heads of the children between boards so as to distort the skull. They were still in the 'stone age' when they were killed off, or died off at the time of the pirates.

During the winter months the climate is as perfect as one could wish. There is very little rain, not too much wind and always a warm sun. The sea is warm and even on the worst days one can stay in the water for as long as one feels inclined. Everywhere there are gorgeous colours that vary with each change of wind and tide.

I was most interested in the type of people. In height they are below the present English average, and their features are small but clear-cut. Their expression is one of determination amounting (I beg their pardons) to obstinacy. They are of the type I have always associated with my idea of the Pilgrim Fathers. May this little settlement long continue to thrive."

In letters to his sister and notes made for his own amusement and records, he passed comment on every aspect of Bahamian life. Something which he found to be of particular interest was the sponging industry.

"The sponging industry, in spite of the rubber substitute, is still an important local industry. The sponges grow on rocks on the banks and a walk round the sponge market will soon make one familiar with the various names such as reef, grass or wool sponge. Many attempts have been made to cultivate the sponge, but although it is quite possible and is experimentally successful, it has never yet been done commercially. They are hooked up by teams of two men working in a dinghy; and a single sloop may serve as mother ship to a dozen or more dinghies. Before being ready of sale the animals are squeezed, washed, dried, clipped to shape, and then baled.

The sloops are some 40 feet in length, and may carry a complement of two dozen or more. The mast, stepped very far forward, is rather longer than the hull and is stayed only up to a point several feet below the top, the upper portion being used only as a 'pretty' and to carry the ensign (sometimes two). The boom is about three quarters of the length of the mast and projects over the stern for some considerable distance.

The accommodation on the sponging vessels is very primitive. All the cooking is done on deck over a wood fire lighted in a wooden box. I do not know why the wooden box does not catch fire. This fire also acts as a navigation light to prevent collision.

The owners are very proud of their ships and some of them are well kept. The sloops that are usually in evidence, however, are generally in a dreadful state of repair. I have often seen a sail that consists more of hole than of sail. The little inter-island sloops are awful; and are so loaded down with passengers and cargo that the dinghies tied on deck are floating when the ship heels over in a breeze. Surprisingly, these vessels seldom come to grief and I was informed that this fact is the cause of all the present trouble in Europe. Providence is so busy looking after Bahamas island sailors that he has no time for anything else."

So taken was Rees by the sponge industry that he decided to apply for the command of a new sloop in the process of being built at Nassau. A short time later however he had changed his mind as he explained in a letter to Muriel:

"Did I tell you I had withdrawn my application to be Master of a Sponge Ship ? She is just about ready to launch and I had a look at her the other day. Not one of my suggestions has been carried out. I begged for a hatch in the engine room so that the engine could be lifted in and out easily for repairs. Two hatches have been cut in the deck through neither of which can the engine be lifted. I should dislike the ship all the time I sailed in her. I very much doubt if she is safe for these waters, but as I am only an airman the sailors do not listen to what I say."

Part of his time was spent at Symonette's Shipyard where he had taken upon himself the task of maintaining the yacht used by the Anglican Bishop of the Bahamas in his rounds of the maritime diocese. The yacht had regular problems with both its engine and hull and, for the former, Rees recommended that the manufacturers should modify certain parts but, as in the case of the sponge ship, his advice went unheeded.

By the summer of 1934, he felt that he had acquired sufficient experience of sailing in the waters of the Caribbean and this, added to the high humidity of a Bahamian summer, prompted him to attempt a second long distance voyage. This time he decided to set a course for the island of Trinidad off the coast of South America, a distance, as the crow flies, of 1350 miles. His record of this voyage has survived and has been included here in almost its entirety.

"Should anyone feel too old at forty (or any other age) and wish to put it to the test, I can recommend sailing a small ship, preferably single-handed, against the trade wind in the West Indies at the commencement of the hurricane season.

Last winter, the Bahamas had provided a most enjoyable experience; but in May nearly all my friends had gone home on leave, or had gone north for the summer. There was some delay about certain stores, and it was only in June that it was possible to leave the Banks.

July to October, inclusive, are considered to be the most dangerous hurricane months, although hurricanes have occurred in every month of the year. Usually in July the hurricanes seem to keep well to the east of the Caribbean Sea; but the trade winds in that and the succeeeding months get stronger, and as somebody in Haiti said - "here in August, we seem to get a hurricane every afternoon." I should hasten to add that no West Indian island admits to being in the hurricane belt lest the Tourists should get frightened; and now-a-days the Islands suffer only from tropical depressions of a greater or lesser intensity.

Early in June I cleared for Trinidad, which is more or less south-east from Nassau in the Bahamas, with the trade wind getting stronger and more regular from that direction every day. The first evening out found my little ship in the sandy bay at the western end of New Providence Island. It is a beautiful place; and fish and crawfish are easy to catch.

Next day was hard work heading into a strong wind and in the evening, with no immediate prospect of shelter

214

ahead, I ran to an anchorage behind a small cay to leeward. Bathing and fishing in the 'blue hole' in the middle of the cay whiles away a day or two. The 'blue holes' look like artificially constructed wells, but communicate with the ocean at a depth, it may be, of 50 fathoms or more.

As the wind showed no sign of either shifting or moderating, the next few anchorages were behind the reef on the western side of the 'Tongue of the Ocean' which was the main route for the old galleons sailing between the Windward islands and Florida. It was on that account that the Pirates at one time (about 1719 AD) made New Providence their headquarters. Here Blackbeard (Teach) had a place, whilst the fort on the opposite corner of Andros is still named after Morgan. No galleon could pass out of the Tongue without being seen from one place or the other. Further south in Andros, the pirates had a big place on the mainland behind Fleur-de-Lys Cay. From their lookout on the hill they could see right across the Tongue to Green Cay, so the southern end was also controlled by them.

What the Pirates did to the old Lucayans, the original inhabitants of the islands, I do not know; but the commencement of the path leading to the fort [at Fleur-de-Lys Cay] was covered with Lucayan rock carvings. Near the patch is Money Rock, also covered with carvings. Two old (dusky) ladies guided me ... to a Lucayan tomb ... and, as soon as we had dug up the first handful of bones they went into hysterics with fright. We had quickly to cover them up again till the old ladies had recovered. The tomb produced nothing but bones and a few bits of Lucayan pottery.

Money Rock was probably used for hauling down the

old ships, as sailors had carved their names on it. A few years ago 'B BILL 1745' was to be seen but nobody now knows where that inscription is.

The 'Tongue of the Ocean' cuts through the middle of the bank, and ends in a vertical precipice. Here I met my first difficulties. Completely misjudging the strength of the tide, I was in deep blue water at nightfall. It was too dangerous to heave-to for the night with all the banks about, so I had to sail on for the channel over the bank. Soundings alter from 800 fathoms to 8 fathoms in a few yards, so striking the edge of the bank was quite exciting work. However, the job was successfully accomplished and as soon as the lead gave me three fathoms, seeing the glimmer of sandbanks all around, I let go the kedge. The wind was fairly strong and the seas steep, so the night was most unrestful.

Holding course along the edge of the bank, the succeeding day more than compensated for the uncomfortable night. The colours were wonderful. Here strips of yellow sand stretch across the 'white' water of the bank and touch the purple edge of the ocean. One bank carrying a depth of only half a fathom, suddenly drops straight into 100 fathoms or so. That evening at Shark Spit, where I saw dozens of sharks, course was altered for Lark Channel. The channel is a blue lane between yellow sandbanks and navigation has to be done by eye. Beating into the wind and overestimating the strength of the current, I sailed unknowingly over the bar at the south end of the channel at dusk. Groping about in the dark with the lead showed me what had happened. There was no going back again so, for a second time, it was necessary to kedge in the choppy sea in four fathoms and pretend to like it.

At dawn, not being sure of my position, a course had to be layed for Long Island by the method used by the Bahama spongers. They look at the sea, look at the sky and then spit in the water. What this disgusting action has to do with it I do not know; but on this morning it worked and I made my landfall with little error and without seeing a single coral head.

After some days of beating into the wind and sailing along the cays I was under the lee of the Cape Verde of Columbus. The colour impression of the land, consisting of sand and rocky cays, had been yellow; but this one was, suddenly, a vivid green. The wind took me around the point and then instantly deserted me. It died away so completely that there was a danger of being washed onto the reef, so the engine had to be requisitioned. In a few hours land had disappeared and, stopping the engine, I drifted slowly through a typical noon. By mid-afternoon the current had taken me almost out of the Passage, so the engine was started again to take me into George Town on Fortune Island.

Here I arrived at dusk to find that recent hurricanes and destroyed all the landmarks - trees, huts and the wireless masts and leading marks. A Haitian gunboat, wrecked on the reef, was represented only by a small black cone, which I mistook for the mooring buoy of the mailboat. Going in slowly by the lead in the dark I felt the coral of the reef touch the keel, and then I backed out. By this time the policeman and the wireless operator were alongside and they guided me to a small sandy patch outside the reef. It was much too open for my liking and the ground much too foul but I wanted a few stores and there was no choice.

One afternoon the wireless operator offered to show

me the sights. Almost as soon as we had started out, the wind shifted to the west, the sea on the reef began to rise and my little ship began to be thrown about. As quickly as possible I got on board, set sail and tried to get the anchor. Nothing doing - the cable was fast around the coral head. Being hove short made no difference, so I took in all the cable I could get and waited for a large wave. When it came along the chain lead on the bowsprit was shot off short as though by a catapult, and that on the stern severely bent. But it was sufficient. The coral head was broken away and the anchor freed. In a few minutes ... the ship was in a perfectly sheltered anchorage for the night.

After the next night in a delightful reef anchorage under the light of Castle Island, a gentle trade wind took me towards Hogsty Reef. The reef is of interest, being the nearest approach to an atoll to be found in the Atlantic. Evening found me becalmed but the engine enabled me to spot the beacon on the reef at sunset. There being a bright almost full-moon, I went in with the lead. It was a hopeless proceeding as the reef, about two miles long in its broadest diameter, is awash except for two small cays at the entrance; and it rises nearly vertically out of 1400 fathoms. However, I was able to pick up the loom of a sandy beach at the entrance and anchor safely

The morrow was the hottest day I have ever experienced being even hotter than Bond Street in July. There was no wind and no shade. Bathing from the larger of the little cays brought small relief as the water was tepid. In the evening a light trade wind arrived and under a bright full moon I set sail for Great Inagua Island. This island is largely salt ponds and swamps and almost at once I was able to smell it although it was a least 40 miles away. The island was well within sight at dawn and mid-day saw me moored in the open road off Matthew Town.

Here I experienced my first dealings with the Haitian authorities. Usually my Bill of Health was given me free, but the consul forced me to pay 5 dollars for it and a further 3 dollars to have my passport visaed (Total £1-12-0).

On the evening that completed my arrangements the wind began to veer into the roads, so under a bright moon I set sail for Haiti, which became visible at dawn, thousands of feet of it. Haiti means mountainous and the first view was most impressive. For several hours after dawn I was becalmed but a good breeze took me into Mole St Nicholas during the afternoon.

I now became a Heaven-sent opportunity. The local policeman came off to give me pratique. I offered him a cigarette. He took the packet and, giving one to his boatman (who also came into my cabin), he pocketed the remainder.

Our conversation was in French, of which language I know little; and the situation was complicated by the policeman who spoke only a patois and who inquired whither I was bound. I told him Trinidad. He repeated the question several times. asking if I meant Port au Prince or Jamaica. Having received the answer Trinidad each time, he settled the question by saying "There is no such place !" and we went on to other business. After some time he went away to call the Port Authorities. They arrived and were the Schoolmaster, who spoke English, the Customs Representative and a friend. The Schoolmaster threatened to search the ship and then wrote out a requisition demanding some of my stores. They asked me more or less directly if I would like to be robbed officially or, as it were, between gentlemen. Being very tired and wishing to get rid of everybody, I chose the latter alternative, having agreed to buy several pence worth of fruit etc. for several pounds.

My visitors left but soon returned with the stores and with my bill of health visaed. The first thing they did was to charge 6 dollars for the visa. They had looked such a lot of ruffians that I had put my pistol in my pocket and I nearly (literally) shot the lot of them out of the ship. Instead I protested, pointed to my Ensign [Royal Welsh Yacht Club] and produced the Admiralty Warrant. They had never seen the Ensign before and they certainly did not treat My Lords with the respect that is their due. Then I had to meet the Schoolmaster's requisition and as soon as they saw my stores the Customs Representative and the friend demanded an equal amount. When that was completed I paid for and took in the fruit. One thing amused me. I had agreed to pay three dollars for corn, expecting to get Indian Corn. What was delivered was a couple of dirty and damaged conch shells (Cornes- the local French name). These I took without protest, owing to my unfortunate habit of keeping my word and even the seller was surprised as he inquired for what purpose I required the dirty shell.

During the night the Representative had thought up some more reasons for getting money out of me and they were back again in the early dawn. ostensibly to give me a clearance (at a price) for other Haitian ports. I resisted several demands, including one for soap for their wives to wash themselves. The night's anchorage had already cost me seven or eight pounds but, as they were leaving the

Representatives demanded a present for their children and I handed over my loose cents, well pleased to be rid of them at any price. As soon as they were gone I set sail, got out to sea, and then hove to for breakfast and a rest.

For a long time I had wanted to see Santo Domingo which was the centre of government [in the Dominican Republic] and is the best example of old Spanish fortifications on this side of the ocean. I therefore layed a course to take me along the western and southern coasts of Haiti.

Some delightful sailing weather saw me under the lee of Cape Dame Marie, the western corner of Haiti. I came in with the evening breeze and kedged under a small cliff in a sandy bay of a beauty that filled the eye to overflowing. On top of the little cliff was a small house, surrounded by its farm, nestling against a grove of palm trees, the whole showing up against a background of vivid tropical greenery. That evening I was entertained by a display of flying by half a dozen pelicans, who dived after shoals of small fish, sometimes singly and sometimes in a formation that would not disgrace Hendon. They never missed their objective.

From here to Santo Domingo is essentially a Cote de Fer [Coast of Iron]. The hurricane season was now well advanced and, although the weather was good, I got tired of reading in the Pilot -"No safe anchorage during the hurricane months". I tried to hurry, but the trade wind, affected by the high mountains, headed me off on each tack as I stood in or out from the shore. Being singlehanded I dared not stand in at night. A gain of 20 miles a day was good going and the drop of wind at night entailed hours of excessive rolling in the long swell.

Although I had intended going straight through, I was enticed into the Baie Aux Cayes after a rough night off Gravios Point. With the best intentions the Pilot, who came to give me pratique at Aux Cayes, directed me towards the inner anchorage. None of the Pilots believes that I draw over 6 feet, as all the local boats are of comparatively shallow draft to take them over the coral heads. I could not get in sufficiently far to shelter behind the protecting reef and spent several uncomfortable days in the rollers. There was a compensation that at night a gentle land breeze brought with it almost flat calm.

The Pilot had told me to make my number to the Customs house next morning at eight o'clock. I arrived on time to find most of the clerks chatting or reading the paper. One was sorting seeds, some of which he was putting into his tobacco pouch, which I thought a strange proceeding. The office clock, also, at that moment, although pointing to twenty minutes past four, struck eleven. I thought I had come to another Mole St. Nicholas but, as soon as the Collector arrived things began to hum and I realised my mistake. The Collector was an American (USA) Official. He was most efficient and helpful and, when he heard about my previous port of call, he promised to take the matter in hand at once.

Aux Cayes is a well laid out town of its kind ... and very little inducement would have made me remain for a long time. Taking a few stores, I continued on my way. On the selected day the sea breeze failed to arrive so, after drifting for some time, I used the engine to take me into the next sheltered anchorage. This was Aquin, an excellent place.

From Aquin there was a stretch of about 100 miles with no safe anchorage and the next few days found me continually being thrown about by the swell and making poor headway against a strong trade wind. As usual the scenery was magnificent and, as the rains were on, there was usually a lightning display each evening and marvelous cloud effects. One afternoon I spotted Cape Rojo, and that evening (it was becoming a habit) in the dark I leaded my way into the calm water under the lee of the cape. And I was very thankful to be there. Next day, during a Make and Mend, the sea breeze under the lee of the cape registered 26 (land) miles an hour by air speed indicator.

On the following morning I was under way good and early and the going was excellent. Suddenly, under the main-sail, a little Dominican motor gunboat appeared, full of sailors and bristling with guns. They shouted and waved and I waved back. Then some of them took off their hats and I, endeavouring to be polite, also doffed mine till I remembered that I was clothed only in my hat. Then, much to my surprise, they uncovered the bow gun and trained it onto me. As quickly as possible I hove to.

Two officers, heavily armed, came aboard and wanted to know where I had come from. I replied "OK", thinking that this was the pronunciation of Aux Cayes and it made them very angry. In return I protested against having a gun trained onto me when I was wearing the blue ensign of my Club; so we were quits. They wanted to see my papers, which I produced, and then they noticed that both my bunks were made up. I always sleep in the lee bunk, but the officers doubted that I was single-handed. Much to my amusement they began to search the ship for a hand (or perhaps a revolutionary agent), not a difficult task and they even peered into all the larger lockers. After all this palaver, we made our adieux as friends and then the interpreter begged for cigarettes. Was that the reason for my being held up?

My intention had been to find shelter under the lee of Alta Vela, the southernmost point of Santo Domingo [Sic]. The wind was now quite strong and the gusts coming round the rock were stronger still. I had to reef right down and, in doing so, tore several hanks off the mainsail, split the headboard, damaged the side and jambed two slides in it at such a height that I could hoist only a double reefed sail. Finding no decent lee at Alta Vela, I sailed to Beata Island and spent the afternoon repairing damage. During the delay the current carried me several miles to leeward, back again under the lee of the island. It was too dark to go searching for an anchorage and, on account of the dangerous rocks, I could not heave to without keeping a watch, so I sailed out to safety into the open, through the Alta Vela Channel. About midnight I had sufficient offing to allow me to lash the wheel so as to get supper and rest. Although the wind had registered 28 miles per hour under the lee of the land and was now considerably stronger, there was no vice in it. The seas, however, were the largest I have ever seen, so large as almost to cease to affect the little ship.

At dawn I was miles out of sight of land which only appeared again, when on the other tack, at about midday. Suddenly I found the tiller lines chafed through and I had to reeve a new wire cable. Being on a directly lee shore the next few days were more uncomfortable than usual but, in due course, I made the landlocked harbour of Caldeira bay ...[where] some odd jobs were completed and the ship cleaned up a bit.

Again, on the day of sailing the sea breeze failed to

come in so I drifted in light airs all day along the coast. At night, the land breeze and the engine speeded me well on towards Santo Domingo (capital). It was an interesting sail as it was done by smell. Standing closely inshore I could not lay the course, and there was no unusual smell. Standing out, I would suddenly run into a belt, about a mile wide, where I could lay the course and where there was a strong and very agreeable scent of flowers. This was at the edge of the land breeze. Passing through the belt, I was in the trade wind where there was a very strong smell of the sea and where I was unable to hold the course I wanted.

At dawn I was just entering Santo Domingo Bay and at sunrise the wind dropped away completely and the swell subsided to an oily calm. Drifting whilst I got breakfast, I restarted the engine and proceeded slowly, as fast as my seven and a half horses would drag me, round the coast, reaching Santo Domingo in the mid afternoon.

As soon as I was inside the river an English speaking pilot parked me alongside the wharf at the customs shed and five hot and very heavily armed officers came off to give me pratique. They were very polite and did their best to make it easy for me to comply with their regulations. They produced fountain pens, and ink spots still show on my settee covers. My shotgun and pistol, with all ammunition, had to be handed in to the Fort for safe custody. Two returns in quintuplicate were required, one showing the registered number of my arms and the other giving my name and destination. Much to my surprise, no charge was made for anything at this port. I found that I should have saluted the town fort on entry and that it was required that I should wear a Dominican ensign during my stay in their waters. Not being able to buy one I had to make it.

Santo Domingo is a very up-to-date and go-ahead town. All places of historical interest are well looked after. Everybody was very good to me and the place was well worth a visit. I wish I could have stayed there longer.

The main track was repaired. When I came to replace it I found that, as it was fitted in England in the winter, expansion would not allow me to get it back in place. It was not until after midnight, when the cool land breeze arrived, that it was possible to finish the job. How the expansion was, and still is, taken up I do not know but it appears to be satisfactory.

The hurricane season was now still further advanced and, as the advice of the British Charge d'Affaires agreed with my inclinations, I left Santo Domingo for the safe anchorages of Jamaica. The Trade Wind had won.

The trip to Jamaica, of no special interest, took rather over a week and, running mostly dead before the wind, I was rushing over the path along which it had been necessary to fight for every inch of headway only a few days previously. Being unable to obtain a chart of Jamaica, I had come to Port Royal by eye. As usual, here again I have found myself amongst friends. The Royal Jamaican Yacht Club kindly looked after my wants and my time is spent refitting and in day sailing.

There are many interesting places near. One of the best is Portland Bight. here, on Goat Island, are the ruins of a typical 'colonial' estate; it is said to have belonged to Sir Henry Morgan, the pirate who afterwards became the Governor of Jamiaca. Galleon Harbour to the north-east is an ideal place, and the 'hurricane holes' cut into the mangroves for the old galleons, are still plainly visible.

Just on the other side of the island is a small cay called Careening Island. It is kidney shaped, protected on the outside by a coral reef but the inner angle is almost steep-to, and the old ships could have been tied up to the mangroves when they required to be hauled down for scraping. Old Sir Henry knew a thing or two about ships.

The tourist place, Montego Bay, was completely spoiled by the bad manners of the inhabitants (as is usual in all tourist resorts near here) and by a steamer who came in at night, dumped a lot of fuel oil, and was away before dawn.

The most delightful anchorage of all was Ocho Rios, the Eight Rivers. The landmark is a waterfall, another waterfall drops into the sea at the mouth of the bay and there are streams all over the place. Being so well watered the place is very green and full of flowers. Not having a chart, I came in with the lead and the local blacks, not recognising the blue ensign, thought I was a Norwegian spy. They were quite concerned about it. One drunk man followed me into a shop insisting that my ship was a yawl. I told him it was a ketch. After a great thought he suddenly said - "I see what you mean. Your sails ketch the wind better."

I had been stung in the ear by a jelly fish and at Port Antonio the matter seemed to be getting serious, the swelling would not go down and I was becoming quite deaf. A local black doctor looked inside the ear and said "There is nothing wrong" and, much to my surprise, from that moment there was nothing wrong. Even more surprisingly, he said that he had done nothing and would accept no fee.

After a trip around the island, there were a lot of odd jobs to be done, and I left Kingston just before Christmas.

A flat calm held me till I was from under the lee of the Blue Mountain, where they grow the coffee. But, as soon as I poked my nose round the corner of the island, I got into a 'Norther'. The wind tore the cringle off the main sail and I found that the ship, having dried in the sun, was leaking in several places. I had to put back to Port Morant for repairs.

The local blacks are a funny people. On the day I arrived [at Port Morant] some of the Fruit Company clerks shouted out that they were coming out to have tea with me. I did not want visitors just then, and did not pay much attention to what they said. In the evening five of them boarded me, went below and sat down. As politely as I could I pushed them back into their boat. Apparently they bore me no ill will as they all brought me presents of fruit when they came to work on the following morning and later on they sent me some recent daily papers which was good of them.

The last 'Norther' had brought a good current through the channel between Jamiaca and Haiti and it took me three days to get across the 50 miles. Each morning I was back in the same place as on the day before. Even then it was the engine that saved the situation. From now onward, I used the engine frequently to get me up against the wind but this time, as far as Tortola. I got into a strong counter current which held me along the coast. In a few days I was back off Santo Domingo capital. The conditions at Alta Vela were bad, as usual, but as soon as the wind saw I meant to get round the point it moderated, and I got excellent sailing conditions from now as far as Trinidad.

After Jamaica, my first real stop was in the Virgin Islands. At Tortola ... I was being shown round one

Sunday afternoon, and my guide said to a black man, who was leaning against his garden wall - "You used to go to church regularly. I have not seen you in church for the last couple of Sundays. How is that ?" The man replied - "Oh. I was baptised a fortnight ago and am saved already. Therefore I need no longer go to church." I liked all the people at Tortola. They are all pleasant proprietors and speak and act as such. They don't beg as the people do in most of the other islands.

From Tortola I went to have a look at Saba, but it was too rough to land. At this island, which is simply a volcanic cone, there is no proper landing; it is necessary to jump out of the dinghy onto the steps cut in the side of the rock. A horse carries you up and down the steps. The people, who are Dutch, speak English and they live in a town on the top of the mountain called Botto. They are mostly sailors, build ships which they launch by lowering over the side of the cliffs and they have the only navigation school in the West Indies. Living on a bare rock, they grow vegetables for their own use, and also for export to the other islands. The place is well worth a visit.

I sailed on slowly and stayed in most of the large anchorages. At St Kitts I met R D Williams of Porth-yr-Aur, who captains the fleet tanker 'War Sirdar'. We talked a lot about olden times. At St Vincent I was surprised to find that the shore boats would not come nearer than shouting distance. The reason was given me by the officers of a schooner who called on me that evening. They were the Tough Captain and the Bucco Mate. Their conversation consisted entirely of the way in which they handled the crew. They had knocked them down the hold with a belaying pin and they had poured the hot soup over the cook whenever it or he had displeased them. That morning the shore boats had annoyed the Mate who had taken pot shots at them with the largest revolver I have ever seen.

St Lucia is a very beautiful island. It had so many sandy coves, hidden anchorages with 'lone trees' etc., that I told myself tales of pirates for days after seeing the place. It was spoiled, as usual, by the people. Some of the shore boats came off and hurled foul abuse at me, quite unprovokedly. I have been called "The father of a hat" by the kafieh-wearing araba and several other names in other parts of the world, but usually there has been some reason for it. Grenada was a good place and I stayed there several days. When I got to Trinidad, I disliked the longshoremen so much that I stayed only one day and decided to go back to Grenada to refit.

Leaving Trinidad, I got three days of calm and the current took me 150 miles to leeward. Not bad going if it had been in the right direction. Not wanting to make the large circuit of the islands so as to get back to windward, I turned round and came to Curacao. I was well repaid by the decision. The conditions of my arrival would have delighted the heart of any boy of any age who likes tales of pirates. The visibility was none too good and suddenly I saw a line of steamers disappearing through an apparently blank wall. There were forts and guns about and the Refinery (the glare from which had been visible all night) was now apparently working overtime to produce a dense black smoke. When I reached the hole in the wall, I found a boom, the pontoon bridge across the entrance. As soon as I appeared the authorities had me in tow and I was tied up at the town wharf so quickly that I did not have time to even turn round and thank the pilot.

They have been good to me here, and I have done quite a respectable refit. For the last few days I have been tied up to the Refinery wharf and crowds of children have been on board. They have broken and pulled off everything that could be broken and pulled off, so that I consider that I am now fit to ride out a gale; and the gale may be a hurricane as I leave tomorrow for the Bahamas." [1]

CHAPTER XIII
War
(1936 - 42)

Shortly after his return from the southern Caribbean, Rees decided to dispose of the *May*. She was a boat designed for the deep waters around the coast of Britain and was therefore unsuited to the shallow banks around the Bahamas. Despite her having been fitted with a set of Bahamian sails which had greatly improved her handling, the depth of her keel caused her to run aground far too frequently with all the problems which that entailed; so far he had been lucky but this could prove to be a major difficulty should he run aground whilst alone on an isolated cay. The obvious solution was to purchase a boat designed for the waters around the islands, ideally a vessel built in the Bahamas.

In November 1936, Rees wrote to his sister that " a young photographer wants to buy my ship. I think I shall sell if he makes a decent offer." The man concerned was Stanley Toogood of Nassau, an Englishman in his early twenties who recalled that at the time he and Rees had a "very congenial friendship ... despite the differences in our ages." Coincidentally, Toogood, who had arrived in the Bahamas after Rees, had heard of the latter's plan to sail the Atlantic in 1933 and had written to offer his services as a crewman. The letter however, arrived too late and Rees had already sailed.

Apart from the need to dispose of the *May,* Rees was

also attracted to Toogood's offer because it included, as part of the deal, a boat which he felt might meet his needs. After some negotiation, agreement was reached between the two, Toogood becoming the owner of the *May* and Rees taking possession of the *Aline B* plus a sizeable sum of cash.

The *Aline B* (or *Aline* as Rees was to call her) had been built at Johnson's Yard in Nassau in the early 1930s for a local man, Maurice Barbess who intended to sail her across the Pacific. She had been named after Barbess' sister and, like the *May,* was a double-ended ketch, having the appearance of a prow both fore and aft but there the similarities ended for the *Aline* was a much smaller vessel finished to a much poorer standard than the *May* . Barbess had sailed her through the Panama Canal and westwards as far as the Gallapagos Islands where he had been taken ill and was forced to return to Nassau where he sold the boat to Stanley Toogood.

For the twelve months which followed his purchase of the *Aline,* Rees appears to have spent most of his time carrying out major modifications to his new floating home.

"I decided to make a modernised copy of the *Goddess Isis* trading between Rome and the East. "Come down to the docks and have a look at the *Goddess Isis*. She has a mast seventy feet tall and they say that she carries enough grain to feed all Athens for over a year. Her Captain is a little old man with a bald pate and a fringe of curly hair. He's an honest fellow and good company." My ship is a little double-ender, and when we had re-decked it to represent the tarpaulin covering the grain, it looked like an egg; but when we had fitted port lights and verandahs to represent the rowers galleries, she looked more like a supercilious whale. She carries only a square sail and split rafee, so that she cannot go to windward. That is accomplished by a little engine to be used only in cases of emergency. The steering is done by rudder bar similar to an aeroplane."

Only an individual like Rees could purchase a vessel because of her suitability for a purpose and her seaworthiness and then modify her so dramatically. The references to the *Goddess Isis* and the rigging which he fitted to the *Aline* indicate that a new interest had appeared in his life; not content with ordinary sailing, he embarked upon a life afloat which was to be difficult to say the least as he intended to try and match the achievements of the sailors from ancient and medieval times. His account of his Atlantic crossing had already shown his fascination with the voyage of Christopher Columbus and it was now his intention to sail around the Bahamas in the wake of the Italian explorer, using a square rigging similar to that which would have been found on the *Santa Maria* in 1492.

The *Aline* was ready by the summer of 1937 and Rees set sail for the island of Conception, where Columbus had landed, which lay directly south-east of Nassau. On the very first day out he ran into difficulties as the wind drove him north-east to Harbour Island, Eluthera and from there, through Current Cut to Hatchet Bay.

"Last season, at this place, I had gone half shares in a melon farm; and had watched the melons till they were nearly ready for market. Then I had to leave the Bay for a few days. On my return my partner showed me a bare field and told me that the little red beetles had eaten all my melons. The little beetles only ate my melons. How did they know that those melons were mine ?"

From there he sailed to the Exuma Cays where, one evening " ...I dropped anchor in a little bay and was immediately hailed by a veritable cast-away. He was starving, and as I could not leave him on the cay I had to sail all the way back to Nassau. So I was exactly where I had started after one month's travelling."

The next few months were spent trying every way to reach the south-eastern islands but to no avail. Rees found it impossible to make any headway against the wind and he refused to use the engine as it would invalidate the experiment. In the end, he had to admit defeat and re-rigged the boat with a fore-and-aft sail - "The last few months have shown me quite clearly what the old Navigators were up against, and I lift my Sou'wester to them."

There now arose the matter of earning a living for the foreseeable future. Living on his capital was convenient enough but it was an ever diminishing asset and, in a letter to Muriel, he outlined his plans:

"I shall go seriously for growing sponges and build a shack on one of the cays in the creek where the sponge farms are situated. If you would care to come out I would build a two roomed shack so that you could watch the sponges growing also."

It was not to be. Not only had Muriel no intention of joining him in the Bahamas but also the days of the sponge industry in those islands were themselves drawing to a close. A then unidentified disease was to all but wipe them out before the end of the decade.

There were to be no more long distance voyages for Rees. Living aboard the *Aline* he cruised amongst the islands becoming something of a local celebrity although few that met him really got to know the man behind the rather reserved public face. Walton Smith, a fellow

Briton, recalls a very shy person who avoided relationships with other people. He would often see Rees walking from Nassau, heavily laden with groceries but, despite the heat and the humidity of a Bahamian summer, he would refuse the offer of a lift in a passing car. To have accepted would have meant explanations and the barrier which he appears to have built around himself would be slightly breached by each such encounter. As with all eccentrics, the truth grows and takes on the form of a minor legend in which one finds it difficult to distinguish between the facts and the embelishments. In his book 'Out Island Doctor', an American Evans Cottman records a meeting with Rees in 1939. What he personally experienced, Cottman noted with reasonable accuracy but that information which he obtained from others was some distance from the truth:

"Next morning Cavill [1] said he was going to take me to visit Captain Rees. The Captain, he explained, was a retired aide-de-camp of King George V and a holder of the Victoria Cross, won for gallantry as a pilot in World War One. Sometime in the 1930s, Rees had bought a twenty-nine foot yacht and set out to cross the Atlantic alone. Originally he aimed for New York but at that latitude the prevailing winds were against him. When his motor conked out before he had gone 500 miles, he hoisted sail, turned south almost a thousand miles to catch the trade winds, rode out a hurricane, and eventually landed in the Bahamas."

So far, Cottman's account of Rees' life is far from accurate although it does show some remote link with the truth and it would be unfair to criticise him as his information was obviously obtained from some third party at a later date. It is highly unlikely that the information came from Rees himself and it would appear that getting any knowledge from him about his early life was almost impossible. Many Bahamian residents knew him for many years before they became aware of his illustrious background. One such man, Lester Brown of Nassau, first met him during the 1930s and, as Rees was referred to as Captain, had no knowledge of any RAF connection until some considerable time later. Eventually he discovered- but not from the man himself, that Rees was the holder of the VC and the story which he heard detailing how the award was earned was far from accurate:

"He was a gentleman. Thoroughly well read and very interesting to talk to. He could discuss any topic and was a marvellous conversationalist. It is hard to imagine him as a man with such a distinguished war record as he gave the impression of being someone who would be unable to kill even a fly."

Cottman's recollections of his actual meeting with Rees and the conditions aboard the *Aline* are worthy of note as they are probably very accurate and provide the only first hand record of his lifestyle at this time.

"We went in Cavill's sailboat, winding between a myriad of tiny uninhabited islands. Captain Rees was anchored off one of these called Mastic Cay [which] belonged to Mr Forsyth, and although there was no house on it, it had been planted with fruit trees and flowers until the island bloomed like a tropical garden. Rees' white yacht in the cove made the picture complete.

The Captain was a big, rawboned Welshman; and if he deliberately lived a solitary life he made up for it when he had company. He was talking before we came alongside and he could get in more words per minute than a speed reader. He clipped the first syllable, or syllables, off most of them, and he spoke the others in such a Welsh accent that I could understand only half of what he said [2]. But obviously Cavill and I were welcome.

I never really appreciated the meaning of the word 'shipshape'

237

until I stepped into Captain Rees' boat. The cabin space was tiny, with every inch of it fitted to maximum use. There was a place for everything, and everything was exactly in its place. There was even a miniature machine shop with a lathe, on which Rees, still talking, turned out a new pipe stem to replace the one Cavill had broken.

The Captain invited us to stay for dinner and we happily accepted. The food was bully beef out of a can, but the service was something else again. The Captain brought out a complete set of sterling silver ... and set to work polishing it. Meanwhile he talked, mixing in a wild collection of ancient British jokes with personal anecdotes about people he referred to only by their first name. It was a long time before I realised he was talking about various members of the British royal family.

Then, with bully beef ready and silver set, Captain Rees dressed for dinner. That is, he changed his torn shorts for an immaculate white pair. Perhaps in deference to his underdressed guests he did not add shirt or shoes."

Rees had the type of personality and a kindness of approach which made him unforgettable and people who met him only briefly during his early days in the Bahamas are well able to recall him fifty years later. The Reverend J M Hutcheson of Nassau remembers the time when, aged only twelve, he and his brother went aboard Rees' boat at Hatchet Bay, Eluthera to try and discover what 'interesting thing' the Captain was up to:

"The late Group Captain showed us how to pump air into the diving bell while he would be submerged in it, and told us that when we felt ourselves getting tired, we must call down to him and he would surface. He was not submerged too long before my brother and I, feeling ourselves getting tired, shouted "Come up ! Come up !" which he did, and he did not go back down.

He took an active interest in exploring, with a cousin of mine, a very large cave situated half way between the settlements of Hatchet Bay and Gregory Town, Eluthera, known as Crossing Hills Cave. After they had returned to the settlement my cousin said "I really had an experience today while exploring with Captain Rees. We went so far into the cave by using torch lights that we entered a room with so many pipes that it looked and sounded like a pipe organ when Captain Rees struck the pipes with the tools he carried. It was the most beautiful sound I have ever heard." As a small boy I always held crossing Hills Cave is awe because we were told by our elders that if we were to enter the cave we would get lost and never be found. Rees was a man I admired very much." [3]

This idyllic existence amidst the tropical islands, pleasing no one but himself, unconcerned about material things and with a responsibility to nobody was, however, destined to change. Even a remote island in the Bahamas was not immune from world news and, as war clouds began to gather over Europe, Rees felt the old loyalties beginning to stir and, on the outbreak of hostilities he was amongst the first to volunteer his services to the RAF. Now aged fifty-five, he was well beyond the age when such service would be expected of him but the idea of remaining in the peace and quiet of the Bahamas was unthinkable if there was the slightest possibility that he could be of any value to the war effort. Not surprisingly, he was judged to be too old and, in the eight years that had passed since he had retired, his ideas would have become outdated. How he must have rued his decision to leave the RAF as men who had been his juniors in rank in 1931 now held positions of high authority, whilst others, older than he, were still on the active list and were about to play major roles in the conflict [4]. Letter followed letter offering his services to the Air Ministry in any capacity and, by way of compensation, he became involved in the recruitment of potential officers and men for the RAF from the volunteers who came forward in the Bahamas. Lester Brown and four other young men with private pilot's licences were accepted for the service but told to remain in Nassau until they received orders to report to Britain. Friends who had admired them when they had volunteered began to laugh as they saw them, weeks later, still walking the streets of the capital. In desperation they turned to the two most influential men that they knew, the Governor General, the Duke of Windsor, and Lionel Rees. Both promised to do what they could and, shortly afterwards, they received their sailing orders. Brown recalls Rees bidding them adieu and assumed that the next time they would meet would be after the war was over. Surely, if young, trained pilots were finding it difficult to gain entry into the RAF then there was little hope for a man of Rees' age, irrespective of his previous experience.

The fall of France during the summer of 1940 and the consequent preoccupation of Britain with keeping the enemy on the far side of the English Channel, led Mussolini to believe that the time was ripe for him to make his move in North Africa. Believing that it would only be a matter of weeks before the Germans were in London, he determined to take the opportunity to seize British controlled territory in Egypt and Somaliland. The government in London however was fully aware of the threat to Britain's lifeline through the Suez Canal to the priceless oilfields of the Persian Gulf and determined to defend Egypt with whatever resources that could be spared.

Under the command of General Wavell, the British troops faced Italian forces which outnumbered them by over four to one. Initially, the Italians met with some success and managed to drive the British forces out of Somaliland but, their successes were short lived and, in early December, the Middle East Command launched its counter strike which resulted in the expulsion of the enemy's forces from Egypt and East Africa early in the New Year.

Whilst British ground forces at home were inactive awaiting the expected German invasion, Dominion and Empire troops were available for operations in Africa. The same could not, however, be said for the air services; the RAF was fully occupied attempting to stem the tide of enemy air attacks against Britain and her maritime supply lines and the strength of the Dominion air forces was negligable at this stage of the war. Although large numbers of recruits were undergoing training in Britain and overseas, there was a severe shortage of officers to fill administrative posts as a stop-gap measure so that others could be released for more active duties. This shortfall was partly made up by the recall to active service of officers who, because of their age, had previously been regarded as unsuitable.

By Christmas 1940, Lionel Rees was back in Britain and having, at his own request, relinquished the rank of Group Captain, he was re-employed into the RAF as a Wing Commander. His experience in the Middle East made a posting to that theatre of operations inevitable and, on 25 January 1941, four days after his return to the active list, he arrived at Heliopolis as a Temporary Supernumerary Officer. Early the following month he was appointed to command RAF El Adem where he remained until late March when he took over as OC RAF Helwan some 15 miles south of Cairo, a station which served as a staging post for new air and ground units arriving in the theatre prior to their posting to the Western Desert. Few remained for any length of time and, whilst personnel came and went, engineers proceeded with the construction of a permanent runway capable of taking the very latest military aircraft. Designed to accommodate under 1,000 men, the station was often overcrowded and this, added to the high turnover of officers and men, was a perfect recipe for administrative disaster as the Station Record Book shows:

"During the past month there have been on the station about 1,300 airmen, continually changing. Some of these were units re-fitting to go out to the Desert, and some were men back from Greece and Crete waiting for re-posting. The result of this floating population was a great degree of disorganisation."

Rees very quickly found that it was almost impossible to maintain any continuity in his staff officers and, consequently, most of the routine administration fell to him. He seems to have been everywhere, doing everything and anything whilst all the time trying to create as pleasant an atmosphere for the young men who were under his command, many of whom were on their first overseas posting. Wing Commander H E Rossiter, then a young RAF officer remembers clearly the first time that he personally came into contact with Rees.

"We arrived at Helwan in a minor sandstorm, after a journey from Suez, very hot, very dusty and very thirsty. This figure marched up to us and said "Drop all your kit gentlemen and follow me." He then led us to the officer's mess where pints of cool beer were laid out. We were all pretty dehydrated and the beer was nectar.

My first personal encounter with him was later when I and my detachment of airmen were having great difficulty in erecting the tents with which we were issued for accommodation.

An imposing figure came striding up to me. I remember my first impression was the rows of medals commencing with the VC ... I had seen nothing like it before, nor indeed since. This figure then, in a most kindly voice, said "Excuse me my boy. I know that you are new out here, may I show you how to pitch a tent in the sand ?" He then proceeded to do so, effectively and efficiently all by himself. I thanked him and then a gust of wind lifted his Wolseley Helmet and sent it tumbling across the sand. I dashed after it and returned it, whereupon he said, again in a kind and fatherly voice, "Thank you my boy but again, I hope you don't mind me advising you ... but if your topie blows off in the desert, never run after it and pick it up." Expecting some weighty advice about the dangers of sunstroke I said, "Why is that sir ?" whereupon he replied "Because some other bloody fool will do it for you" and strode off leaving me dumbfounded and at a complete loss for any form of repartee.

From my own recollections I would certainly describe Rees as kindly, considerate and, to a very young officer, a typical RAF/RFC 'Uncle' figure, able to command because of his bravery and eccentricity rather than as a disciplinarian. Whether he was efficient as a Station Commander I would query. He seemed to be just anxious to do all he could to help the war effort in any capacity. Indeed, he seemed to take on all the extraneous duties to relieve other junior officers of the work. He was PMC, Bar Officer, Mess Secretary etc.. I went to pay my mess bill on being posted ... he was then sitting in the Mess Secretary's office typing out mess bills, one fingered, on an old battered typewriter. He thanked me for having the courtesy to pay during normal duty hours as so many others had kept him working into the night to settle up. He was one of the last great eccentric characters for which the pre-war RAF was noted." [5]

Although some considerable distance from the front line, Helwan was not always a peaceful station. Following the evacuations from Greece and Crete, those Egyptians who were pro-Axis in their sympathies felt that the time was ripe for them to show their true colours and the station came under fire from snipers, resulting in the death of one civilian worker. As the Allies began to meet with some success, particularly after the advance into Syria to destroy the Vichy French forces there, the sniping ceased as abruptly as it had started. Occassionally an enemy aircraft would venture over and attempt to drop bombs on the numerous military targets in the area and such events were dreaded by Rees' adjutant as, instead of taking cover during the raid, the Wing Commander would insist that they drive around to plot any bomb damage, particularly to the runway. Fortunately neither was injured and the adjutant was quite relieved to be posted away.

By November, the construction work had been completed but the airfield could not become operational as it was discovered that the runway was too short and lengthening took a further month. In order to deceive the enemy, a dummy landing ground was constructed four miles to the east. The station was officially taken over for flying on 17 December and, by early 1942, squadrons of every type and nationality were flying in and out of Helwan.

With the station fully operational and with an ever increasing flow of officers arriving from Britain, the Air Ministry decided that Rees' services were no longer required and on 27 February he handed over command to Group Captain G R O'Sullivan. Once again, his age was to debar him from serving and he was ordered to take transport back to Britain.

Due to the heavy losses sustained by the RAF and the Royal Navy in the Mediterranean region, it had become customary for transport flights from Egypt to travel overland to West Africa and thence to Gibraltar. This was the route home which Rees took and the aircraft in which he was flying landed at Takoradi in the Gold Coast after a journey of nealy 4,000 miles from Cairo, broken up by short halts for fuel and rest; a total flying time of 19 hours. When the journey was resumed, Rees was not aboard having gone 'missing' at the last moment. He had found a job which needed doing and, in his own inimitable way, he had simply got on with it without reference to a higher authority.

That same month, the Air Ministry had announced the establishment of the Royal Air Force Regiment in order to standardise the defence of RAF establishments and stations both at home and overseas. This applied to the West Africa Command as much as to any other and a number of personnel were distributed to each station with little or no thought being given to their training, duties or command. As one officer recorded in his memoirs:

"The trouble had its roots in the official Air Force idea ... that the Regiment was merely one of the 'trades' of the Air Force. A station far from civilisation wanted some cooks. very well, send them out half a dozen. Let them cook, and the senior administrative officer of the station would look after them. They wanted some RAF Regiment, well, send them eight aι.d a sergeant, and let them get on with it. A section of regular soldiers with several years of training and discipline behind them, and with an exceptionally good NCO in charge, might, if left in peace to their military life by the RAF station commander, have survived this for a time without losing their cohesion. But these men of the RAF Regiment were, many of them, little above recruit standard in their training, and no higher in their discipline. The men belonged to no unit or sub-unit of the Regiment and their supervision depended upon whether a Regiment officer happened to be considered necessary on the establishment of the station or RAF unit concerned. They were owned by no flight or squadron and, as far as their military side went, were nobody's child." [6]

These units had simply been formed from any personnel engaged in full-time ground defence duties for the RAF. In fact, even in late 1942, some men were unaware that they had changed units and, in some cases, also changed service.

At Takoradi there was a small section of the RAF Regiment without a commanding officer. Rees had quickly identified the problem and appointed himself to the position of Station Defence Officer - quite unofficially and without pay. "Full of enthusiasm and the love of training, he took charge of the squadron ... with no other officer to help him and kept it something more than 'ticking over'"[7].

The problem which he faced was a daunting one. The men under his 'command' appeared to lack even the basics of military training and many were unfit for duty. Poor medical examination procedures back in Britain had resulted in men being posted to the Gold Coast who were totally unsuited to the conditions which were testing even for the fittest serviceman. Ably assisted by an efficient Flight Sergeant, Rees drew on his experiences of over forty years and tried to create a cohesive force out of what could best be described as a shambles. Gradually, some semblance of order was established and, on the arrival of the Command Defence Officer [8] in August, and the appointment of junior officers to each unit, the Regiment began to function as a military unit.

Rees appears to have thoroughly enjoyed himself at Takoradi, no doubt thinking back to his earlier service in West Africa in the days before the First World War. As in Egypt, there was always a constant stream of personnel flowing through the station en route to other theatres of operations and he regularly came across old friends and acquaintances. Lester Brown, who had waved goodbye to him in Nassau, arrived in 1942, in command of a squadron of Blenhiem Vs, en route to the Middle East. Delayed by bad weather, Brown wandered into the Officer's Mess, one of the few 'civilised' aspects of life at

Takoradi, and was amazed to see Rees standing at the bar and the two relived earlier, more peaceful days in the Bahamas.

In West Africa, as indeed everywhere, Rees seems to have made a profound impression on those that he met. Lieutenant-Colonel Sherbrooke-Walker had very fond memories of him.

"Takoradi, with its huge airfield and little army of RAF, was the principal place from our point of view, and our 'Gold Coast Squadron' of some hundred and twenty men was concentrated here under the charge of a remarkable character - one of those men I have known ... who leaves one better but humbler, for having known them.

Rees had been a station commander in the Middle East, but on reaching the alloted span he was retired from the Air Force and sent home. But the authorities were counting without their Rees. Like the good old soldier he was, he refused to 'die', and, dropping off his aircraft at Takoradi ... remained there ... until the slow but remorseless 'personnel] machine overtook him. Modest and unassuming to a degree, and with delightfully courteous manners ... it was only by chance that one discovered he owned a string of decorations, headed by the VC.

Rees showed me round everywhere and to keep up with his long and energetic stride I had to put my best foot forward. He knew every tree and bird and always carted a supply of pennies in his pocket for the village children when he went further afield.

It was a sad day when he was allowed to tarry no longer and went on his way home to his coral island - no doubt to take up once more his hobby of sailing the oceans alone in a small boat. O ! Si sic omnes !" [9]

The "remorseless machine" caught up with him in November, 1942 and he handed over command of his unit to Major J B Moffat. He left the service on 20 November, assumed his old rank of group Captain (Retired), and headed back to the Bahamas.

CHAPTER XIV
Andros
(1942 - 55)

Returning to the Bahamas with a world war still raging , Rees found the inactivity forced upon him frustrating in the extreme. He was disappointed to discover that there was no role for him at the RAF training bases which had been established at Oakes and Windsor Fields and he had little choice but to try and pick up the pieces of the life which he had left nearly two years previously. Living on Blue Hill, New Providence, in what can only be described as a wooden cabin, he set about making the *Aline* fit for sailing and, when his friend and 'landlord' Herbert McKinney suggested that he might care to sail south to Crooked Island to carry out some survey work, Rees jumped at the opportunity to resume his nomadic life afloat. Although not a qualified surveyor, his military training gave him more expertise than the average layman and his descriptions of McKinney's property and the lifestyle of the inhabitants of the island show clearly not only his ability to observe but also his sense of humour:

"This is the first impression of Crooked Island, & you are getting it because the sun has burnt my lips and back so badly that I am taking a day in the shade.

I reserve the right to alter every statement and any resemblance to places or people is purely coincidental.

First of all the bad. Forsyth was quite right. The place is a desert; & it will take both time & money to do anything with it. The ground has been so burnt over that the country is a cross between the top of Vesuvius & Berlin. Wherever you look smoke is rising from the farms.

The people that I have met are quite the best in the Bahamas & are like the people of Tortola, Virgin Islands. Although very African, they appear to be better educated than most, their huts are cleaner & there is no begging. Wherever I have been I have been invited into the houses & given some orangeade & cakes."

It was during this trip that he appears for the first time to have expressed an interest in the agriculture of the islands (or, in some cases the lack of it) and formulated some opinions on how it should be carried out particularly regarding the practice, which was common throughout the islands, of burning away the undergrowth. At Crooked Island he saw evidence of an alternative method of farming:

"The brother of Mr Moss of Mosstown called on me with a present of fresh vegetables and eggs. Another brother of Mr Moss has a beautiful farm. Citrus planted in rows, a patch of Bananas whose leaves are green & fresh in spite of the drought. Plenty of sugar cane & onions, beets, tomatoes & cabbage planted in beds. The ground has been levelled off and tons of seaweed have been carried onto the farm. It shows that a farm can be made, but it is probably a very hard job.

The Commissioner showed me a letter he wrote about change of headquarters to Hope Great House, in which he suggested that Long Cay residents be transported to Crooked Island. They all go to church here & it might be pointed out that a man who burns a farm cannot really love God. Therefore God will punish him to the third and fourth generations.

I suggest that every man who is moved from Long Cay to Crooked Island be given his land - and also an equal amount which he must NOT touch till after the third and fourth generation. This means that in 100 years each family moved will have land with 1 inch of earth on it & a growth of some use. I don't know if a government can take such a long view of such matters."

He concluded his report by informing McKinney:

"If this letter has bored you, you cannot get at me to smack me in the eye or anything & I cannot get out of the Sound (Turtle Sound) till next moon with a south wind. I can't guess when that will happen." [1]

His conviction that the burning of the undergrowth was detrimental to good farming seems to have gripped him with an almost crusading zeal and, shortly after his return from Crooked Island, he established himself on a small cay at Andros where, after seeking advice from the Bahamas Agricultural Board, he set about practising what he had preached. He devoted a great deal of time and an enormous amount of energy to the task and later reported the results of his endeavours in the Nassau Guardian:

"I have made my farm for one year and kept it up for one year, working single-handed. When I say 'made', I mean it literally. Everything is growing in sand, seaweed etc., that I myself have carried. The Cay has been so badly burned that there is no humus on it, and it takes a little tree two years to get its roots down into fertile earth.

I am quite independent of rain, as a member of the Board showed me how to bore for water. I have six wells on my little patch, one of which is 30 feet deep, and was dug in two days.

Should I need help, the Trade Winds will pump all the water I require, and I shall farm as they do in Palestine and other parts of the world.

On the Cay, I found a few dying trees, covered with love vine. This year one grapefruit tree gave me 700 fruit, an orange 600, a lime 2,000. All my trees are clean, as the Board told me about Lady Birds.

My first Corn was planted under instructions I got out of the Nassau Guardian and a radio broadcast from ZNS. At the same time a farm was being burned on a Cay opposite mine. My corn gave me a 2,000 to 1 return. My opposite number got a few bearing stalks giving about 200 to 1. I thank the Board. My dillies, salved in accordance with information furnished by the Board, gave me the best dillies I have yet seen and are at this moment laden down with young fruit. My peas are the best in the vicinity, and my potatoes, planted as the Board said, are giving excellent results. All sixty of my young trees are doing well, and one seedling planted by me has already borne fruit.

As a matter of interest I might say that I dig my beds with an eight-pound hammer." [2]

His continual reference to the advice which he received from the 'Board' leads one to think that his farming experiment might even have been sponsored by them as a means of persuading the out-islanders to abandon their old traditional methods in favour of a more scientific approach. Whatever influence, or lack of it, which he may have had on the islanders, the editor of the Nassau Guardian was certainly impressed and extolled his achievements:

"It is important to note that ... Group Captain Rees chose for his agricultural experiment the most unpromising land, the fields of a 'stony cay'; that he has challenged the recalcitrant soil of such an islet and has so far broken down its resistance so as to draw from it what, in the circumstances, can only be called more fruitful harvests. All this by the lone efforts of one man, let it be remembered. This amateur farmer - winning fast towards professional status - has further proved that the Bahamian farmer need not be totally dependent upon our erratic rainfall. The example of Group Captain Rees a modern Cincinatus cultivating the Bahamian soil, is an inspiration to all Bahamians, and, will, we trust, cause many of them to follow the lead he has given." [3]

Strong, if rather poetic words which, because of their style, would probably have fallen upon ears as deaf as the rocky cays were barren. How relevent Rees' experiment was in reality is questionble as his farm was only developed for a limited period and, if so successful, it is strange that the ideas were not universally adopted, if nowhere else than at least on Andros where its value would have been obvious and clearly visible to all.

It is generally accepted that a man's desire to cultivate the land is the first step towards the establishment of a more sedentary lifestyle. Arable farming of any description is a long term process and the fruits of one year's labours are often not available for harvesting until a lengthy period of time has passed. Certainly, in the case of Rees, the days of wandering around the islands seem to have come to an end by 1947. The Anglo-Iranian Oil Company which had been carrying out test drilling for oil at Deep Creek on Andros had decided to close down their operations as the geology of the region made its extraction impractical. The task of winding up the drilling site was given to Rees and, it was whilst he was there that he met Sylvia Williams who was, very quickly, to have a profound effect on the remaining years of his life.

Sylvia was the eighteen year old daughter of Alexander and Mary Williams of Pinders, a small settlement near Mangrove Cay. Despite being of pure-blooded West African descent and almost illiterate, she was attracted to this elderly Welshman who seemed so wise, well-educated and gentle. Officially, she became his housekeeper but, very soon, the two were emotionally involved and neither the wide gulf between their ages not the even wider cultural differences appeared to matter. In the end, perhaps inevitably, Sylvia discovered that she was pregnant and there appears to have been no question that Rees should do anything but the honourable thing and, consequently, on 12 August 1947, they were married by the Civil Commissioner for Andros.

News of the marriage shocked white 'society' in Nassau; he was a man who could have had his choice of the many eligible ladies in the capital, so why had be chosen a black Androvian? They all reached the same conclusion, that Sylvia had laid a trap for him into which he had fallen. No-one could accept any other explanation; it was unthinkable to them that he could have entered into such a marriage of his own free will. He must have felt obliged to have married the girl "having got her into trouble". That, they said, was taking "the manners of an officer and a gentleman too far". A friend, Walton Smith, who was living in Miami, returned to Nassau for a holiday and found the news of the marriage "hard to believe, since he [Rees] was extremely shy and even politely hostile to women". Many believed that the marriage would not last and that Rees would "very quickly come to his senses". [4]

Was the opinion of Nassau 'society' correct or was it simply racism which was so prevalent in the 1940s and indeed is only just below the surface in the Bahamas today ? Might Rees not have married Sylvia without coercion, for some other perfectly normal reason. If it was not for love perhaps it was because he was simply delighted at the thought of becoming a father at the age of 62. Despite Smith's comment, there is evidence to suggest that Rees was far from being averse to female companionship and that it had been his love of his independence and the style of life which he had always led which had steered him away from matrimony in the past. Something had evidently happened which had made him change his mind and it was probably nothing more sinister than the advancing years. Perhaps he yearned for the stability and security of family life which seems to have been denied to him even by his own parents. The person closest to him, his sister Muriel, was on the far side of the Atlantic and, despite his requests, she had emphatically refused to join him in the Bahamas. Certainly, throughout his life he appears to have related well to children and the absence of any of his own may have been a cause of great frustration; he who had done and seen so much had no-one to whom he could pass on his experience and knowledge. The fact that neither he nor Muriel had married meant that the family line was about to come to an end and this may well have influenced his actions. Or, it may simply be that he had fallen for Sylvia who, because of her age brought an ageing man a last reminder of youth. We will never know the true reason as the only person with at least part of the answer, Sylvia Rees, has chosen to remain silent .

The marriage may have caused scandalous gossip in Nassau but on Andros it was quite acceptable to the community which had an almost naive but endearing simplicity in its attitude towards life; it was fine for him to have married a girl so many years his junior as he was a gentleman and had plenty of money. One elderly Mangrovian lady went so far as to say, in that bluntly honest style of the Caribbean, "...so long as he could do the job - there would be no problems". He had long since been accepted into their midst and had acquired a reputation as something of a sage, a man to whom others less knowledgeable could turn for advice and assistance. Whenever the Mangrovians had a problem it was to the 'Captain' that they turned and he assumed the role of an unofficial leader in the community. Over forty years later, he is still highly thought of by those who knew him and he is still spoken of with great reverence.

Almost as soon as they were married, Rees set about constructing a home for his new wife and eagerly expected child. On the ridge above Mangrove Cay, near Sylvia's home at Pinders, he built a one-roomed house of very simple design with corrugated iron walls and roof, a drain in the centre of the earth floor and the sleeping accommodation curtained off from the living area. For water, he sank his own well and a small generator supplied electricity, a rare commodity in Mangrove Cay in the 1940s. The basic construction work was carried out by the local population with Rees supervising and personally producing the more technical items such as the blades for his windcharger. By European standards the house was primitive but on Andros it was regarded as the latest in modern out-island accommodation [5].

In March 1948, Sylvia gave birth to a son whom they named Ailean Lionel (the first christian name being a variation on the name of Rees' boat) and, over the next five years, there were two more children, a daughter, Aline and a second son, Olvin. As his eldest son grew older, Rees taught him the basics of the few machines and gadgets which the family owned and, when out walking, tried to create in him an awareness of the landscape. Cyrus Sharer, a young American post-graduate student, visited Mangrove Cay in the early 1950s and has fond memories of the Rees family, headed by this highly intelligent elderly man who seemed to delight in the company of his small son, taking every opportunity to teach him those skills which he regarded as essential. Today, only Allen (as Ailean has come to be known) of the three children has any real recollection of his father and those early days on Mangrove Cay.

"My life was carefree and full of days wandering the beaches with my father. He would always talk to me as if I was an adult, I think he wished I was older, so that I could understand much more of the things he was telling me. We talked about his days in North Africa and his life in the RAF. I do remember that he was obsessed with the idea of sailing. It must have been a big disappointment when he finally got ill and could not sail as much as he would have liked. My father spent many hours studying Greek, and reading classic books. In the evening at 6.00 pm, he would listen to the BBC on the shortwave radio which was powered from storage cells which were charged from a wind generator.

Our house was the first to have electric lights, due to the generator. The plumbing for the house was derived from 55 gal. storage tanks which had to be filled each day. Water had to be pumped manually to a height of approximately 20 feet so that water pressure could be generated in the plumbing. We had a well stocked workshop. Most of the furniture was made by hand in this shop. Before I entered school, I was at least two years ahead of children of my own age and this became somewhat of a problem; kids do not know how to react to others who 'know it all'.

My father was an honest and passionate man; a gentleman until the minute of his death." [6]

Sadly, this picture of tropical bliss was not to last and Rees' time with his new family was to be very short. Despite being old enough to be the children's grandfather, he had hoped to spend many years in their company but it was not to be as during the early 1950s he became unwell and the illness was eventually diagnosed as leukaemia, a disease which could not be treated locally. Gradually, the debilitating nature of the illness meant that he became less able to do those things, like sailing, which had given him great pleasure. In what must have been very difficult circumstances, he sold the *Aline* to a partnership of the Commissioner for Andros and Mr McPhee who operated her as a ferry between Mangrove Cay and Nassau. In 1953, as a desperate attempt to try and arrest the advance of the disease, Rees returned to Britain where he was admitted to the RAF Hospital at Uxbridge [7] where he received treatment but it could only delay the inevitable. He realised that he was dying and that his ties were now in the Bahamas and so he made his farewells to his homeland. Unable to make the journey to Caernarfon, he wrote to the Mayor and Corporation:

"The doctor tells me that I shall soon fade away and that I shall take no further interest in life in a few weeks time. I should therefore (in case the diagnosis is correct) like to make my adieu to the Mayor, aldermen, councillors and burgesses of Caernarvon.

In the same way as other people I have had my difficulties. I have met them during the last war, and whilst sailing and just in the ordinary way of life. When things have been really bad I have often said to myself, "What would a freeman of Caernarvon do about this ?"

The answer has come to me that a freeman of Caernarvon would just get on with the job. This I have done and the difficulties have disappeared."

This time however, the difficulties were not going to disappear and the doctor's prognosis was, unfortunately all too accurate. A few weeks after he had returned to the Bahamas he was back in a hospital bed, being admitted to the Princess Margaret Hospital in Nassau on 20 May, 1955. Sylvia, in the tradition of Andros, wanted to remain with him in the hospital and only after considerable difficulty, was she persuaded to leave and appear at the official visiting times. His friends in the capital would call and the members of the Royal Air Force Association arranged for the installation of a radio to help him pass the days of enforced idleness. The matron, Miss Denise Dane, recalls that he was a very sick man but that his mind and memory were both very good and he spent his days preparing for the inevitable. To Mrs Mallie Lightbourn, Chairwoman of the War Graves Commission for the Bahamas (and the daughter of his long time friend Herbert McKinney), he sent a request that he be buried in the RAF Cemetery but, even with such a sombre request, he was still able to add a touch of humour, commenting that as he was so much against absentee landlords he did not intend to leave vacant for very long any land which he might be granted. For his family, he drew up a short and simple will which summed up everything that was important to him:

"I leave everything I possess to my wife, Sylvia Rees. I hope that she will keep my books, instruments, tools in good condition, in trust for my children.

I hope that any land which we possess will be kept in proper condition, in trust for the children, that it will not be destroyed by burning and by being allowed to erode." [8]

The care of his children he placed in the hands of the church in the hope that both they and their mother would be protected until they were better able to care for themselves. He was obviously aware of the bad feelings which his marriage had aroused and attempted to ensure that his family would not suffer after he was gone. Even today, controversy still exists about these final years and the two communities, at Mangrove Cay and Nassau, both claim a different truth. Perhaps Miss Dane has summed it up best:

"We had all heard of his great career and it distressed most people that he lived in such reduced circumstances in one of the out-islands. We all felt that a hero like Group Captain Rees should have had a happier ending but he may well have preferred things to be as they were." [9]

Rees declined gradually and died as 10.45 on the morning of Wednesday, 28 September, 1955. As was the custom in the tropics, the funeral was arranged for later the same day and the small cortege left the hospital at 4.30 pm. He was buried, with full military honours, in the RAF Cemetery with members of the RAF Association acting as pall-bearers and the Royal Bahamas Police providing a Guard of Honour and a firing party. The mourners were few and consisted mainly of immediate family and a few close friends.

Today, the RAF Cemetery in Nassau is a blaze of colour, the low stone wall which contains an area of bright green crab grass also keeps check on the tropical undergrowth. All around, the Bahamian national tree, the Poinciana, provides a dramatic backdrop of brilliant red and the air is filled with the sound of tropical insects. Neat rows of white stone tablets lie of the grass, each bearing brief details of young men who died in the service of their country, mostly during the Second World War. Two graves however, are different and lie next to each other on the left as one enters the cemetery; one is the last resting place of Hilary St George Saunders, famed writer of RAF history and the other is that of Lionel Rees who did more than most to create that history.

Let the last words be those of an anonymous poet:

"May he rest in peace" in the Good Tomorrow
One of those fond and foolish fools
Who, scorning fortune and fame
Turn out with the rallying cry of their schools
Just eager to play the game."

NOTES

Chapter I

1. The spelling of the name Caernarfon has undergone a number of changes during its history. The two spellings Carnarvon and Caernarvon are used in the names of organisations, newspapers and quotes where they were originally spelt that way. In the text the name is recorded in the modern Welsh spelling of Caernarfon.
2. Hilton *Nine Lives* .

Chapter II

1. Later Air Vice Marshal The Rt. Hon. Sir Frederick Sykes, GBE, GCSI, GCIE, KCB, CMG, PC.
2. Later Lieutenant General Sir David Henderson, KCB, KCVO, DSO.
3. It was fortunate that Captain Ross Hume, the pilot of this machine managed to ditch in the sea without serious mishap as his observer was Captain Hugh Dowding, the future Commander in Chief of Fighter Command during the Battle of Britain in 1940.
4. Later Marshal of the Royal Air Force Sir John Salmond, GCB, CMG, CVO, DSO.
5. The latter was located on the Thames estuary at Dartford Creek.
6. In this instance 'gunner' means armourer. The pilot of the machine was 2nd Lieutenant Montagu Chidson and

his observer was Corporal Martin.

7. German records show that this machine did receive damage to its floats and fuselage but managed to reach its base safely (although the gunner was wounded by anti-aircraft fire as they crossed the Flanders coast). Both were awarded the Iron Cross the next day.

Chapter III

1. Later Air Marshal Sir Patrick Playfair, KBE, CB, CVO, MC.

2. Later Air Commodore Andrew George Board, CMG, DSO, DL. He resided at Glan Gwna, near Caernarfon in his latter years.

3. Algernon John Insall, brother of Gilbert Insall VC, was one of the founders of the Imperial War Museum Photographic Department. He became a noted aeronautical writer between the wars and published his memoirs of the First World War under the title *Observer*.

4. A J Insall, *Observer*.

5. Ibid.

6. Letter held by No.11 Squadron, RAF.

7. There are various spellings of this aerodrome's name. I have used that which is shown on the current issue of the Michelin road map.

8. Insall, *Observer*.

9. Insall, A.J., *The First Fighter Squadron*, Popular Flying, February, 1935.

10. Later Wing Commander G W P Dawes, OC RAF in the Balkans, 1918.

11. Letter held by No.11 Squadron, RAF.

12. A J Insall, *Observer*.

13. This is how Esterre is spelt in the official

documentation of this mission but, as Esterre is over 50 miles north of Peronne, it would appear to be an error. It is more likely to have been Estrees, which is only 5 miles south east of Peronne.

14. Archie was the nickname given by the RFC to the German anti-aircraft defences and is believed to have originated from a popular music-hall song of the time, 'Archibald, Certainly Not!'.

15. London Gazette, 29 October 1915. Rees also received his first Mention in Despatches in the same issue of the London Gazette.

16. No. 11 Squadron had moved its base to Villers Bretonneux during September.

17. The brother of A J Insall, also of No. 11 Squadron.

18. Interview recorded by Barrington Gray.

19. In 1917, Gilbert Insall escaped from his prisoner of war camp at Strohen and, after a journey of nine days, crossed the frontier into Holland. Returning to the RFC he did not see further combat service. He retired from the RAF in 1945 with the rank of Group Captain.

20. The quadrant mounted Lewis gun attached to the upper wing of the Nieuport was able to fire upwards at an angle of 80 degrees, a feature which other fighters of the time did not possess.

21. In the House of Commons on 24 January 1916, it was stated that during the previous four weeks 1227 British machines had overflown enemy territory whilst only 310 German machines had crossed the British lines. During the same four week period the RFC and RNAS had employed 138 machines on bombing raids whilst the enemy had used no more than 20.

22. See page 69, Chapter IV for definition of a tractor aircraft.

23. The author of this remains anonymous but there is some evidence which would suggest that Rees may have been responsible. If this is indeed the case then his ideas and views had matured considerably during the intervening two years.

Chapter IV

1. What Fokker actually did was modify the interruptor gear invented by the Swiss engineer Franz Schneider in 1913.
2. Later Squadron Leader E L Conran, RAF (retired 1921).
3. Major Lanoe George Hawker, VC, DSO, was killed in action on 23 November 1916, the eleventh victim of Manfred von Richthofen. His death was unquestionably caused by the lack of power in the DH2 rather than by Richthofen's superior skill as a pilot.
4. Insall A J *Great British Fighter Pilots*, War in the Air.
5. Later Wing Commander Gwilym Hugh Lewis, DFC. A fellow Welshman, he is the last survivor of the original pilots of No.32 Squadron and the author of *Wings Over the Somme*.
6. It was not the custom at this time for squadron commanders to lead their men in the air. Rees had been granted permission to fly but was forbidden to cross the front line when the squadron arrived in France.
7. Rees published rigging manuals for both the DH2 and the Vickers FB5.
8. Interview with the author, July 1986.
9. Recalled in a letter to the author by Mr R Beach, a fitter with No. 11 Squadron on its formation in 1916.

10. I am endebted to Wing Commander William Fry, MC, for particulars of this machine. He is probably the last survivor of the small handful of pilots that flew the Bullet in the war.

11. Later Marshal of the Royal Air Force, Viscount Trenchard, GCB, DSO, DCL, LLD, generally known as the 'Father of the Royal Air Force'.

12. There would appear to be some confusion over the identity of this pilot as some records show that it was Lieutenant Bath whilst others say that it was 2nd Lieutenant Hunt.

13. Each Brigade was made up of Corps Wings (who were involved in reconnaissance, photography and artillery co-operation on the corps front) and Army Wings (equipped with faster aircraft they carried out the reconnaissance and combat patrols over a wide area, often far behind enemy lines).

14. 2nd Lieutenant Reginald Arthur Stubbs, Royal Munster Fusiliers, attached RFC, was the son of George and Annie Stubbs of Walton-on-Thames. He was aged 25 and had been an undergraduate at Keeble College, Oxford and hoped to take holy orders after the war. He was buried in Quatre-Vents Military Cemetery, Estree-Cauchy, Plot 2, Row A, Grave 1.

15. Lewis' father, Hugh Davies Lewis, was knowledgeable about flying and had obtained his Royal Aero Club Certificate (No. 2269) in January 1916 when aged 50. According to his son, he was determined not to fight in any trenches should the Germans ever land in Britain and possession of a pilot's licence might enable him to play a part in the air defence of the country.

16. 2nd Lieutenant Owen Thomas, Royal Welsh Fusiliers, attached RFC, was the son of Brigadier General

Sir Owen Thomas, a prime mover behind the scheme to create a Welsh Division and its first commanding officer (he was MP for Anglesey from 1918-23). 2nd Lieutenant Thomas was killed on 29 July 1918, whilst instructing another pilot, 2nd Lieutenant A J Cairns, in night observation; his aircraft caught fire after a parachute flare became stuck in its tube. His two brothers were also killed in the war.

17.   On 21/22 June, the two Vickers Bullets flown by Rees and Hellyer were exchanged for two DH2 Scouts.

18.   Lieutenant John Clark Simpson was the son of James and Leila Simpson of Gwelph, Ontario, Canada. He was buried in Vermelles British Cemetery, Plot 4, Row F, Grave 24. The village is mid-way between Bethune and Lens. He was aged 26. His entire combat had been witnessed by ground units who subsequently submitted a report on the action to the RFC.

19.   Auntie Katie was Mrs Catherine Moore of Greenhall, High Blantyre, Rees' mother's widowed sister. Since his mother had died in 1911, she had taken on the role of surrogate mother to him.

20.   Later Lieutenant Colonel T A E Cairnes, DSO. On Rees' departure from No.32 Squadron, the senior Flight Commander, Captain Gilmour, had become acting CO but, later that same day, he received a bullet wound in the head in a combat with a Fokker and, as a consequence, he was hospitalised for a week. Cairnes assumed the command of the squadron on 7 July 1916.

Chapter V

1.   Whilst staying at the Station Hotel their cover was ruined by no less a person than Balfour himself who gave

his autograph to the hotel liftboy.

2. *The World*, 10 June 1917.

3. *Air Travel*, October 1917.

4. Letter from Brigadier General George O Squier, Chief Signal Officer, US Army to Lieutenant General G T M Bridges, CMG, DSO, 18 May 1917.

5. Hiram Bingham was perhaps best known in his peacetime capacity as an archaeologist and explorer. He published his recollections of the events of 1917 in his autobiographical volume *An Explorer in the Air Service*.

6. Later General Henry Harley 'Hap' Arnold, General of the United States Air Force.

7. For his services in the United States Lionel Rees was created an Officer of the Most Excellent Order of the British Empire (Military Division), London Gazette, 3 June 1919.

Chapter VI

1. Robert Smith-Barry had established a flying school at Gosport where officers were taught how to instruct. It had a remarkable effect on British flying tuition and formed the basis of all future RAF instruction.

2. Figures compiled from official Allied and German communiques which, although probably far from accurate, do clearly show the steep rise in casualties.

3. Some of the hanger buildings erected at this time are still standing at Ayr.

4. Spring, Elliot White, *War Birds - Diary of an Unknown Aviator*.

5. Ibid.

6. Later Major James Byford McCudden, VC, DSO and Bar, MC and Bar, MM, Croix de Guerre. He was

unofficially credited with having destroyed fifty-two enemy aircraft in combat. He was killed in a flying accident in July 1918.

7. Later Major Edward Mannock, VC, DSO and two Bars, MC and Bar. He was killed in action on 26 July 1918 and is unofficially credited with having destroyed seventy-three enemy aircraft in combat. Some students of his career place his score at well over one hundred enemy machines destroyed.

8. Later Wing Commander James Ira Thomas Jones, DSO, MC, DFC and Bar, MM, Cross of St George (Russia). He was unofficially credited with the destruction of forty enemy aircraft. His experiences at Ayr are described in his book *Tiger Squadron.*

9. The instructor was a man named Ortmeyer who had over 300 hours experience in the USA where he had instructed on the Curtis biplane.

10. Macmillan, Norman, *Into The Blue.*

11. It would appear that the American pupil pilots had a great deal to be dissatisfied about. Having been amongst the first US airmen to cross the Atlantic they had not been commissioned. The American commander in Europe, General Pershing, had decided that pilots did not warrant officer status and wanted then all to be sergeants. He was also in favour of abolishing flying pay. Some of the pilots who had been given commissions were threatening to resign unless the same privilages were given to their comrades.

12. During the Second World War, when Ayr was again used as a training station for pilots, a number of fatal accidents occurred and it was rumoured that shortly before each crash a ghostly biplane fighter was spotted over the area. A memorial, located on the golf course,

records the names of those who were killed during the First World War.

13. An extension of the Smith-Barry School at Gosport.

14. The Royal Air Force, the world's first independent air force, had come into being on 1 April 1918 and had assumed control of all RFC and RNAS units.

15. For his services in the instruction of pilots for both the RFC and the RAF, Lionel Rees was awarded the Air Force Cross, London Gazette, 2 November 1918

Chapter VII

1. Later Air Vice Marshal W L Freebody, CB, CBE, AFC.

2. The previous recipients of this honour were:- Sir William Preece, Mr J H Bodvel-Roberts, Rt. Hon. David Lloyd George, Sir John Pritchard-Jones, Sir Charles Assheton-Smith, Mr Owen Jones.

3. Later Air Vice Marshal Sir Charles Longcroft, KCB, CMG, DSO, AFC.

4. Later Marshal of the Royal Air Force, Viscount Portal of Hungerford, KG, GCB, OM, DSO, MC.

5. Later Air Chief Marshal Sir George Mills, GCB, DFC.

6. Later Air Chief Marshal Sir Theodore McEvoy, KCB, CBE.

7. Later Marshal of the Royal Air Force Sir Dermot Boyle, GCB, KCVO, KBE, AFC.

8. Later Air Vice Marshal Sir Geoffrey Worthington, KBE, CB.

9. Air Vice Marshal Wilfred Leslie Freebody, CB, CBE, AFC.

10. Air Vice Marshal A D Gilmore, CB, CBE.

11. Later Air Commodore Ward, CB, DFC.
12. Later Air Chief Marshal Sir Arthur Barratt, KCB, CMG, MC, DL.
13. Later Flight Lieutenant F W L C Beaumont. He resigned his commission in 1938 only to rejoin the service as a Pilot Officer in the RAFVR in 1939. He was killed on active service during the Second World War.
14. Flying Cadet V O Gillmore (1922) and Flying Cadet H H Aspinall (1924).
15. Later Air Vice Marshal John Gerald Franks, CB, CBE.
16. This idea has been revived, with some success, at modern airports where 'bird strikes' are a constant cause of concern to airline pilots.
17. Letter to the author from Lady Joan Portal, 1986.
18. Air Vice Marshal Sir Richard Jordan, KCB, DFC.

Chapter VIII

1. Later Air Vice Marshal Stanley Vincent, CB, DFC, AFC, DL.
2. O.C. Transjordan Frontier Force.
3. On 25 April, a DH9a piloted by Flight Lieutenant Philip Wigglesworth (later Air Marshal Sir Philip Wigglesworth, KBE, CB, DSC) failed to return to its base but managed to make a safe landing in the desert.
4. Group Captain Rees' report to the Chief Secretary, Jerusalem, on the occupation of Azraq, 14 May, 1927.

Chapter IX

1. Later Air Vice Marshal John G Franks, CB, CBE.
2. Insall later discovered the ancient city of Seleucia in

Mesopotamia using the same method.

3. The Geographical Journal, Vol LXXIII, No 6, June 1929, Royal Geographical Society, *Air Photographs of the Middle East,* p.511.

4. Natural History Magazine, Vol XXIX, No 1, 1929, *Early Man in North Arabia,* Henry Field.

5. Antiquity, No 3, 1929, *The Transjordan Desert ,* Group Captain L W B Rees, VC.

6. Letter to the author.

7. Later Air Vice Marshal Percy Maitland, CB, CBE, MVO, AFC.

8. Letter to the author. Dr Betts is the co-author, with S Helms, of *The Desert Kites of the Badiyat Esh-Sham and North Arabia,* published in Palorient Vol 13.1, 1987.

9. Palestine Exploration Quarterly, Jan -April 1948, *The Route of the Exodus. The First Stage. Ramses to Etham.* by L W B Rees.

10. Notes prepared by Rees for a lecture which he gave at East Molesey, 1 February 1933.

Chapter X

1. Later Sir Alec Kirkbride, KCMG, Kt, CVO, OBE, MC.

2. Brabazon Rees Lodge, RAOB, Grand Lodge of England, No. 6009 (Transjordan).

3. Command of Plaestine and Transjordan was given to Group Captain 'Pip' Playfair, MC, a former member of No.11 Squadron in 1915.

Chapter XI

1. Today, this sword is on public display in the VC

gallery at the RAF Museum, Hendon.

2. In 1934, the Cruising Club of America awarded Rees their 'Blue Water Medal' for the most outstanding sailing achievement of the year. This award is now displayed in the Royal Welsh Yacht Club, Caernarfon.

Chapter XII

1. 11 May 1935.

Chapter XIII

1. Percy Cavill, a reknowned Australian swimmer who was living on Andros. Cavill is credited with having developed the Australian Crawl swimming stroke. He was a close friend of Lionel Rees.

2. There is no evidence that Rees ever spoke with a Welsh accent. His public school education and military career would almost certainly have removed from his speech any trace of his origins. What Cottman had mistaken for a Welsh accent was probably a very refined English accent.

3. Letter to the author.

4. Squadron Leader Portal, who had served under Rees at Cranwell, rose to become Marshal of the Royal Air Force, Lord Portal of Hungerford. He was Chief of the Air Staff from 1940 until the end of hostilities. Captain Hugh Dowding, formerly of No. 6 Squadron (1914) was AOC Fighter Command in 1940 when 58 years of age.

5. Letter to the author.

6. Lieutenant Colonel Ronald Sherbrooke-Walker (later Colonel). He had served as a pilot in No.22 Squadron during the First World War and had rejoined the army

(after serving in the Territorial Army) on the outbreak of war in 1939. He was the author of *Khaki and Blue*.
7. Ibid.
8. Ibid.
9. Ibid.

Chapter XIV

1. Letters from Rees to Herbert McKinney, held by Mr A McKinney, Nassau.
2. Nassau Guardian, 8 January 1948.
3. Ibid.
4. Letter from Dr Walton Smith to the author.
5. The house still stands today but, although the property of the Bahamian Department of Education, it is unoccupied and is slowly disappearing behind a curtain of uncontrolled undergrowth.
6. Letter to the author.
7. Ironically, one of the foundation stones of this building had been laid by Rees when he was OC No.21 Group in 1929.
8. Probate Office, Nassau.
9. Letter to the author.

MAPS

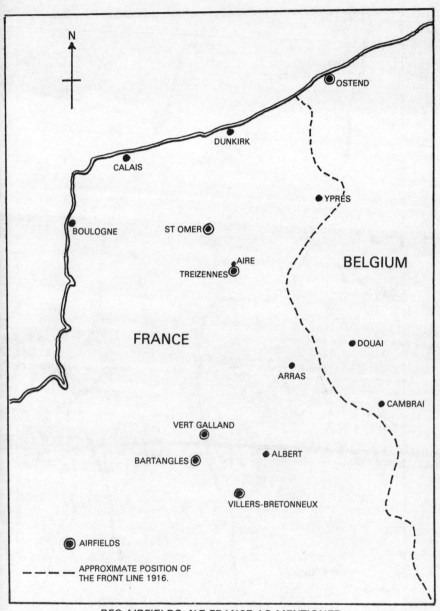

RFC AIRFIELDS, N E FRANCE AS MENTIONED
IN THE TEXT

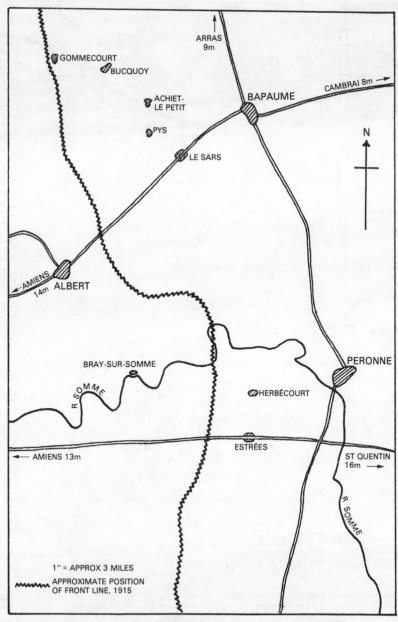

MAIN AREA OF OPERATIONS, No 11 SQUADRON, RFC, 1915

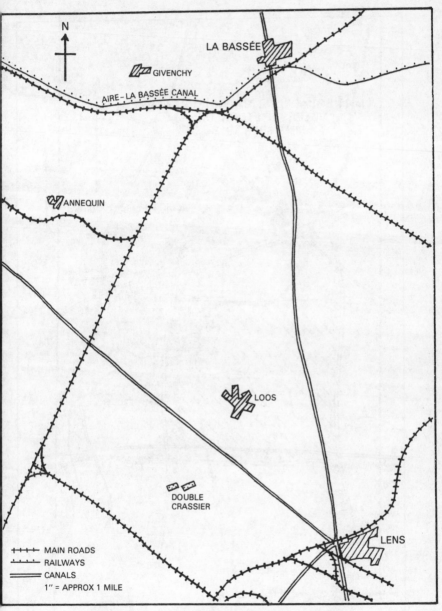

AREA OVER WHICH REES FOUGHT HIS VC ACTION
1 JULY, 1916

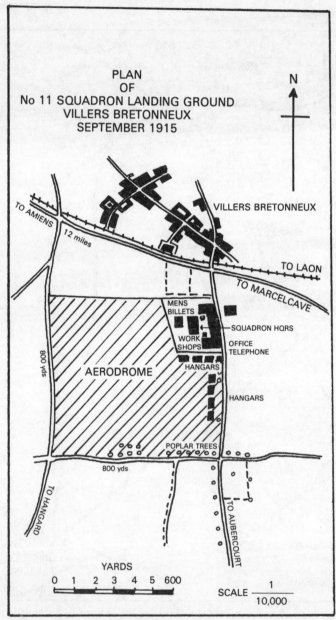

RE-DRAWN FROM THE ORIGINAL. PRO. AIR 1/2395/255/2

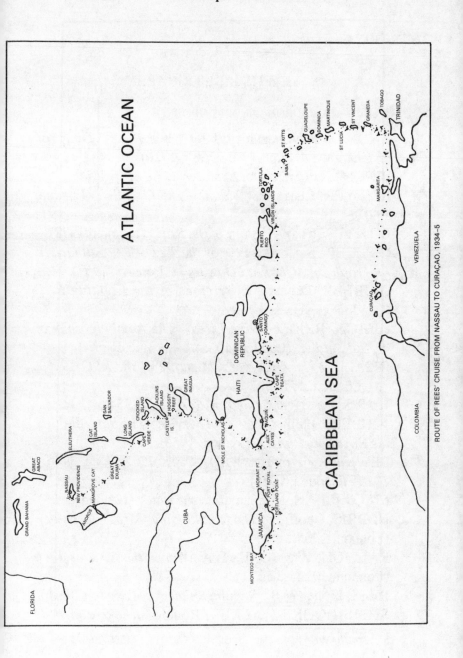

ROUTE OF REES' CRUISE FROM NASSAU TO CURAÇAO, 1934–5

SELECT BIBLIOGRAPHY

ANON [SPRING, Elliot White] *War Birds - Diary of an Unknown Aviator* (New York, 1926).

BINGHAM, Hiram *An Explorer in the Air Service*

BOWYER, Chaz *For Valour - The Air VCs* (London, 1978).

BOWYER, Chaz *History of the RAF* (London, 1977).

COLLIER, Basil *Leader of the Few - The Authorised Biography of ACM Lord Dowding* (London, 1957).

GRIBBLE, Leonard R *Heroes of the Fighting RAF* (London, 1941).

HILTON, Richard *Nine Lives - The Autobiography of an Old Soldier* (London, 1955).

INSALL, A J *Observer - Memoirs of the RFC 1915 - 18* (London, 1970).

JONES, Ira *Tiger Squadron* (London, 1954).

JOUBERT, Philip *The Third Service - The Story Behind the Royal Air Force* (London, 1955).

LEWIS, Gwilym H *Wings Over the Somme 1916 - 1918* (London, 1976).

MACMILLAN, Norman *Into the Blue* (London, 1929).

NORRIS, Geoffrey *The Royal Flying Corps - A History* (London, 1965).

RALEIGH, W & JONES H A *War in the Air Vols 1 - 6* (London, 1922 - 37).

REES, Lionel W B *Fighting in the Air* (London, 1916).

SHERBROOKE-WALKER, Ronald *Khaki and Blue* (London, 1952).

WILLIAMS, W Alister   *The VCs of Wales and the Welsh Regiments*   (Wrexham, 1984).

WINTER, Denis   *The First of the Few - Fighter Pilots of the First World War*   (London, 1982).

WOOD, Eric   *Thrilling Deeds of British Airmen* (London, 1917).